D0296700

N

UNIVERSITY OF GLAMORGAN
LEARNING RESOURCES CENTRE

Pontypridd, Mid Glamorgan, CF37 1DL
Telephone: Pontypridd (0443) 480480

Books are to be returned on or before the last date below

ONE WEEK LOAN

-3. DEC. 1992

9 NOV 2000

14. JAN. 1994

1 1 DEC 2000

1 6 FEB 2004

1. MAY 1994

2 7 APR 1998

This book has been retained for research purposes. Information contained within may not be CURRENT LAW

22. 2. 06

LAW, STATE AND SOCIETY

EXPLORATIONS IN SOCIOLOGY

*A series under the auspices of the
British Sociological Association*

Law, State and Society

Edited by Bob Fryer, Alan Hunt, Doreen McBarnet
and Bert Moorhouse

THE POLYTECHNIC OF WALES
LIBRARY
TREFOREST

CROOM HELM LONDON

CAT. 2
34 :301
WALD

CAT 2
340-115
LAW

© 1981 British Sociological Association
Croom Helm Ltd, 2-10 St John's Road, London SW11

British Library Cataloguing in Publication Data

Law, state and society. – (Exploration in sociology).
  1. Sociology jurisprudence – Congresses
  I. Fryer, Bob   II. British Sociological
  Association   III. Series
  340.1'15
  ISBN 0-7099-1004-5

226453

Printed and bound in Great Britain by
Redwood Burn Limited
Trowbridge and Esher

CONTENTS

NICOS POULANTZAS

The editors were deeply distressed to learn of the death of
Nicos Poulantzas in September 1979. Nicos opened the 1979 British
Sociological Association with a plenary session on 'law and the
capitalist state'. We wish to pay tribute to the memory of someone
who contributed widely to both the intellectual and political
concerns of the present.

1 LAW, STATE AND SOCIETY

Bob Fryer, Alan Hunt, Doreen McBarnet and
Bert Moorhouse

The 1979 British Sociological Association Conference on Law and
Society set out to achieve three aims, reflected in the choice of papers
for this volume: first, to develop theoretical explorations in a field
which had for so long been theoretically underdeveloped; second, and
closely related, to encourage *theoretically informed* empirical investigation, as a conscious move away from what Campbell and Wiles have
called the 'socio-legal' approach,[1] focusing on pragmatically identified
'problems' and purporting to adopt a theoretically neutral empirical
methodology; third, to redirect the focus of research from criminal law
towards civil law and deeper underlying questions of the form of law.
Criminal law may have been the logical focus for a sociology of law
revived through radical criminology.[2] But the roots of the sociology of
law go back much further to the grand theorists, Marx, Weber, Durkheim, and to the core of sociological theory.

Indeed the concerns of the sociology of law converge with the most
important questions confronting contemporary sociology for reasons
other than its historical roots. The sociology of law in Britain has barely
reached the level of a recognised sub-discipline of sociology. It occupies
a marginal place in the organisation of academic sociology and just as
precarious position on the fringe of legal education. Yet the very fact of
its late achievement of sub-disciplinary status has meant that it has not
become entrapped in the self-protective specialisation which both protects and immunises many sociological sub-disciplines from the wider
concerns of the social sciences as a whole. One major consequence of
sub-disciplinary specialism manifests itself in the tendency for the sociology of law to become narrowly linked to the requirements of facilitating reforms in the administration of the legal process to such an
extent that concern with the social and political context within which
the legal system is located has received much less attention. It is thus
significant that some of the work that has had the greatest impact on
the field has come from people who are not 'sociology of law'
specialists. Important examples of such interventions have been the
very provocative discussion of 'the rule of law' by E.P. Thompson in
the conclusion of *Whigs and Hunters*, in which he has insisted on 'the
unqualified human good' embodied in the rule of law in opposition to
the prevailing tenor of Marxist discussion which has relegated the rule of
law as bourgeois ideology.[3] Similarly the work of Stuart Hall and his

colleagues in *Policing the Crisis* articulates an explicitly Gramscian perspective to the theorisation of law.[4] The issues there raised are taken up
and discussed by Philip Corrigan and Derek Sayer in their paper which
opens this volume.

However, the convergence with mainstream sociology is perhaps
most clearly the product of one important feature of the recent
development of the sociology of law: the extent to which it bears the
theoretical imprint of Marxism. This does not imply that *all* work in
the field is Marxist oriented. There are other methodologically radical
departures from the 'socio-legal' approach,[5] such as the ethnomethod-
ological and phenomenological critique. However, much of the work
which could legitimately claim to be influencing the direction of
research within the field as a whole is written under the influence of the
theoretical presence of Marxism. Now this approach to identifying the
impact of a particular intellectual current should not be taken as
implying that Marxism is of importance solely because it is (or is
presented as) a 'general theory'. Indeed part of the later argument will
seek to stress the developing convergence between empirical and
theoretical concerns within the field.

The 'convergence' is manifest in four central themes present in
contemporary sociology of law:

1. the coercion-consent dichotomy;
2. the ideological dimension of law;
3. legality and the form of law;
4. law and the state.

The 'rediscovery' of structural conflict by sociology since the
1960s, epitomised by the work of Alvin Gouldner, manifested itself at
the most general level in 'conflict sociology' and in a temptation to
effect the simple negation or reversal of the dominant paradigm. However necessary it may have been to install structural conflict into the
concerns of an increasingly complacent sociological enterprise, the
inadequacy of the simple substitution of the supposition of 'conflict',
counterposed to normative consensus, soon became apparent. The
recognition of the inadequacies of conflict sociology were for some
time masked by the focusing of attention on elements of social structures and institutions in which the presence of conflict was most
readily apparent; this was particularly pronounced in the development
of sociological consideration of deviance, crime and law over the last
decade. The liberation from the complacent assumptions of the
normative integrationist assumptions of the prevailing orthodoxy
revealed itself in enthusiastic insistence on the conflictual face of
deviance, crime and law.[6] One of its immediate consequences was to

direct the attention of radicals towards a sociology of law that focused almost exclusively on criminal law and ignored the whole body of civil law exhibiting a more apparently consensual face.

The search for a theoretical grounding for conflict sociology reinforced a tendency already present which released a fresh interest in Marxist sociology.[7] However, it must be stressed that the process of adoption of Marxism was a contradictory development since the theoretical and conceptual structure of Marxism is one which is to a greater or lesser extent divergent from the theoretical base of conflict sociology. One important consequence was that the form of Marxism adopted, at least in the early stages of the process of transition from conflict theory to Marxism, was a rather naive and instrumental version of Marxism, which treated law exclusively as a coercive apparatus wielded at will by a malevolent ruling class.[8]

The developments that were taking place within general Marxist theory brought to light the problems inherent in the dichotomy between 'coercion' and 'consent'. This is most sharply apparent in the debates engendered by the explosion of interest in the theoretical potential of the Marxism of Antonio Gramsci.[9] Gramsci insisted on the central part played by the 'mobilisation of consent' (hegemony) in the reproduction of capitalist social order and of the integral role of law in these processes. Such an insistence accorded well with a recognition of the political inadequacy of trying to understand the persistence of capitalist relations as a result of coercion or conspiracy. An immediate consequence was to provide a theoretical base for the rejection of the instrumentalist theory of law that had almost universally been regarded as synonymous with a Marxist theory of law. Undoubtedly the appropriation of Gramsci in discussions of Marxist theory of law resulted in a one-sided emphasis on the consensual dimensions of the function of law. Yet little advance is achieved through Perry Anderson's insistence on reinstating the role of coercion, state and domination in Gramsci's Marxism. The central problem remains: how to conceptualise social processes that involve both 'coercion' and 'consent' without lapsing into 'either-orism'; that is *either* consent is the dominant element *or* coercion is paramount. In other words the process of the reproduction of social order is conceptualised as taking specific historical forms along a continuum from 'coercion' to 'consent'. Essentially the same dualism is involved in Althusser's distinction between ideological state apparatuses (ISA) and repressive state apparatuses.[10] It hardly needs to be underlined that the dichotomy between coercion and consent had a central importance for all theoretical discussion of law not only within the Marxist tradition but also in non-Marxist sociology of law and in jurisprudence. Similarly this dualism goes to the very root of the wider sociological concern with the processes of social order. Thus the current concerns of the sociology of law exhibit a basic congruence with wider sociological problems and at the same time provides a fertile arena of exploration for attempts to overcome the limitations of the dualistic presentation of the problem.

The second arena of convergence revolves around the relationship between law and ideology, again manifested most visibly in work within the Marxist tradition, but equally present, if not always couched in the same terminology, in non-Marxist sociology.[11]

A key role in the development of contemporary Marxism has been played by debates concerning ideology. The importance of ideology in Marxist sociology stems from its theoretical function of providing the linkage between the conceptualisation of the 'objective' structures and processes, and the subjective experience of individuals. The recent developments in the theorisation of ideology have gone a long way towards breaking away from the determinist equation of ideology = appearance = falsity = false consciousness. The importance of Althusser, whatever other controversies surround his essay on *Ideology and Ideological State Apparatuses*,[12] lies precisely in the fact that he insisted upon ideology as a real relationship. Taken alongside the theoretical trends which have been concerned to break with economic reductionist versions of Marxism, the result has been that the concept 'ideology' has become one of central importance not only in Marxist sociology but in sociological theory in general.

Law and legal relations demonstrate both the reality and effectivity of ideology. Legal relations are constituted in and through ideology. There is no better field of analysis than this to undertake the examination of fundamental ideological categories, the subject, equality, rights, justice, etc., etc., whilst at the same time to be forcefully made aware that such ideological elements are not mere glosses or mystification but have quite specific and determinant effects in the social, political and economic contests and struggles that find their way before the courts. Thus, for example, 'justice' is no more the self-evident reality of every Western democracy than it is a deceitful manipulation of the ruling class; rather its reality is the result of complex social struggles which manifest themselves in important shifts in the legal and political construction of justice. Two essays in this collection focus upon the ideological dimension of law. Pat Allatt's essay on stereotyping and the family explores the role of ideology in first marking the whole substantive content of social security legislation in the post-Beveridge era and then the role that such ideologically forged legislation plays in reinforcing and legitimising the ideological constructs. Mike Brogden on the other hand explores the contradictory and volatile popular conceptions of police and policing.

The ideological dimension of law is closely related to issues

surrounding the *form of law*. This constitutes a third area of convergence and focus of current attention. In this field the convergence is
surprisingly wide since it links the concerns of mainstream sociology
of law with what have been some of the most influential developments
in jurisprudence. The important focus of theoretical liberalism within
the sociology of law is with the quest for the elusive role of 'legality'
or with what Selznick identifies as the quest for the 'distinctively
legal'.[13] The same preoccupation lies at the heart of Roberto Unger's
concept of 'legal order'.[14] This concern with the uniqueness of law,
explicitly focused on the concern with 'a special ideal — the rule of
law',[15] also provides the frame of reference for post-war jurisprudence
epitomised by the confluence of the concerns of Hart and Fuller and
the liberal theory of justice of Rawls. Iain Stewart draws upon this
jurisprudential tradition in his paper 'Sociology in Jurisprudence' to
problematise the way in which sociology has conceptualised law.

   This proximity between liberal sociology of law and modern jurisprudence is perhaps not surprising, but what is less obvious, and
probably more controversial, is the proximity of these concerns to
those of contemporary Marxist theories of law. At the point in its
development when Marxist theories of law arrived at a common recognition of the inadequacies of an instrumentalist conception of law as the
unproblematic tool of the ruling class to be deployed in the protection
of its class interests, then attention necessarily becomes directed
towards a concern with the attempt to come to grips with the 'distinctively legal'. If law is no longer conceived as an instrument then
'legality' emerges from the shadows as a constitutive element of law.
This changing focus of concern has clear political roots in the dual process which is characterising the contemporary left in Western Europe.
On the one hand the displacement of the traditional division between
revolution and reform manifests itself in the coming together, albeit
hesitantly, of political traditions that can be identified for our present
purposes as Euro-Communism and left social democracy, both positions
sharing a common critique of the 'actual socialism' of Eastern Europe.
One important element of this critique is the insistence on the
necessary place of some conception of 'the rule of law' in the socialism
of the future. We say *some form* of the rule of law because it does not
necessarily incorporate what constitutes a major element of that
concept in classical liberal theory, namely the doctrine of the separation of powers. The second strand in this process is the commitment to
a radical or participatory democracy embracing a plurality of interests
and political forces which, once purged of an adherence to a one-
dimensional conception of the passage from 'bourgeois' to 'proletarian
democracy', necessitates the rule of law as a guarantee of this pluralist
conception of socialism.[16]

The major theoretical vehicle in which the concern with 'legality' has been explored by Marxists has been through the analysis of the *form* of law. A major expression of this development has been the rediscovery of the writings of Pashukanis who argued that the bourgeois character of law stemmed not from the substantive content of its rules but from its very *form*, which was itself a necessary expression of capitalist commodity relations. Since law is inescapably bourgeois in form, socialist and communist societies in abolishing capitalist relations must also abolish law or rather ensure that it 'withers away'. There has been a veritable explosion of both translations of and commentary upon this early Soviet jurist.[17] The rediscovery of Pashukanis is not accidental; he provides a powerful exemplification of a mode of analysis which has been widely employed in recent years. It owes much to a thorough and theoretically attentive reading of Marx's *Capital* which has become a precondition for most recent Marxist analysis. Form analysis starts from Marx's chapter on commodities and derives the form of law (and of the state)[18] from the nature of the social relations resulting from the centrality of commodity relations in capitalist societies. The commodity relation constructs the relations between economic actors (as buyers, sellers, employers, workers, etc.) as relations between 'legal subjects', a fetishised form of the real or concrete economic agents. Legal subjects are conceived as the possessory bearers of rights, analogous to commodities as the bearers of value. Law, as relations between legal subjects, is thus the form though which abstract equivalence is established between atomised economic subjects.

Two consequences, one positive and the other negative, stem from this theoretical framework. The positive element is that, in focusing attention of the specific form of law, it breaks with the instrumentalism (law as instrument of ruling class) of vulgar Marxism. In so doing it invites us to analyse the real effects of legal relations as constitutive elements of social relations whilst at the same time being able to grasp the real roots of 'legality' (rights, liberties, rule of law, due process, etc.) which are in turn a condition of the effectivity of law. Yet on the other hand by imposing an identity, legal form = commodity form, it erects insurmountable barriers to grappling with the problem of the 'form of law/forms of law'. The derivation of the form of law from commodity relations produces a general correspondence between law and private or contractual law.[19] As a result it creates considerable difficulties for the analysis of forms of law which do not correspond to the commodity/contractual ideal type. Thus the analysis of both public law and criminal law is rendered extremely difficult; since they do not correspond to the unitary essence they are treated as being secondary;[20] hence the law of corporate forms can only be dealt with as a fictional form of the essential relation. Not only is specific analysis of divergent forms of law impeded, but there is an ever-present tendency to lapse back into the formalism, characteristic of traditional jurisprudence, of a concern with law-in-general, 'the Law'. It is for this reason that the designation of the problem in terms of form of law/ forms of law helps guard against lapsing into an essentialist conception of law, law-in-general, and against an empiricist approach to particular laws without attention to their systematic integration (not necessarily complete and without contradiction) as 'law'.

The fourth and final field of convergence between the concerns of the sociology of law and those of general sociology is found in the relationship between law and the state. The relationship between law and the state is arguably the central and at the same time most difficult question confronting the sociology of law. The relationship between law and the state has been an absent dimension of the sociology of law. Or to be more accurate, the overwhelming weight of sociology of law has been founded on unexamined assumptions about this relationship subsumed within the doctrine of the separation of powers. The radical critique of the sociology of law has as a result tended to place considerable emphasis upon the failure of sociology of law to grapple with the law-state relationship. One consequence is that it has encouraged a critique based on negation or reversal of conventional wisdom,[21] and adopted a naively instrumentalist conception of law, which failed to grapple with the complexity of the law-state relationship.

One of the most important developments within Marxist theory over the last decade has been in the field of the theory of the state. Its intellectual and political inspiration lies in the attempt to escape from the inherent limitation of instrumentalism which reduces the state to a tool of a class and which assumes the identity of the dominant economic class(es) and the 'ruling class'.[22]

Despite the difference between Poulantzas and Miliband,[23] their now famous debate clearly recognised one thing: rejecting the simple equation of class power and state power produces a whole set of new and significant problems. As a consequence the primary focus in these debates and the subsequent discussion has been on the relationship between classes and the state. In the course of this discussion the analysis of the relationship between the institutions of the state has been touched upon but rarely explored in any depth. Yet this is precisely the key question involved in any discussion of the relationship between law and the state. The rejection of positions that conflate law and state does not justify an uncritical or formal acceptance of the classical doctrine of the separation of powers. Poulantzas helpfully suggests the need to distinguish between institutional separation and the processes whereby one institutional level gains 'dominance' over other levels.[24] Yet there persists in Poulantzas a tendency to explore questions about law through a procedure, which avoids this simple location of the processes of domination/subordination within the state; he focuses instead on a dualistic treatment, contrasting the institutional or state character of law and the ideological dimension of law.[25]

Yet what is absent in this treatment, and even more so in Miliband's,[26] is any attempt to deal with the structural location of legal systems in capitalist societies. What is of critical importance is to grapple with the way in which Poulantzas' general thesis concerning the function of the state as 'the factor of cohesion between the levels of a social formation'[27] is made manifest through the specific institutional location of law within the state. The fact that Poulantzas' discussion is couched in terms of the 'function' of the state does not, in itself, justify the conclusion drawn by some that he is adopting a functionalist perspective. Nevertheless, such an accusation would have come to have substance if law was analysed as operating to provide one element, for example that of legitimation of the general function of the state since it would import an *a priori* functional integration of state institutions.

The question of the relationship between state and law is only just beginning to be posed. It is perhaps a small pointer to the importance of the question that the British Sociological Association has over such a short period given over its annual conference to the themes of the state (1977) and law (1979) in which the type of questions posed above emerged. The upsurge of sociological attention to the state in recent years is likely to continue to explore the problems of the location of law since it so self-evidently exhibits features of autonomy, whether relative or absolute, and yet its institutional location is unambiguously part of the state. The significance of these issues is reinforced by a wider-ranging concern with the changing form of the capitalist state in which an expanded role is played by law and legislation as the direct and immediate agency of economic and social policy. The papers in this volume by Bob Fryer dealing with state intervention in the labour market through redundancy payments legislation and by Chris Whelan on the use of coercive state power in industrial disputes reflect this increasing concern with the examination of the relationship between law and the state.

The four areas of debate and controversy surveyed are ones which find their place in the essays collected in this volume. It is the persistence of these themes in current discussions within the sociology of law which accounts for the importance of these discussions in the general debates within sociology, and thereby lifts the sociology of law above its more restricted sub-disciplinary status. One important result is that the sociology of law is an expanding field of interest in Britain. A further important consequence of this widened interest is the much

greater attention being given to problems of the theoretical framework
within which the field can best develop; in contrast to the earlier
empiricist character of British sociology of law which was most concerned with very specific analyses of the internal mechanism of the legal
process, the underlying thrust was the concern with reforming the
administration of law and specifically with overcoming the gap between
legal ideal and legal practice (the gap made famous by American realist
jurisprudence between 'law in books' and 'law in action').[28] The rapid
expansion of Marxist interventions has undoubtedly stimulated a theoretical debate that had previously been absent.[29]

Yet at the same time the Marxist intervention, which has in the main
operated at a relatively abstracted theoretical level, is increasingly
turning its attention to empirical investigation. The turbulent debates
amongst Marxists since the late sixties have subsided to some degree in
a climate which proposes that the further resolution of the theoretical
debates must be worked through in relation to empirical studies; hence
the growing repetition of Lenin's dictum that Marxism is 'a concrete
analysis of a concrete condition'.[30] Because of the general emphasis
upon the historical dimension of Marxist method, and the well-
established tradition of Marxist history in Britain, it is not therefore
surprising that historical studies have been the most obvious product
of this new turn in Marxist analysis. Of particular importance in this
respect is the work of Edward Thompson and his colleagues,[31] and a
similar interest has been occasioned by the Marxist response to
Foucault's analysis of imprisonment and discipline.[32] A stage of
detailed historical studies is likely to become a more pronounced
feature. The papers by David Sugarman and Roger Cotterrell in this
collection are significant expressions of this new concern with the
historical analysis of law; they both exhibit a keen awareness of the
need to go beyond the narrowly empiricist and institutional styles of
legal history and thus of the centrality of theory in historical research.
Indeed David Sugarman's paper discusses many of the wider theoretical
problems raised in this introduction and in the paper by Corrigan and
Sayer.

The historical analysis of the effectivity of law has a parallel in an
already established tradition within the sociology of law, usually
referred to as 'emergence studies', in which attention is focused upon
the formation of individual legislative enactments. The element which is
sometimes hidden under the 'emergence' label is that between studies
concerned with the actual formation of emergence of the enactment
and those which then go on to study the effectivity or impact of the
legislation in question. The latter focus tends to be less well developed
in British research. It should further be noted that whilst the individual
legislative item provides a ready definition of research focus it tends to

suggest that what is significant for the sociology of law is the impact or effectivity of that which is 'new'. This orientation tends to define as being of no special importance to the sociology of law the study of the effectivity of ongoing areas of law. This is not the case with regard to the criminal law and procedure, but remains rather startlingly so for most of the civil and public law.

The potential that exists is for a considerable extension of work that focuses explicitly on concrete or empirical problems, but is more fully conscious of the theoretical issues that underpin the analysis of the effectivity of law. The essays collected in this volume mark a step towards this integration of theoretical and empirical concerns.

Notes

1. C.M.Campbell and P. Wiles, 'The Study of Law in Society', *Law and Society Review*, 10 (4) (1976), pp. 548-78.
2. See I. Taylor, P. Walton and J. Young, *Critical Criminology* (Routledge and Kegan Paul, 1975).
3. E.P. Thompson, *Whigs and Hunters: The Origins of the Black Act* (Penguin, 1977); see in particular the section on 'the rule of law' in concluding chapter, pp. 258-69.
4. S. Hall, C. Critcher, T. Jefferson, J. Clarke and B. Roberts, *Policing the Crisis: Mugging, the State, and Law and Order* (Macmillan, 1978).
5. The distinction between 'sociology of law' and 'socio-legal' is widely used in the literature. Whilst the distinction has a plausibility and a certain limited use it should not be allowed to pose as an adequate classificatory device. Its great fault is to reproduce the very widespread error of distinguishing between 'theoretical' and 'empirical' sociology as if it were the case that empirical sociology was in some sense non-theoretical. As in the wider field so in the study of law and society, there are no theoretically neutral empirical studies.
6. This 'revelation' of conflict finds its clearest expression in such authors as Richard Quinney, *The Social Reality of Crime* (Little, Brown, Boston, 1970) and William Chambliss, in W. Chambliss and R. Seidman, *Law, Order and Power* (Addison-Wesley, 1971). For a critical discussion of this radical tradition see A. Fraser, 'Legal Theory and Legal Practice', *Arena*, 44-45 (1976), pp. 123-57 and J. Young, 'Left Idealism, Reformism, and Beyond' in B. Fine *et al.* (eds), *Capitalism and the Rule of Law* (Hutchinson, 1979).
7. It is important to stress that whilst there existed a tendency for conflict to 'adopt' Marxism as an available and articulated theory this should not be taken to imply as some have done that the latter is simply an extension of the former. This trend is found in both the supporters (see W. Chambliss, 'Functional and Conflict Theories of Crime' in W. Chambliss and M. Mankoff (eds), *Whose Law? Whose Order?* (Wiley, 1976)) and opponents (see J. Hagan and J. Leon, 'Rediscovering Delinquency: Social History, Political Ideology and the Sociology of Law', *American Sociological Review*, 42 (1977), pp. 387-98) of conflict sociology. Against these trends it is necessary to insist (but not to develop the argument fully) that this adoption of Marxism only became possible because of the quite separate resurgence that can be traced back to the political and intellectual developments within Marxism in Western Europe.

8. See for example R. Lefcourt, *Law Against The People* (Random House, 1971).

9. See in particular P. Anderson, 'The Antimonies of Atonio Gramsci', *New Left Review*, 100 (1977), pp. 5-78, and Hall *et al.*, *Policing the Crisis*, Chs 7 and 8.

10. L. Althusser, 'Ideology and Ideological State Apparatuses' in *Lenin and Philosophy* (New Left Books, 1971).

11. P. Berger and T. Luckmann, *The Social Construction of Reality* (Allen Lane, 1967).

12. Althusser, 'Ideology and Ideological State Apparatuses', pp. 121-73.

13. P. Selznick, *Law, Society and Industrial Justice* (Russell Sage, New York, 1968), p. 5.

14. R. Unger, *Law in Modern Society* (Free Press, 1976).

15. Selznick, *Law, Society and Industrial Justice*, p. 3.

16. For an illustration of these features of recent socialist debate see K. Coates and F. Singleton, *The Just Society* (Spokesman, 1977), and E.P. Thompson, 'Introduction' to *The Review of Security and the State* (Julian Friedmann, 1978), and Jock Young's insistence on the importance of 'socialist legality' in 'Left Idealism, Reformism and Beyond', pp. 11-28. From a very different tradition see the discussion of socialist legality in G. della Volpe, *Rousseau and Marx* (Lawrence and Wishart, 1978).

17. For translations of Pashukanis see C. Arthur (ed.), *Law and Marxism: A General Theory* (Ink Links, 1978), and for a more extensive selection P. Beirne and R. Sharlet (eds), *Pashukanis: Selected Writings on Marxism and Law* (Academic Press, 1980). These replace the earlier and very defective translation in J. Hazard (ed.), *Soviet Legal Theory* (Harvard University Press, 1951). For critical discussion of Pashukanis see the Introductions to the above and P. Hirst, *On Law and Ideology* (Macmillan, 1979), S. Redhead, 'The Discrete Charm of Bourgeois Law', *Critique*, 9 (1978), and S. Picciotto, 'The Theory of the State, Class Struggle and the Rule of Law' in Fine *et al.* (eds), *Capitalism and the Rule of Law*.

18. See, for application of form analysis to the state, J. Holloway and S. Picciotto, *State and Capital* (Edward Arnold, 1978).

19. It is not the intention to deny the significance of contractual relations and contract law; indeed contractual conceptions provide a dominant ideological framework through which both legal and social relations are constructed; but this importance must not be extended so as to invest the commodity-contract relation with essentialist properties as the determinant form of the all juridic relations.

20. For the elaboration of this argument concerning the analysis of criminal law and public law by Pashukanis see, respectively, Redhead, 'The Discrete Charm of Bourgeois Law' and Hirst, 'Pashukanis and the Legal subject' in *On Law and Ideology*.

21. For an analysis of the role of 'reversal' and 'negation' in radical literature see A. Hunt, 'The Radical Critique of Law: An Assessment', *International Journal of the Sociology of Law*, 8 (1980), pp. 33-46.

22. The influence of instrumentalist views of the state amongst Marxists is particularly significant because it was a field in which Marx himself had produced, in practical form, such masterly historical studies as *The Eighteenth Brumaire of Louis Bonaparte* and *The Civil War in France*.

23. See the republication of the original *New Left Review* (nos 58 and 59) exchanges in J. Urry and J. Wakeford (eds), *Power in Britain* (Heinemann, 1973) and continued in *New Left Review*, 82 and 95, and in R. Miliband, *Marxism and Politics* (Oxford University Press, 1977).

24. N. Poulantzas, *Political Power and Social Classes* (New Left Books, 1975), pp. 303-7.

25. Ibid., p. 348, in which juridical-political ideology is identified as 'the dominant region of the dominant capitalist ideology'.

26. R. Miliband, *The State in Capitalist Society* (Quartet, 1973), pp. 124-30. Law is dealt with only through a discussion of the judiciary and under the unproblematic conception of 'servants of the state'. Miliband's conclusion that 'the dominant economic interest in capitalist society can normally count on the active goodwill and support of those in whose hands state power lies' (p. 130) reduces the effective integration of state functions to the 'goodwill' of 'servants' united by common background and outlook. This position is retained in *Marxism and Politics* where he explicitly states his assumption that 'a common social background and origin, education, connections, kinship, friendship, a similar way of life, result in a cluster of common ideological and political positions and attitudes, common values and perspectives' (p. 69).

27. Poulantzas, *Political Power and Social Classes*, p. 44.

28. Campbell and Wiles, 'Study of Law in Society', pp. 549-60.

29. Grace and Wilkinson, *Sociological Inquiry and Legal Phenomena*, can be clearly seen as an attempt to grapple with the emergence of radical theories of law and to state a claim for subjectivist sociological theory in the field.

30. V. Lenin, 'Kommunismus', *Collected Works*, vol. XXXI, p. 166.

31. Thompson, *Whigs and Hunters* and D. Hay *et al.*, *Albion's Fatal Tree: Crime and Society in Eighteenth Century England* (Allen Lane, 1975).

32. M. Foucault, *Discipline and Punish* (Allen Lane, 1975); see also M. Ignatieff, *A Just Measure of Pain* (Macmillan, 1978) and D. Melossi, 'Institutions of Social Control and Capitalist Organisation at Work' in *Capitalism and the Rule of Law*, pp. 100-17.

2 HOW THE LAW RULES: VARIATIONS ON SOME THEMES IN KARL MARX

Philip Corrigan and Derek Sayer[1]

. . . every form of production creates its own legal relations, forms
of government, etc. In bringing things which are organically related
into an accidental relation, into a merely reflective connection, they
display their crudity and lack of conceptual understanding. All the
bourgeois economists are aware of is that production can be carried
on better under the modern police than e.g. on the principle of
might makes right. They forget only that this principle is also a legal
relation, and that the right of the stronger prevails in their 'constitutional republics' as well, only in another form.

> Karl Marx, *Grundrisse* (1858, p. 88)

[The buying and selling of labour power.] There alone rule Freedom, Equality, Property and Bentham. Freedom, because both
buyer and seller of a commodity, say of labour-power, are
constrained only by their own free-will. They contract as free agents,
and the agreement they come to, is but the form in which they give
legal expression to their common will. Equality, because each enters
into relation with the other, as with a simple owner of commodities,
and they exchange equivalent for equivalent. Property, because
each disposes only of what is his own. And Bentham, because each
looks only to himself. The only force that brings them together
and puts them in relation with each other, is the selfishness, the gain
and the private interests of each.

> Karl Marx, *Capital* I (1867b, p. 176; compare 1867a, p. 280)

The primary concern of this paper is with how historical materialism
can help us understand the natural-seeming rule of law and transform it
into conscious and collective rule by the people. We start, but do not
stop, with Marx's work.[2] Our discussion is, we hope, not without
relevance to the current 'conjuncture' in Britain, which is being defined
from one side as restoring 'Law and Order' and on the other as 'Defend
Legality!' We should not take the prevailing — and increasingly tech-
nicist — definitions of such terms in the form in which they are
'provided' for us. On the contrary, we should seek to establish how
limited is the range of the acts to which we are 'encouraged' to apply
these narrow conceptions of justice and legality, and how many are
the fundamentally vicious, cruel and unequal social relations which are

placed firmly outside these vocabularies and in the realms of 'misfor-
tune' and/or 'economic necessity'. When aged people die through
socially preventable diseases, cold or hunger, we ought to be shouting
'*Murder*!' When social assets are 'hived off' and rendered into private
capital, we should be shouting '*Theft*!'

I

Capital, I contains some of Marx's fullest discussions of specific bodies
of law: labour legislation from the 1349 Statute of Labourers to the
Factory Acts of his own time. We begin here, not because we can find
in these discussions a cut and dried Marxist theory of law, but rather
the opposite. These laws, and Marx's observations upon their passage,
offer considerable resistance to the easy generalisation and accompanying avoidance of history which attend even the best of Marxist
theorising in this area.[3] That is to the good: any half-way adequate
theory of law (or anything else) needs to be grounded in just such
awkward and empirical particulars.

However much capital may now rule through the 'silent compulsion' of 'the "natural laws of production" ' (1867a, p. 899) — and
arguably Marx exaggerates, in these passages, the extent to which it
ever can or does — things were not always thus. 'It is otherwise during
the historical genesis of capitalist production. The rising bourgeoisie
needs the power of the state', that 'concentrated and organised force of
society, to hasten, as in a hothouse, the process of transformation of
the feudal mode of production into the capitalist mode, and to shorten
the transition' (1867a, p. 899-900; cf. pp. 382, 915-16). 'Force', Marx
adds, 'is the midwife of every old society pregnant with a new one. It is
itself an economic power' (1867a, p. 916; cf. Engels, 1890b). And its
use, he makes clear, is 'an *essential* aspect of the so-called primitive
accumulation' (1867a, p. 900, our italics). 'The *governments*, e.g. of
Henry VII, VIII etc. appear as conditions of the historic dissolution
process [of the feudal mode of production] and as makers for the conditions of existence of capital' (1858, p. 507, our interpolation). The
conditions in which the 'natural laws' of political economy could
operate had to be forcibly *constructed*. Laws of a most unnatural kind
bore very directly on that struggle: 'grotesquely terroristic laws',
'bloody legislation against the expropriated' (1867a, p. 899, 896) the
passage of which did not merely mark, express, sanction, confirm or
codify the economic power of the rising bourgeoisie, but was integral
to its creation.

Capital being the social relation it is, 'the expropriation of the agri-
cultural producer, of the free peasant, from the soil is the basis of the

whole process' (1867a, p. 876). If the law — to indicate, not for the last time, something of the complexity with which we are dealing — initially sought to curtail such depredations (see 1867a, p. 879-81), it ended up orchestrating them:

> The advance made by the eighteenth century shows itself in this, that the law itself now becomes the instrument by which the people's land is stolen . . . The Parliamentary form of the robbery is that of 'Bills for Inclosure of Commons' . . . (1867a, p. 885)

This does not *merely* represent a legal gloss on *de facto* theft. Enclosure Acts are part of a wider, and centuries-long, transformation of communal and feudal into *private* property, within which not only who owned what but what it meant to be an owner were turned upside down.[4] It is a far cry from feudal tenure to the *jus utendi et abutendi*, from the complicated network of personal lordship and servitude, substantial right and obligation, which enmeshed lord and serf, to the substantially rightless but formally free wage labourer voluntarily contracting with his or her chosen employer. Property did not have just to be seized, it had to be *constituted*. Legitimation, here, means more than mere ratification:

> The form of landed property with which the incipient capitalist mode of production is confronted does not suit it. It first creates for itself the form required by subordinating agriculture to capital. It thus transforms feudal landed property, clan property, small-peasant property in mark communes — no matter how divergent their juristic forms may be — with the economic form corresponding to the requirements of this mode of production . . . it divorces landed property from the relations of lordship and servitude, on the one hand, and, on the other, totally separates land as an instrument of production from landed property and landowner . . . Landed property thus receives its purely economic form by discarding its former political and social embellishments and associations, in brief all those traditional accessories, which are denounced . . . as useless and absurd superfluities by the industrial capitalists themselves, as well as their theoretical spokesmen, in the heat of their struggle with landed property. (1865, p. 617-18)

We shall return to this 'purely economic form' of property below.

The dispossessed, meantime, had also to be jollied into playing the proletarian part for which Nature had clearly intended them. 'It is a matter of historic record', Marx notes, that, whether by inclination or for want of an alternative, they tried 'begging, vagabondage and robbery

... but were driven off this road by gallows, stocks and whippings, onto the narrow path of the labour market' (1858, p. 507).[5] He details various of the cruel, but doubtless effective, statutory instruments of 'the discipline necessary for the system of wage-labour' (1867a, p. 899) — branding, mutlilation, flogging, hanging — in Chapter 28 of *Capital*, I, which is wholly given over to the theme. The same work enumerates, in comparable detail, the legislative panoply which fixed wages, extended the workday, and outlawed workers' combinations through five long centuries.[6] Thus, in large part, was 'a working class which by education, tradition and habit looks upon the requirements of that mode of production as self-evident natural laws' (1867a, p. 899) made.

II

Marx's discussions of the Factory Acts have somewhat different emphases. Here, it is less what is done to the working class than what the working class does to capital which claims his attention. And we see another side of the law altogether. Marx certainly sees factory legis-lation as both generally 'appropriate' to the conditions of developed capitalist production and, in certain cases, of clear benefit to capital. Chapter 15 of *Capital*, I discusses at length the various ways in which the 'industrial revolution . . . is . . . helped on by the extension of the Factory Acts' (1867a; p. 605).[7] More generally, Marx avers that factory legislation is 'just as much the necessary product of large-scale industry as cotton-yarn, self-actors and the electric telegraph' (1867a, p. 610);

> these highly detailed specifications, which regulate, with military uniformity, the times, the limits, and the pauses of work by the stroke of the clock, were by no means a product of the fantasy of Members of Parliament. They developed gradually out of circum-stances as natural laws of the modern mode of production. (1867a; pp. 394-5)

One might cavil at 'natural laws'. But, Marx immediately adds, 'their formulation, official recognition and proclamation by the state were the result of a long *class struggle*' (ibid., our italics). And it is this class struggle which forms the central thrust of his account.

'The legal limitation and regulation of the working day', he writes, was 'wrung step by step in the course of a civil war lasting half a century' (1867a, p. 409; cf. ibid., p. 413). Factory Acts had to be *imposed* by labour on capital, and they were felt and fought as an imposition: 'Capital never becomes reconciled to such changes — and this is admitted over and over again by its own representatives — except "under the pressure of a General Act of Parliament" ' (1867a, p. 610). 'Nothing characterises the spirit of capital better than the history of English factory legislation from 1833 to 1864' (1867a, p. 390). It is, in *Capital*'s account (1867a, b, Ch. 10, sec. 6), a history of considerable (and carefully traced) complexity, of vying intra-class interests (big and small capital, industrial and manufacturing capital, capitalists and state servants),[8] of shifting inter-class alliances and battle-lines, of trickery, perfidy and opportunism. But it is above all a history, as Marx sees it, of intransigent, outraged and jealous defence of its 'freedom' to contact by capital, in the face of unremitting and ever-increasing popular pressure for its statutory limitation. The Ten Hours Bill is for Marx emphatically a *'working men's measure'* (1864, p. 345).

Importantly, it is not just the fact of a working-class victory Marx celebrates but what it betokens. He describes the Factory Acts as a triumph for 'social control' (1867a, p. 411), by which he means something rather different from (and measures his distance from) the modern 'radical' sociologist. He is speaking of control by society over the 'private interest' of capital, conscious and collective regulation of its hitherto unhampered *jus utendi et abutendi*. Factory legislation, he writes, represents 'a first conscious and methodical reaction of society against the spontaneously developed form of its production process' (1867a, p. 610). The Ten Hours Bill had something to exalt it beyond 'the immense physical, moral and intellectual benefits hence accruing to the factory operatives' (though, take note, Marx *is* very much aware of the latter):

> This struggle about the legal restriction of the hours of labour raged the more fiercely since, apart from frightened avarice, it told indeed upon the great contest between the blind rule of the supply and demand laws which form the political economy of the middle class, and social production controlled by social foresight, which forms the political economy of the working class. Hence the Ten Hours Bill was not only a great practical success: it was the victory of a principle; it was the first time that in broad daylight the political economy of the middle class succumbed to the political economy of the working class. (1864, p. 845-6)

The legal objectives of the contending classes have their roots in different worlds. Liberal freedom from control faces socialist freedom *as* control; we see here a wholesale conflict of entire political and moral economies. In however partial, limited, or disorted a way, Marx discerns in the Factory Acts the imprint of the political economy of the future.

III

Alongside these discussions of particular bodies of legislation, there exists in Marx a sustained critique (in the fullest materialist sense: attempt to unearth the historical conditions and boundaries[9]) of the rule of law as such, which we need to consider before drawing any conclusions on the basis of the above. The beginnings of this critique lie in that *Rheinische Zeitung* experience of the force of 'material interests' which led Marx to withdraw to his study in the spring of 1843 and re-examine Hegel's *Rechtsphilosophie*,[10] and it is developed through various writings of the next three years. It receives its clearest formulations in *The German Ideology*, especially in the understudied Part II. But it is not a phenomenon of Marx's early years alone: its themes are thoroughly congruent with those which dominate his later political writings, especially after the Paris Commune of 1871.[11] And it is implicit, as Pashukanis (whose perceptiveness is all the more remarkable in view of his probable lack of access to many of the relevant early texts[12]) has argued, in the fundamental supposedly 'economic' analysis of *Capital* itself. This critique is more difficult to present, for by comparison with the analyses considered so far it remains rudimentary and unsatisfactory. Others have noted that Marx arrived at a theory of the relation of law and the modern state to capitalism before his analysis of the latter was far advanced (Colletti, 1975; Draper, 1977). It shows: his grasp of the connections he is asserting remains one which is, by *Capital*'s standards, relatively abstract and philosophical. But it remains a considerable, and largely neglected, starting-point.

Pashukanis begins his text by remarking Marxists' tendency to treat law entirely from the viewpont of its (class) content, and neglecting to explain why this content should take specifically legal forms in the first place. Exactly the same is true of most Marxist discussions of what Marx describes as 'the *modern* state – based on *freedom of labour*' (1846, p. 205). Whilst the class content of state activity is more or less convincingly demonstrated, why bourgeois rule should take (*inter alia*) the specific form of an institutionally distinct state at all is rarely explained.[13] But Marx does provide at least the beginnings of an explanation of both.

It is well known that Marx anticipated the transcendence of the state with Communism. He makes clear, in a number of places, that this does not mean the disappearance of *any* public power; rather, in the words of the *Manifesto*, 'the public power will lose its political character' (1848, p. 505).[14] He means, first, that it will cease to be an instrument of class rule. But he also, in our view, means something more than this. 'Separation', he writes in *Theories of Surplus Value*, 'appears as the normal relation in this society . . . in this society *unity* appears as accidental, *separation* as normal' (1863, Part I, p. 409). What, for Marx, gives the modern state its specifically *political* character is as much its *separation* from 'civil society', its constitution as a distinct polity in apparent opposition to the sphere of the private and personal, as its class character pure and simple. And, he argues, the rule of law is precisely the form of social regulation best suited to such circumstances. But before we elaborate on that, we need to clarify what is meant here by 'separation'.

Some of Marx's most uncompromising denials of the independence of law and politics from 'the production and reproduction of real life' can be found in exactly those texts which develop his analysis of the state/civil society separation furthest, especially *The German Ideology*;[15] while fifteen years later he was to summarise the conclusions of just this body of work in the stark claims of the 1859 *Preface*. He cannot plausibly be interpreted, therefore, as conceding to law and state any substantive or real autonomy. 'Separation' must be understood within the boundaries of his wider and oft-repeated attack on any such notions. Happily there are clear and (relatively[16]) consistent formulations throughout the relevant literature which allow us to do just this. In brief,[17] Marx's argument is not that law and politics are separate from production and its relations as such, but rather that in commodity production the social relations of production *themselves* take the forms of apparently exclusive political and economic spheres. 'Polity' and 'economy' are in other words but different facets of one and the same set of production relations. One of Marxism's most common, and theoretically *and* practically crippling errors has been to collapse *production* into 'the economic' as defined *within* that (phenomenally persuasive) separation. Consider carefully the grammar of the following pronouncements:

Civil society embraces the whole material intercourse of individuals within a definite stage of development of productive forces. It embraces the whole commercial and industrial life of a given stage, and, insofar, transcends the state and the nation, though, on the other hand again, it must assert itself in its external relations as nationality and *internally must organise itself as* state. (1846 p. 89, our italics)

This conception of history . . . relies on expounding the real process of production ·. . . and comprehending the form of intercourse connected with and created by this mode of production, i.e., civil society in its various stages, as the basis of all history; describing it *in its action as* the state . . . (1846, p. 53, our italics)

In fine, 'the hitherto existing production relations of individuals are bound also to be expressed as political and legal relations' (1846, p. 363).

Marx gives these general assertions a clear historical reference with his observation that 'the term "civil society" emerged in the eighteenth century, when property relations had already extricated themselves from the ancient and medieval community. Civil society as such only develops with the bourgeoisie . . . ' (1846, p. 89). An earlier text, *On the Jewish Question*, connects commodity production, the modern state and the rule of law even more closely: 'the establishment of the political state and the dissolution of civil society into independent individuals — whose relations with one another depend on law', Marx writes, 'is accomplished by *one and the same* act' (1843, p. 167). Max Weber draws attention to the same set of connections in his study of what he (instructively) calls the 'national citizen class' in his neglected and brilliant *General Economic History*.[18]

For his part, Marx explains these 'separations' in terms of private property and the division of labour (which he sees as 'identical expressions' for 'the power of disposing over the labour-power of others' (1846, p. 46; cf. ibid., pp. 64, 206, 230-1; 1847b, pp. 318 *et seq*.)):

> The material life of individuals . . . their mode of production and form of intercourse, which mutually determine each other — this is the real basis of the state and will remain so at all stages at which division of labour and private property are still necessary . . . The individuals who rule in these conditions — leaving aside the fact that their power must assume the form of the state — have to give their will — a universal expression as the will of the state, as law. (1846, p. 329; cf. ibid., p. 46)[19]

We cannot pursue Marx's analysis fully here. It should be admitted, however, that even in the comparatively materialist formulations of *The German Ideology* (let alone the taut aphorisms of the *Jewish Question*) its statement remains relatively abstract. In brief, Marx argues that in general where individuals are separated (and, as *Capital* was later to exemplify,[20] in competition) through the division of labour then the only form in which real or illusory communal interests can be expressed or secured is through 'practical intervention and restraint by the illusory "general" interest in the form of the state' (1846, p. 47). It is the strictly historical *bellum omnia contra omnes* that is the anarchy of commodity production which calls forth Leviathan. And in particular, he contends, the state is 'the form of organisation which the *bourgeois* are compelled to adopt, both for internal and external purposes, for the mutual guarantee of their property and interests' (1846, p. 90, our italics). He elaborates — and in the process shows how what are now known as Badman (law as coercion) and Goodman (law as consent) theories of legal relations can be tackled in a materialist manner:

> the fact that they [the individuals who rule in these conditions] enforce their own will in the form of law, and at the same time make it independent of the personal arbitrariness of each individual among them, does not depend on their idealistic will. Their personal rule must at the same time assume the form of average rule. Their personal power is based on conditions of life which as they develop are common to many individuals, and the continuance of which they, as ruling individuals, have to maintain against others, and, at the same time, to maintain that they hold good for everybody. The expression of this will, which is determined by their common interests, is law. It is precisely because individuals who are independent of one another assert themselves and their own will, and because on this basis their attitude to one another is bound to be egotistical, that self-denial is made necessary in law and right, self-denial in the exceptional case, and self-assertion of their interests in the average case. (1846, p. 329)

The bourgeoisie is unique among ruling classes in the extent to which it is, so to speak, divided against itself. The rule of law — 'equality in the conditions of competition' (1867a, p. 621)writ large — is the form in which, at the cost of individual self-limitation, it can none the less formulate and impose something approaching a class will. To put the same point the other way, 'it is precisely because the bourgeoisie rules as a *class* that in the law it must give itself a general expression' (1846, p. 92, our italics). Further division of labour — specialised civil servants, politicians, lawyers, etc. — is in its turn, of course, implicit in these social forms themselves (1846, pp. 343, 357).

Capital without doubt offers a much more precise (and historically specific) exposition of the 'totality of *bourgeois* relations of production' in which, by the mid-1840s, Marx already knew '*private property* . . . consists' (1847b, p. 337; cf. 1847a, p. 197). As Pashukanis above all has demonstrated, it accordingly offers the possibility (and in occasional passages, like, say, those commenting on factory owners themselves agitating for standardisation of factory legislation, the reality) of a correspondingly more concrete grasp of the why and wherefore of the specific legal forms assumed by those relations. But it does not, in our view, alter the essentials of Marx's analysis as developed here, his characterisation of the state/civil society separation and attendant rule of law as *par excellence* social relations of commodity (note: *not* simply capitalist[21]) production.

IV

In general, then, Marx analyses specifically legal forms of regulation —
i.e., the enforcible adjudication of disputes between contending parties
on the basis of an established body of rule and/or precedent, a form the
criminal law shares — as having their material groundwork in the privat-
isation of civil society which reaches its zenith in capitalist commodity
production. He also offers some sharp observations on these forms
themselves which call for further mention.

   The German Ideology berates the unfortunate Max Stirner for
knowing nothing about

> the medieval mode of production, the political expression of which
> is privilege, and the modern mode of production, of which *right* as
> such, *equal* right, is the expression, or about the relation of these
> two modes of production to the legal relations which correspond to
> them. (1846, p. 327)

This opposition between privilege and (equal) right is fundamental to
Marx's analysis of the rule of law. Integral to the rise of generalised
commodity production, he argues, is the wholesale destruction of
particular, concrete and substantial privileges of distinct estates within
the feudal polity, and their replacement by universal, but at the same
time abstract and formal rights of legal subjects as such; incidentally,
an extremely bloody and protracted affair, involving not merely the
legal levelling of lords but equally the abrogation (and often the crim-
inalisation) of common and customary rights of the people.[22] Going
along with this is the increasing institutional specialisation of the law:
'two completely different systems of production form the basis of the
individuals where court and administration are separate, and where
they are combined in a patriarchal way' (1846, p. 316n; cf. ibid.,
p. 342; Weber, 1918, p. 82).

   We may best exemplify by reference to Marx's discussion of what he
with some justice regards as the paradigm of bourgeois right, the *jus
utendi et abutendi.* The *utendi* is any possessor's right to use and
abuse his possessions without let or hindrance. As such, it represents
property in what appears to be its simplest and most universal form: as a
direct relation of person and thing. We will return to this appearance
shortly; for the moment, it is the nature of Marx's critique that we wish
to emphasise. *Capital* argues thus against Hegel:

> Free private ownership of land, a very recent product, is according
> to Hegel, not a definite social relation, but a relation of man as an
> individual to 'Nature', an absolute right of man to appropriate all
> things . . . [Hegel] makes the blunder at the outset of regarding as
> absolute a very definite legal view of landed property — belonging to
> bourgeois society — [and] understands 'nothing' of the actual nature
> of this landed property. This contains at the same time the
> admission that 'positive right' can, and must, alter its determinations
> as the requirements of social, i.e. economic, development change.
> (1865, p. 615n)

This recalls *The German Ideology*'s attack twenty years earlier on
Stirner's identical misconceptions about 'owning' (1846, p. 206; cf.
ibid., pp. 228f.). Both he and Hegel make the mistake of treating
juridical forms 'not as *historical* but rather as eternal categories' (1865,
p. 615, our italics).

For the right of property to be *definable* with this simplicity[23]
— abstractly and universally, without reference to the nature or
standing of either owner or object owned — supposes, so Marx argues,
definite historical conditions that were long and often violent in the
making. The *utendi* summates a social order in which individuals on the
one hand, and their possessions on the other, have been 'freed' from the
complicated web of localised and definite privileges and obligations —
'in brief all those traditional accessories, which are denounced . . . as
useless and absurd superfluities' — through which their intercourse had
previously been organised:

> In civil law the existing property relations are declared to be the
> result of the general will. The *jus utendi et abutendi* asserts on the
> one hand the fact that private property has become entirely inde-
> pendent of the community, and on the other the illusion that private
> property is itself based solely on the private will, the arbitrary
> disposal of the thing. (1846, p. 91; cf. 1865, p. 615f.).

For the majority, it needs once again to be interjected, that 'freeing'
was very much a mixed blessing. Marx's accounts of, for instance, the
doings of the Duchess of Sutherland (1853a; 1867a, pp. 890-5) show us
some of what had to be done to *enforce* a reality of which the *utendi*
could in due course make self-evident descriptive and moral sense. The
facts he reports (and their like) have lost none of their power to stun.
Nor, we might remember, have the Sutherlands and *their* like lost much
in the way of the 'ancestral' properties thus constituted.

Marx extends his argument in various places (notably the *Jewish
Question*) to comprehend the Rights of Man *per se*. The abstract legal

subject, with universal (and thus equal) legal rights, is but the juridical
counterpart of his schizoid dweller in the world of the commodity,
bourgeois and *citoyen* (see 1843, pp. 160-8; nor should the invariable
masculinity of the rights celebrated in these abstractions be allowed to
pass unremarked). Bourgeois right, whether *de l'homme* or *du citoyen*,
is of its very essence a pure right, a right defined independently of the
particulars of empirical circumstance or the facts of real difference. Of
course, such formal emphasis on equality before the law can and does
coexist with substantive clustering and grouping which facilitates
systematic inequality: at any given point in time not inconsiderable
numbers (and classes) of people — lunatics, criminals, blacks, Roman
Catholics, women, those who do not own real property, and their ilk
— have always been excluded in law from the full rights of (sane, law-
abiding, white, Anglo-Saxon, protestant, male and propertied) 'Man'.[24]
But these are, precisely, exclusions, and there is — in more than a figur-
ative sense — a world of difference betwen this and, say, the feudal
state of affairs. Similarly, Marx is obviously correct when he points
out that so long as factual inequalities persist such 'equal' right is
necessarily *'a right of inequality, in its content'* (1875, p. 16). Law is
class (and colour, and gender) law as much because of as despite its
equal application. But what interests us, for the time being, is the form
itself. When Marx sardonically observes that 'the most fundamental
right under the law of capital is the equal exploitation of labour-power
by all capitalists' (1867a, p. 405; cf. ibid., pp. 381, 621) he is not
just making a cheap jibe, but a fundamental point about what equity
can amount to in the bourgeois polity. In a mode of production predi-
cated on private property, division of labour, and all the ensuing separations of individual and social, private and public, 'civil society' and the
state, what equity could there be that does not have the general form
of 'equality in the conditions of competition' (1867a, p. 621)? The
divorce of form from content fundamental to bourgeois right and the
indifference to real difference which constitutes legal impartiality
perfectly mirror — and sanctify — that set of separations.

From here Marx moves swiftly to an analysis of what such legal
forms and vocabularies can accomplish. Classes rule ideologically as well
as materially, and the ideologies through which they seek to normalise
their rule are rarely merely false. Basic to their hegemony (but see
Edward Thompson's remarks on the pitfalls of this category, 1965,
pp. 72-4, 1977a; cf. Corrigan, Ramsey and Sayer, 1979a, Pt II, essay
4) is the idealisation of the material *facts* of their dominance, the
attempted translation of 'the relations which make the one class the
ruling one' (1846, p. 59) into what *Capital* calls 'natural, self-understood
forms of social life' (1867, p. 75; cf. 1867a, p. 168). Classes rule most
securely through the achievement of the Obvious, wherein the condi-

tions of their dominance become the taken-for-granted categorial
and moral frameworks through which people apprehend 'reality'. It
needs immediately to be stressed that this *is* an achievement: not only
did it have to be fought for (against alternatives that had first to be
smashed); it *remains* fragile and precarious, demanding unceasing
maintenance (against new forms of those same alternatives, which
will gum up the works . . .). We have touched a little on some of what
was involved in naturalising the conditions of capitalist production
above. A book like *Policing the Crisis* shows the maintenance men still
very much on the job.

Law, for Marx, is central to this front of the class struggle, giving
enforceable definition and fixity to the wider moral classifications of
capitalist production. Integral to the law is a moral topography, a
mapping of the social world which *norm*alises its preferred contours —
and, equally importantly, suppresses or at best marginalises other ways
of seeing and being. This amounts, in sum, to a *coded denial of experience*. As we argued four years ago:

> the production relations of capitalism constitute a repertoire of
> experiences, languages do not merely name but constitute the world
> within which people work, also 'offering' explanations of any
> abrasion between expectation and experience . . . A ruling class will
> always try to ensure that everybody says and knows what, in
> practice, the majority do not and cannot experience. But that
> dominated class — and this is the dimension which is overlooked —
> will experience what it appears cannot be said (at least in public
> discourse). That makes that experience private; but also immoral,
> infidel and heathen. (Corrigan and Sayer, 1975, p. 28; cf. 1978)

There is, as we discuss later, a gap between experience and the
encouraged forms of expression. For Marx and Engels,

> the conditions of existence of the ruling class . . . [are] ideally
> expressed in law, morality, etc., to which [conditions] the ideolo-
> gists of that class more or less consciously give a sort of theoretical
> independence; they can be conceived by separate individuals of that
> class as vocation, etc., and are held up as a standard of life to the
> individuals of the oppressed class, partly as embellishment or recog-
> nition of domination, partly as a moral means for this domination.
> (1846, pp. 419-20)

The ethereal *dramatis personnae* of the legal repertoire are in fact
idealisations of mundanely concrete and historical kinds of individual
related in quite definite ways. In 'this society of free competition, the

individual *appears* detached from the natural bonds, etc., which in
earlier periods make him the accessory of a definite and limited human
conglomerate' (1857, p. 83, our italics). All the characteristic forms
of law — its boundaries of public and private, its notions of interest and
adjudication, its conceptions of right, liability and equity — presuppose
and seek to regulate relations between such apparently detached
individuals. But the appearance is just that: 'the epoch which produces
this standpoint, that of the isolated individual, is also that of the
hitherto most developed social (from this standpoint, general) relations'
(1857, p. 84). As with the *utendi*, so more generally: apparently the
simplest and most natural of categories (of property, of subjectivity, of
right and liability), 'the most general of abstractions arise only in the
midst of the richest possible concrete development' (1857, p. 104).
This is the world the law *takes for granted*.

Elsewhere, Marx uses the term 'fetishism' to describe how political
economists metamorphose 'the social, economic character impressed on
things in the process of social production into a natural character
stemming from the material nature of those things' (1878, p. 229). We
might usefully speak of a similar fetishism attendant on the vocabularies and forms of law. 'Man as a member of civil society, *unpolitical*
man, inevitably appears . . . as the *natural* man. The *droits de l'homme*
appear as *droits naturels*' (1843, p. 167).[25] Like property as defined by
the *utendi*, the legal subject appears as natural, primeval, original, and is
thus conceivable in vocabularies that are formal, abstract and universal,
only within definite social relations and following a long and bloody
history. But this very formality, abstraction and universality of legal
categories (and the seeming timelessness of the rituals they articulate)
mask the relations and bury the history. The very forms of law, in sum,
threaten to accomplish much. In them the moral topography of the
bourgeois universe is extended into a premise of any human sociation
(or at least, civilisation) whatsoever. At the same time, and by the same
acts, vocabularies in which we could voice the substantive particularities
of social experience — of class, of gender, of place — are declared, quite
literally, out of court.

V

Let us begin to try and pull some of these threads together. To start
with, it is clear that for Marx law was no mere superstructure.[26] We
have argued that he saw the phenomenal and categorial separations of
the 'economic' from the 'political' and 'legal' in commodity-producing
society as characteristic forms of existence of production relations
themselves. But even if this is rejected, his acknowledgement of the

indispensability of state action through the law to the genesis of capital
is enough to establish that he did not regard law as *per se* a secondary
and derivative phenomenon. This does not, in our view, testify to a
conflict between Marx's more general assertions and his empirical and
historical analyses. We suggest rather that the first should be read in the
light of the second. Part VIII of *Capital*, I does not invalidate the 1859
Preface's conclusion that 'neither legal relations nor political forms
[can] be comprehended . . . by themselves . . . on the contrary they
originate in the material conditions of life' (1859), or *The German
Ideology*'s corollary 'there is no history of politics, law . . . etc.' (1846,
p. 92; cf. ibid., pp. 37, 91). It provides the means for interpreting such
propositions. And what it suggests is that for Marx law and state cannot
be understood apart from the making and sustaining of particular
modes of production, because they are an essential part of the relations
between people through which such production is alone carried on.
Law and state, in short, are constitutive of particular ways of making
things: by no means epiphenomena of some notionally pure 'economic
base' existing elsewhere – the latter is a reification and a myth – but,
in Edward Thompson's words, 'deeply imbricated within the very basis
of productive relations which would have been inoperative without
this law' (1975, p. 261).

No more did Marx see the law as an unproblematic ruling-class
instrument, manipulable at will. It is not, in any case, merely an instrument: the whole thrust of the above analyses is to expose the thinglike
appearances which succour this delusion as forms of definite social
relationships. Nor is it so readily manipulable. Marx's celebration of
the Factory Acts is sufficient testimony to what he thinks the people
can do through the law, while to acknowledge, as he does, universalisation of rights and liabilities as (at the very least rhetorically) central
to its forms is to point to the severe limits of any such naked class
manipulation. This is not to deny the class origin of judges and magistrates or the existence of sometimes obviously partisan legislation and
judgements – who could, living in Mrs Thatcher's Britain? – nor to
endorse social democracy's view of the law as another kind of instrument, one that is sufficiently powerful and at the same time sufficiently
neutral to bring about the socialist transformation of society. Nor is it
to gainsay Marx's observations concerning the inequity of applying
rigorously equal standards to the congenitally unequal. We will return
to this below. It is to make the point, again with Thompson, that:

> if the law is evidently partial and unjust, then it will mask nothing,
> legitimise nothing, contribute nothing to any class's hegemony. The
> essential precondition for the effectiveness of law, in its function as
> ideology, is that it shall display an independence from gross manipu-

lation and shall seem to be just. It cannot seem to be so without
upholding its own criteria and logic of equity; indeed, on occasion,
by actually being just. (1975, p. 263)

Engels long ago acknowledged that 'law must not only correspond to
the general economic condition and be its expression, but must also be
an *internally coherent* expression' (1890b; cf. 1890a, 1893, 1894). We
cannot occlude the ruling class and the judiciary quite so easily. There
is a certain gap — maybe even a necessary gap, following our argument
in III above — between (to use Basil Bernstein's terms[27]) the 'powered'
and the 'controllers', the class whose rule is established by capitalism's
relations of production and (one of) the mechanisms through which the
reproduction of those relations is achieved. We can measure their
distance in the way we could all *see* that Sir John Donaldson's
Industrial Relations Court was not a proper court — which episode
says a lot in itself about how the law rules. This is not to reintroduce
the independence ('relative' or otherwise) of law from the relations of
production. It is simply to appreciate the constraints imposed by the
specificity of the forms those relations take.

To the extent that capital rules within and through the law — and
it would be as well to remember that it does not always or everywhere
do so — the specific forms and procedures of law circumscribe its
freedom and constrain its modes of action. A materialist analysis of
how and why the law — as opposed to capital or the state — rules
might, we suggest, do a lot worse than begin by following Marx in his
recognition of both the *force* of law, its internality to the relations of
capitalist production, and the vital kernel of *truth* in its protestations
of (certainly, bourgeois) equity. We might then begin to understand one
part of our history. The law has historically been a major battleground
of working-class struggle because, bluntly, it *is* important. It is
important whether capital rules unfettered or hedged about by factory
legislation. It is important whether the state rules through the courts or
through torture chambers and concentration camps — or, to take an
instance not too far from home, through tanks on street corners, the
suspension of *habeas corpus* for years on end and 'modified' rules of
evidence in political trials. Law is important precisely because it is
not a mere 'superstructural' gloss on some capitalist power residing
elsewhere, but constitutive of the very modalities of its exercise.

Intellectuals have sometimes been inclined to forget this. Marx did
not; and nor, more to the point, do those whom it most affects.
Workers' movements have *had to* take the law very seriously indeed,
because law — and its absence — has very material effects on workers'
lives. Minimally, it is a defensive matter: rights, because they are not
natural, have to be fought for and need to be *guarded*. Anyone inclined

to doubt this might look, *inter alia*, at a number of recent pieces on picking of juries and suspects' rights.[28] That is not to mention the legislative feast we are undoubtedly in for on the ancient theme of dangerous combinations. Maximally, it is a matter, if not of legislating the socialist commonwealth — that has to be collectively and self-consciously accomplished, it cannot be donated — then certainly of extending territory captured (however temporarily) from the capitalists. The relevant points here are exactly those emphasised by Marx in his discussion of the Factory Acts. First and foremost, the law used in this way *has* considerably transformed for the better the lives of working-class men and women in Britain over the last 150 years. There is a certain kind of intellectual for whom the changes in education, housing, health and transport can be totally disregarded in favour of a reified and ultimately despairing model of 'social control'. We reject this stance utterly, and for reasons that are analytic as well as political and moral. It is this basis in historical experience — in *know-ledge* of the force of law — that, far more than any 'false consciousness' (or the wearisome 'corporate' instincts of the British working class), accounts for the strength of social democracy. Its promise of the trans-formability of the world through politics and law has had at least enough experiential support to make plausible the charges of betrayal or failure of nerve where expectations have not been fulfilled; more than enough, one might hazard, in the face of the available 'revolu-tionary' alternatives (both Communist and Trotskyist). Second, as Marx noted, the law used thus *does* represent a forcible imposition of social mores on capital, albeit in forms which blunt, dilute and at times come close to obliterating their working-class content. Legal forms of regula-tion are indeed alien and (in the fullest sense) alienated vehicles of socialist purposes, since they are designed precisely to govern societies in which production is *not* consciously, collectively or democratically administered for the common wealth. Still, the posing by Owen and the Ricardian socialists of 'Society' against 'the Individual' was and remains a classic moment of socialist theory, capturing a reality experienced by collectivities of workers in many forms of struggle and daily life. The single representative of the enemy — employer, landlord, rentier, polit-ician, bureaucrat — against the group, the collective, the class, the people — this is central to the imagery of socialism. It is an incono-graphy we neglect at our peril.

These things have been said before — recently by Maureen Cain, by Alan Hunt, and with eloquence and urgency by E.P. Thompson[29] — and they need to be said again. But they are not *all* that needs to be said.

VI

When the 'blue locusts' were first imposed on working-class communities they often met strenuous resistance.[30] If that resistance is
remembered at all today it is likely to be only to confirm how badly
the constables were needed. There is an unspoken paradigm through
which we are 'encouraged' to comprehend such events:[31] that of an
Original Vacuum filled by timely state — or commercial — provision.
In this case the presumed vacuum is a state of lawlessness: which term,
not irrelevantly for our argument, has since come to be synonymous
with a general breakdown of order. The history of education, or of
welfare services, or of arts and leisure facilities, is commonly viewed
through the same prism. The result is a twofold distortion. First,
provision was never made simply into a vacuum but against existing and
potential working-class (and other) alternatives, which were in the
process — or, often, independently and specifically — marginalised,
absorbed or suppressed. Second, that provision always came in definite
social forms which differed from these alternatives and actively contributed to their destruction. Education, for instance, was provided in
the form of schooling following decades of state assault on various
independent working-class organisations through which people had
sought to educate themselves.[32] The provision of 'order' through
policing is no more neutral a donation. The resistance, we suggest,
testifies less to the innate criminality of the lower orders than their
defence of other ways of ordering human communities: ways
embedded in an alternative political and moral economy.

There is, in sum, another part to our history. The sort of 'respect'
for the law discussed in our previous section is not infrequently coupled
with a pervasive and energetic contempt for The Law — the police often
being identified with/as The Law — and its rule. We know the foregoing example was emblematic. Nowadays the police are more likely to
be accepted. Yet it should not be imagined that we are talking only of
'the past', and acceptance (as a fact of life) should not be mistaken for
endorsement. The contempt survives, albeit in forms which are — to
adapt Bernstein again — less elaborated: in jokes, aphorisms and sayings,
stories, traditions, taboos and images rather than explicit ideologies.
We are again in the presence of that gap between class experience and
the forms available for its public expression, which blinds so many
intellectuals to all but the obvious phenomena of 'apathy' and
'reformism'. The contempt is evident in the extent to which 'The Filth'
is still — after 150 years — not welcome in working-class communities;
in a continuing and widespread reluctance to involve 'The Law' in what
are regarded as intra-community affairs; or in the (eloquent) *expecta-
tion* that coppers will be bent. The brutal deaths of Liddle Towers and

Jimmy Kelly provoked a good deal of anger on Tyneside and Mersey-side: not much shock.

This contempt too has its roots in material experience. First, there is immediate, personal experience. If you are working class this is likely to be overwhelmingly experience of the receiving end of the law (beginning with growing up on streets where 'doing nothing'[33] is taken as *a sign of trouble*[34]). Second, there is a wider, class, historical experience, sedimented in and communicated through the humour, the anecdotes, the values, the routines, which can compass and comprehend that personal experience. The lessons of many lifetimes of 'brushes with the law' form a part of the cultural resources through which working-class men and women define themselves and the world around them. We do not refer only to the grand symbols of the labour movement — Taff Vale and the Tolpuddle Martyrs, Saltley gates and Grunwick — though these are important; nor even just to the wider popular imagery of, say, the Great Train Robber — pulling a fast (and big) one — and of the sentences it occasioned. It is less the particular experience*s* than the collective *experience* which remains long after they have been forgotten — the *knowledge* which results and which is expressed in a diversity of ways — that we are trying to point to. In it the past does indeed live in the present.

We are suggesting that alongside the tactical seriousness[35] displayed in all working-class approaches to law there exists just as practically grounded an awareness of the ultimate poverty of bourgeois right, which amounts, in sum, to a strategic contempt: contempt minimally for the hypocrisy of the law's protestations of fairness and equity, the old old refrain of one law for the rich and another for the poor. But also more than this: a contempt for the limits of law which has its roots in popular notions of justice which are at the same time more inclusive and more substantial than their bourgeois legal counterparts. In a sense socialism is the elaborated statement of this contempt. The poor have always known that, to be real, rights must be material. Which brings us back to Marx and Engels, and *their* contempt for the 'narrow horizon' (Marx, 1875, p. 17) of bourgeois right: 'as far as law is concerned, we with many others have stressed the opposition of communism to law, both political and private, as also in its more general form as the rights of man' (1846, p. 209; cf. 1853b, p. 185). This is *not* mere ultra-left hyperbole (or intellectuals' abstraction). It is just such a strategic elaboration of an enduring and authentically popular strand in what Thompson calls the 'sub-political' or Williams the 'pre-emergent' forms of working-class consciousness. Marx and Engels are giving political voice to a truth which is widely known without necessarily or always being explicitly recognised: law *is* an essential relation of commodity production the rule of which — preferable as it undoubtedly is to lawless tyranny — is not yet the rule of the people, and the justice of which is less than equitable. And they articulate this, crucially, *in opposition to* another attempted 'elaboration': that 'offered' by the forms of law themselves.

For law, too, is centrally concerned with classification and framing. Ideologies of law as 'society's moral code' or 'common sense writ large' conceal a fundamental truth. The dominant material relations of capitalism do ground a morality — or, to be more accurate, what we referred to above as a moral topography: they operate as the hidden organising principle of ostensibly descriptive and technical classifications which are in fact shot through with evaluations. And law does draw much of its authority, in Weber's sense — and hence much of its power — from its embeddedness in this wider moral fabric. We need not labour what every lawmaker knows, save perhaps to stress that we are not resurrecting that marvellously self-subsistent 'consensus' once so beloved of sociologists. The classifications in question — as Don Quixote long ago discovered[36] — are materially grounded and historically contingent. We wish more particularly to emphasise the *active* indeed often the vanguard role of law within this wider context of moral classification. For law is not merely the passive reflection of the moral and material framework which overarches it. There is a dialectic to be observed.

These moral classifications are themselves the object of (attempted) class and state regulation. Since they *are* materially grounded — in experiences, moreover, which vary as to class, and gender, and colour, and all the other material 'classifications' capitalism reproduces — they are not infinitely malleable. There is a hard material core to the experience of the majority which time and again resists 'encouraged' classification; which may cause uncertainty, unease and self-doubt, but which *can* provide the foundation for new ways of seeing.[37] But there is nothing automatic here. The character of social consciousness is only ever partially determined by its raw material: like any other artefact it has had to be worked and shaped, its substance given form. This forming *is* a class struggle: on the one side, to give that material core voice; on the other, to regulate (variously: incorporate and absorb; interpret and distort; deride or deny; outlaw or taboo) its expression and exorcise its threat. Law is absolutely central to this regulation. It is at once a remarkably coherent elaboration of the moral essentials of bourgeois civilisation — the rule of law lies at the very heart of bourgeois culture (if not always of capitalist practice) — *and* a uniquely powerful vehicle for their propagation, backing immense authority with the physical force of the state. It is, in sum, the major means through which the boundaries of preferred moral classifications can be regulated: defined, emphasised, focused, nuanced, shifted.[38]

Law works on and with wider moral classifications to 'encourage'

some ways of seeing (and being) and outlaw others. This is most visible
in statute law, or in judicial decisions of clear policy intent. The
coercive machinery sanctioned by the 1966 and 1971 Social Security
Acts, for instance, 'works' far less through the (minimal) money it
saves the DHSS in detected frauds than by the way it mobilises existing
moral resources — some of them, it should be said, working class and
even proto-socialist — to make 'Scrounger' a descriptively plausible and
morally pertinent category in which to place those of our fellow human
beings who are currently 'surplus' to capital's requirements. This is, or
at any rate ought to be, a sociological commonplace. Less often
remarked is a coding that operates more insidiously, more pervasively
and at a deeper level: less through this or that statute, judgement, or
exemplary sentence than cumulatively; not in particulars at all so much
as in the entire gamut of what rules as The Law. As we tried to show in
IV above, precisely the most fundamental, general and abstract of legal
categories — law's grammar, so to speak — articulate (even while
concealing) relations that are irreducibly bourgeois. *This* is the wood we
so often miss as we stumble about in the tactical thickets.

The law, *per se*, codes — and codes violently. Law rules least noticeably yet most directly through its forms: through the ways in which it
'encourages' us to present and represent ourselves. Law rules by
seeming to be above (even while quietly employing) material
differences and celebrating pure individuality and equality. What we
seek to establish is that *such* equality hurts. It is in fact doubly violent.
First, the terms and rituals of law do violence to the majority in
exactly the way Bernstein over twenty years ago showed 'Standard'
English to: they force people to express themselves in codes that rule
out the core of what constitutes their lives. For individuality is not
pure (or equal): it is their material differences that make people who
they are. Second, the paradigm of individuality which law sanctifies as
the universal human essence (with its timeless 'common sense') is in
reality an idealisation of a (bourgeois) state of being most of us *cannot*
aspire to. Not only can we not signify our own mundane experiences
within the forms of law; we are also struck dumb and made to feel
stupid by our distance from this fictive ideal. Mr Peachum (of *The
Threepenny Opera*) said much the same thing more succinctly when he
gave it as his opinion that the law is made for the exploitation of those
who do not understand it.

This is *not* a matter of 'deprivation', and increasing access is not
enough. To win in this 'game' will *always* be at immense cost, since
winning implies speaking a language and playing a part which systematically denies the identity and power of working-class people. Class
victories at law are articulated in forms which actively, insistently and
rigorously denegate their class character and origins. Law must indeed

be taken seriously.But a major part of that taking seriously must lie in recognising that law as such is an alienation of social powers that need to be reappropriated if the people are to rule. When the latter keep their distance from The Law, it is a class distance.

Notes

1. This paper was originally presented in slightly different form to the 1979 Conference and has benefited from discussion at that presentation. It draws heavily on our work with Harvie Ramsay: *Socialist Construction and Marxist Theory* (Macmillan and Monthly Review Press, 1978: cited as *SCMT*); *For Mao* (Macmillan and Humanities Press, 1979 cited as *FM*); and 'The State as a Relation of Production' (originally presented to 1977 BSA Conference, published in revised form in P. Corrigan (ed.), *Capitalism and State Formation* (Quartet, 1979)). We also draw on Corrigan, 'State Formation and Moral Regulation in 19th Century Britain' (PhD thesis, University of Durham, 1977) and Sayer, *Marx's Method* (Harvester and Humanities Press, 1979). We would like to thank Piers Bierne for comments.
2. Cain and Hunt, 1979, is a valuable and welcome anthology of the writings of Marx and Engels on law: though one inclined in our view to under-represent what we identify as the latter's *strategy* of contempt for its rule.
3. Pashukanis (1929; cf. Arthur, 1976; Redhead, 1978) for instance presents a dazzling analysis of the connectedness of bourgeois legal and economic forms. But it is an analysis which is overwhelmingly formal and pays little attention to their history. Poulantzas likewise – notwithstanding important shifts in his recent writings – separates, in best structuralist fashion, investigation of the origin of social forms from that of their functioning. A simlar strategy is evident in Collins, 1979 and Picciotto, 1979. Leaving aside the question of the empirical adequacy of purely formal or 'synchronic' analyses – the facts often prove to have a mulish 'irrationality' in face of the schemata – the effect of ignoring history is to obscure the *accomplished* – and therefore the fragile and precarious – character of these forms, and efface the *alternative* forms against the challenge of which they were constructed. We cannot, even methodologically, sever social forms and 'structures' from the class (and other) struggles through which they are brought into being *and sustained* without doing great violence to our understanding. Social forms *are* class struggles.
4. We extend these remarks below and provide documentation. Marx's awareness of the wholesale transformation goes back to his first brush with 'material interests' in 1842 (Marx, 1842a: cf. note 10 below) and extends through discussions in *The German Ideology, Grundrisse* and *Capital*: see, *inter alia*, 1846, pp. 63-4, pp. 89-92, 206-8, 228-31, 342-3, 362-4, 372-3; 1858, pp. 471-514 *passim*; 1865, Chs 37, 47 *passim*; 1867a/b, Part 8 *passim*; cf. Ditton, 1977; Linebaugh, 1976; Lazonick, 1974, 1978; Hammen, 1972; Mayer, 1959; and similar accounts.
5. Corrigan and Corrigan, 1978, offers an extended discussion of the making and sustaining of the labour market (until 1870) which makes use of Marxist resources and modern historiography; Corrigan and Corrigan, 1977, examines the modern relations between labour and the state. See Beier, 1974; Chambliss, 1964; Slack, 1974; Thompson, 1967, 1975; Vorspann, 1977; Malcolmson, 1973; Silver, 1967; Bailey, 1978; Pollard, 1963, 1965, for discussions of labour discipline/vagrancy from the fourteenth to the nineteenth century.

6. Marx, 1867a/b: see especially Chs 10 and 28.

7. Corrigan, PhD, Ch. 3 (discussion of Leonard Horner) shows how (a) factory legislation was trans*formed* into a service for vanguard capital, (b) inspection-in-general worked to favour *particular* forms of capitalist enterprise. Similar ways in which technical/administrative regulation alters social/cultural form have been noted in relation to e.g. fire regulations and music halls.

8. See also Corrigan, PhD, Chs 3 and 4; Blelloch, 1938; Foster, 1974. It is important to see the Factory Acts within a wider and crucial moment of state and thus legal reconstruction. Such 'moments' can be understood at various levels (Raymond Williams constantly returns to the same period to examine the novels; Edward Thompson gives us the 'pre-emergent forms' to use Raymond Williams's exceptionally useful concept) – we suggest that they are the times when the *codes* are changing. Others would have to include the 1530s and the English Revolution in all its phases. In the present century the 1960s seem to have a particular significance in contrast to the explicit 'Reconstruction' after the 1914-18 and 1939-45 wars. Cf. Paul Corrigan, 1979c.

9. See Sayer, 1979a, Chs 5 and 6; 1979b; *SCMT*, Ch. 1; for elaboration.

10. Marx discusses this, 1859; Draper (1977, Part 1) is among the few commentators who give this experience due weight. Cf. especially Marx, 1842a, b.

11. See especially Marx 1871a, b, c, above all the sections dealing with the internal organisation of the Commune; and 1872, 1874 and 1875, especially pp. 14f. and Part 4 of the latter; cf. Draper, 1962, 1970; Ollman, 1978; *SCMT*; *FM*.

12. Marx's critique of Hegel's *Rechtsphilosophie* was first published in 1927, the Paris Manuscripts and *The German Ideology* in 1932. If Pashukanis used the MSS he makes no mention of the fact. His own book was first published in 1924, the last revisions being made in 1929.

13. Holloway and Picciotto, in the Introduction to 1978, are a notable exception: though much of the material translated in their volume, for all its suggestiveness, suffers badly from the formalism discussed in note 3 above.

14. In other respects Marx specifically repudiated the proposals in the relevant section of the *Manifesto*, after the experience of the Commune, precisely because of their *Statism*: see Marx 1872; cf. all texts cited in note 11 above, and Corrigan, PhD thesis, Ch. 2, plus Engels, editorial note of 1885 (*Collected Works* 10, p. 285).

15. See Marx, 1846, pp. 37, 91, 92.

16. Sometimes in these texts – as also occasionally in later ones like *The Eighteenth Brumaire* (the relevant parts of which he implicitly corrects, however, in *The Civil War in France*) – Marx comes close to speaking of the state really being independent when no single class clearly rules: see e.g. 1846, pp. 90, 105. But in general he is adamant that such occasions are appearances of independence or are untypical of bourgeois rule.

17. We develop this argument very much more fully in 'The State as a relation of production'; see also Corrigan and Sayer, 1975. Cf. Godelier, 1978; Gellner, 1979.

18. Weber, 1920, Part IV. Although Weber agreed with Trotsky (the words he agreed with are quoted in Deutscher, 1954, p. 320) that 'Every State is founded on force' he always stressed the relationship between force and legitimacy: 'The State is a relation of men dominating men, a relation supported by means of legitimate (i.e. considered to be legitimate) violence' (1918, p. 78). Gramsci's well-known statement is congruent with this: 'The State is the entire complex of practical and theoretical activities with which the ruling class not only justifies and maintains its dominance but manages to win the active consent of those over whom it rules' (1934, p. 244).

19. The journal *Radical Philosophy* has done much to illuminate the material grounds of legal philosophising (cf. Skillen, 1977, Ch. 1 and pp. 97f.). See Hart, 1958, 1961; Devlin, 1959, 1962, 1965; the summary volume by Dworkin (1977) is very useful; the whole hidden market for labour and capital emerges in the debate over Rawls (1972; Barry, 1973; Daniels, 1975). More general is the debate over 'sovereignty' interestingly specified in a *Times* editorial (19 April 1975): varied approaches are Laski, 1930; Schaar, 1970; Nicholson, 1973; Yaney 1966. The best historical discussions are Kiernan, 1965 and Part IV of Weber's *General Economic History*; cf. Corrigan, PhD thesis, Chs 3 and 4; MacFarlane, 1974; Frankel, 1970; Deutsch and Senghaas, 1975; and Nozick, 1975. Hume, 1977, pp. 205f., 'Political Society', is a major starting-point used by Bentham, Austin and Green and countered by Marx in *The German Ideology*. The idea of the law as refined common sense is very strong: see e.g. the obituary for A.L. Goodhart (*The Times*, 11 November 1978). The state (and national interest) complement common sense such that the needs of the former can deny the latter, can deny 'natural justice' as with the Agee and Hosenball cases or the Presidential Order in India extending the Internal Security Act (27 June 1973, quoted in *The Times*, 17 July 1973) which simply removes all rights for any 'person (including a foreigner)'.

20. See *Capital*'s discussion of manufacturers themselves agitating for standardisation of factory legislation in furtherance of equality in the conditions of competition: 1867a, pp. 381, 393, 621f. Cf. Foster, 1974 and notes 7 and 8 above.

21. This is crucial for socialist construction (as Pashukanis also argues) *inter alia* because it implies (a) the utopianism of attempting to introduce 'proletarian law' by fiat and (b) the need for continued struggle under socialism to overcome, with their conditions, legal forms as such. It also underlines again that legal forms and the rule of capital cannot simply be elided: though the former may reach their zenith in societies founded on the capitalist mode of production – the most 'advanced' form of commodity production and division of labour – they are not *only* found there, nor is there any good reason why they should be.

22. See, above all, Thompson, 1963, 1967, 1971, 1974, 1975, 1977a, and Hay *et al.*, 1975. A valuable review essay of this and related literature is W.G. Carson and J. Ditton (1979). Cf. notes 4 and 5 above.

23. There are close parallels here, also noted by Pashukanis, with Marx's analysis of the classical economists' category of labour (1857, pp. 103-5). On the latter, and historical categories in Marx generally, see Sayer, *Marx's Method*, Ch. 4 and elsewhere.

24. Gender differences have been studied by Smart, 1976; Sachs and Wilson, 1978; Hagan *et al.*, 1979; and see here Coote's analysis of the Equal Employment Commission in *New Statesman*, 1 December 1978, and letter, ibid., 15 December 1978. See also Robertshaw and Curtin, 1977; Humphries, 1977; Barker, 1978; Kuhn, 1978; McIntosh, 1978; Corrigan and Corrigan, 1978; Thane, 1977; Thompson, 1977b; Hill, 1978; Alcock, 1979 – these are all discussions of different facets of familial form. Further information can be obtained from the journals *m/f; Women's Studies; Feminist Review*; and the volumes *Women Take Issue* (Hutchinson, 1978) and *Feminism and Materialism* (Routledge, 1978), plus Bland, McCabe and Mort, 1978; Wainwright, 1978; and Harrison and Mort, 1978. A current group 'excluded' from the citizenry (and full legal rights) are migrant workers: see Corrigan, 1976; Berger and Mohr, 1975; Guyot *et al.*, 1978.

25. In this connection it is worth noting – especially given recent attacks by Hindess and Hirst and others – that Marx considered it a *fruitful error* to think that money is merely a symbol because 'under this error lurked a presentiment that the money-form of an object is not an inseparable part of the object, but *is*

simply the form under which certain social relations manifest themselves. In this sense *every commodity is a symbol*, since, in so far as it has value, *it is only a material envelope of the human labour spent on it'* (1867b, p. 90). In other words (cf. Corrigan & Sayer, 1975, 1978) it is better to err on the side of realising that things were *made* and can be *different*.

26. At least not in any accepted sense: we have set out our own view of what we think Marx was attempting with his (unfortunate) metaphor in our other writings.

27. Despite the problem of a seeming formalism and abstraction in his work (on which Bernstein is not silent: 1977b, p. 2) it is a major resource, on which we have drawn heavily in this paper. We would like to acknowledge the help of Mike Smee in this connection. Pat Carlen (1976) also makes excellent use of his formulations; cf. some of the 'deep structure' of Phil Cohen's work or Stuart Hall's, 1978a. This is, perhaps, also the point at which to indicate our major debt to the work of Edward Thompson and Raymond Williams (whose direct and sharp materialism is evident in his recent *Politics and Letters*). All have a lifelong concern with *class*: see Bernstein, 1977b, p. 181; 1977a; Thompson, 1976 and 1979 interviews, and of course his 1963 work – one of the best *theoretical* resources we have – and Williams, 1956; 1958; 1961, Part III; 1973, pp. 363f.; 1977b, Part II. Class is also a category central to much of the work of Stuart Hall and the CCCS: cf. Hall, 1978b, c and *Radical History Reivew*, no. 19, 1979.

28. See Thompson, 1978c, d, e; Kettle, 1979. It seems entirely to the point that within years of the ending of any property requirement for jury service (itself introduced as part of the bourgeoisification of justice in 1665, formally abolished in 1972 – a nice *three-century* run) attempts were made to alter the 'rules of the game' away from juries towards other actors in the drama of justice. The staging posts of these alterations are indicated in Harriet Harman and John Griffith's NCCL pamphlet *Justice Deserted* (pp. 14 on) and in an earlier comment by Geoff Robertson (*New Statesman*, 10 December 1976).

29. Cain, 1977; Hunt, 1977; Cain and Hunt, 1979, especially Introduction to Ch. 6; Thompson, 1975, pp. 258-69; 1978 c, d, e.

30. See in particular Storch, 1975, 1976; or for exemplification of how the regulation and classification we address in this section took place, the work of David Jones and Alan Bainbridge on mid-nineteenth century Wales: Jones, 1974; 1976b; 1977; Jones and Bainbridge, 1979 and references.

31. See Corrigan, 1979, and Lazonick, 1978, for fuller discussion of this, and references there.

32. See *inter alia* Paul Corrigan, 1979a; Corrigan and Gillespie, 1974, and references there; Johnson, 1970.

33. See Paul Corrigan, 1975, 1979b; and Paul Willis's work.

34. The title of Taylor *et al.*, 1976; cf. Paul Corrigan, 1979a, 1980. Not to be confused with Deputy Assistant Commissioner David Powis's *The Signs of Crime*, which is a manual for 'thief-catchers' which comes complete with a commendation from Sir Robert Mark when he was Police Commissioner for the Metropolis. This warns us to 'Watch out!' for people with 'disdainful or contemptuous smiles. Yes, smiles! Really good thieves sometimes betray themselves with a joint glance together of silent, smiling amusement immediately after a successful theft . . . ' (p. 66). *This* is of course exactly how 'doing nothing' does become 'a sign of trouble'; normal and generalised forms of behaviour (smiling . . .) are converted into grounds for suspicion because of a context. In its way it is a microcosm of how the law rules. One of the major strengths of the 'deviancy' writing was to focus on the construction of 'normal' crimes, criminals, 'events', and so on from primary acts of classification and negotiation and their secondary

support (or erasure) by the administration of justice and the reporting of events
by the media.

35. The tactical seriousness/strategic contempt formulation we employ here
is taken from Mao Tsetung's remarks in Moscow in 1957; *Selected Works* 5,
pp. 517-18.

36. See Marx, 1867a, p. 176n.

37. See Corrigan and Sayer, 1975. It is worth noting here that the key
problem for *any* oppressed group has always been first of all to establish (collective) *identity*, to recognise an *Us*: consider such organising slogans as 'black is
beautiful' or 'sisterhood is powerful'. The classifications buttressed by law
fragment, disrupt and deny both the particularity and the collectiveness of such
struggles. Cf. Mao's remarks on 'the Number One Authority under Heaven'
(1941, p. 21). As we have argued (*SCMT*, p. 163; *FM*, p. xv) it is often against
'Marxist' methods of work that these necessary struggles have first to be waged.
Cf. Michéle Barratt *et al.*, 1978, pp. 16f. on 'heroes and icons' and Sheila Row-
botham on 'the power of definitions and icons' in *Beyond the Fragments*
(Newcastle Socialist Centre, 1979, pp. 34f.).

38. Durkheim — currently a much underestimated theorist of law, state and
morality — knew this well: 'This is what *defines* the State. It is a group of sui
generis officials, in whose bosom are elaborated representations and volitions
which bind the collectivity, although they are not the work of the collectivity. It
is not exact to say that the State incarnates the *conscience collective*, for the
latter extends beyond it on all sides . . . The representations deriving from the
State are always more self-conscious, more conscious of their causes and their
ends . . . These representations are distinguished from other collective representations by their higher degree of consciousness and reflection . . . The State . . .
does not think for the sake of thinking . . . but in order to regulate [diriger] the
collective conduct. This does not alter the fact that its essential function is to
think' (1900, pp. 61-3; our translation).

References

Abrams, P. (ed.) (1978) *Work, Urbanism and Inequality*. Weidenfeld and
    Nicolson
Alcock, P. (1979) 'Legal Ideology, the Family and the Position of Women', Paper
    to BSA Conference
Arthur, C.J. (1976) 'Towards a Materialist Theory of Law', *Critique*, 7
Bailey, P. (1978) *Leisure and Class in Victorian England*. Routledge and Kegan
    Paul
Bankowski, Z. and Mungham, C. (1976) *Images of Law*. Routledge and Kegan
    Paul
Barker, D.L. (1978) 'The Regulation of Marriage'. In G. Littlejohn *et al.* (eds)
    Power and the State. Croom Helm
Barratt, M. *et al.* (eds) (1978) *Ideology and Cultural Production*. Croom Helm
    (1979)
Barry, B. (1973) *The Liberal Theory of Justice*. Oxford University Press
Beier, A.L. (1974) 'Vagrants and the Social Order in Elizabethan England'. *Past
    and Present*, 64
Berger, J. and Mohr, J. (1975) *A Seventh Man*. Penguin
Bernstein, B. (1958) 'Some Sociological Determinants of Perception'. In *Class,
    Codes and Control*, vol. 1 (1971)

—— (1959) 'A Public Language'. In *Class, Codes and Control*, vol. 1 (1971)

—— (1971a) Introduction to *Class, Codes and Control*, vol. 1 (1971)

—— (1971b) *Class, Codes and Control*, vol. 1. Paladin (1973)

—— (1975) 'Class and Pedagogies: Visible and Invisible'. In *Class, Codes and Control*, vol. 3 (1977)

—— (1977a) Introduction to *Class, Codes and Control*, vol. 3 (1977)

—— (1977b) 'Aspects of the Relations Between Education and Production'. In *Class, Codes and Control*, vol. 3 (1977)

—— (1977c) *Class, Codes and Control*, vol. 3. Revised edition, Routledge and Kegan Paul

Birmingham Centre for Contemporary Cultural Studies. Women's Study Group. (1978) *Women Take Issue*. Hutchinson

Bland, L., McCabe, T.M. and Mort, F. (1978) 'Sexuality and Reproduction: Three 'Official' Instances. Ch. 4 of M. Barratt *et al*.

Blelloch, D. (1938) 'A Historical Survey of Factory Inspection in Great Britain'. *International Labour Review*

Bowden, T. (1978) 'Guarding the State'. *British Journal of Law and Society*, 5 (1)

Bunyan, T. (1976) *The History and Practice of the Political Police in Britain*. Julian Friedmann

—— (1977) 'Tyranny in the UK 1977'. *Time Out*, 10 March

Cain, M. (1977) *Optimism, Law, and the State . . . European Yearbook of Law and Sociology*. Nijhoff, Amsterdam

—— and Hunt, A. (1979) *Marx and Engels on Law*. Academic Press

Carlen, P. (1976) *Magistrates' Justice*. Robertson

Carson, W.G. and Ditton, J. (1979) 'The Tyranny of the Present'. Mimeo

Central Office of Information (1976) *The Legal System of the British Isles*. HMSO

Chambliss, W.J. (1964) 'Sociological Analysis of the Law of Vagrancy'. *Social Problems*, 11

—— (1975a) 'Towards a Political Economy of Crime'. *Theory and Society*, 2

—— (1975b) 'The State, the Law, and the Definition of Behaviour as Criminal or Delinquent'. Ch. 1 in *Handbook of Criminology*. Rand-McNally

Cohen, P. (1977) 'Legal Subjects in the Working Class City'. Paper read at University of Sheffield, Centre for Criminological Studies

—— (1979) 'Turn Out Your Pockets: Some Personal Observations on the Political Science of Police'. Mimeo (from author, University of London Institute of Education)

Colletti, L. (1975) *Introduction to Karl Marx Early Writings*. Penguin

Collins, H. (1979) 'The Marxist Theory of the Form of Law'. Paper to BSA Conference

Commons, J.R. (1924) *Legal Foundations of Capitalism*. University of Wisconsin Press (1957)

Corrigan, Paul (1975) 'Doing Nothing'. *Working Papers in Cultural Studies*, 7/8

—— (1978) 'Deviance and Deprivation'. Ch. 5 in Abrams (1978)

—— (1979a) *Schooling the Smash Street Kids*. Macmillan

—— (1979b) 'Out With the Lads . . . ' *New Society*, 5 July

—— (1979c) 'The Local State'. *Marxism Today*. July

—— (1980) *Education, Reproduction, Inequality*. Fontana

—— and Corrigan, P.R.D. (1977) 'Labour and the State'. Paper to BSA Conference. Partly published in revised form as Paul Corrigan, 'The Local State'

Corrigan, Philip R.D. (1976) 'Feudal Relics or Capitalist Monuments . . . ' *Sociology*, 11 (2) (1977)

—— (1977) 'State Formation and Moral Regulation in 19th Century Britain'. PhD thesis, Durham University; revised version forthcoming in 2 vols. Macmillan

—— (1979) 'Capitalism's Cultural Revolution'. Mimeo
—— (ed.) (1979) *Capitalism and State Formation: Historical Investigations.* Quartet
—— and Corrigan, V. (1978) 'State Formation and Social Policy until 1871'. In *Social Work and the State.* Arnold (1979)
—— and Gillespie. V. (1974) *Class Struggle, Social Literacy, and Idle Time.* Brighton, Labour History Monographs (1978)
——, Ramsay, H. and Sayer, D. (1978) *Socialist Construction and Marxist Theory: Bolshevism and its Critique.* Macmillan/Monthly Review Press
——, Ramsey, H. and Sayer, D. (1979a) *For Mao.* Macmillan/Humanities Press
——, Ramsey, H. and Sayer, D. (1979b) 'The State as a Relation of Production'. In P.R.D. Corrigan (ed.) (1979) (Revised version of paper to BSA 1977 Conference)
—— and Sayer, D. (1975) 'Moral Relations, Political Economy and Class Struggle'. *Radical Philosophy*, 12
—— and Sayer, D. (1978) 'Hindess and Hirst: a Critical Review'. *Socialist Register*
Critchley, T.A. (1967) *A History of the Police in England and Wales 1900-1966.* Constable
Daniels, N. (ed.) (1975) *Reading Rawls.* Blackwell
Denning, Lord (1979) *The Discipline of Law.* Butterworth
Deutsch, K. and Senghass, D. (1975) 'The Fragile Sanity of States'. In *New States in the Modern World.* Harvard University Press
Deutscher, I. (1954) *The Prophet Armed.* Oxford University Press
Devlin, Sir P., Lord (1959) *Enforcement of Morals.* Oxford University Press
—— (1962) 'Law, Democracy and Morality'. *University of Pennsylvania Law Review*, 119 (635)
—— (1965) Revised edition of *Enforcement of Morals.* Extracts in Dworkin (1977)
Ditton, J. (1977) 'Perks, Pilferage and the Fiddle'. *Theory and Society*, 4
Donajgrodski, A. (ed.) (1977) *Social Control in Nineteenth Century Britain.* Croom Helm
Draper, H. (1962) 'Marx and the Dictatorship of the Proletariat'. *Etudes de Marxologie*, 6
—— (1970) 'Death of the State in Marx and Engels'. *Socialist Register*
—— (1977) *Karl Marx's Theory of Revolution*, Part I. Monthly Review Press
Durkheim, E. (1900) *Leçons de Sociologie: Physique des Moeurs et du Droit.* Istanbul Faculté de Droit/Presses Universitaires de France (1950)
Dworkin, R.W. (1977) *The Philosophy of Law.* Oxford University Press
Edelman, B. (1979) *Ownership of the Image: Elements for a Marxist Theory of Law.* Routledge and Kegan Paul
Engels, F. (1890a) Letter to Bloch, 21-22 September. In *Selected Correspondence.* Moscow (1975)
—— (1890b) Letter to Schmidt, 27 October. Ibid.
—— (1893) Letter to Mehring, 14 July. Ibid.
—— (1894) Letter to Borgius, 25 January. Ibid.
Foster, D. (1974) *Class Struggle and the Industrial Revolution.* Weidenfeld and Nicolson
Foucault, M. (1975) *Discipline and Punish.* Allen Lane (1977)
Frankel, J. (1970) *National Interest.* Macmillan
Friedmann, W. (1950) 'The Function of Property in Modern English Law'. (Review of Renner 1928/1949.) *British Journal of Sociology*, 1
Gellner, E. (1979) 'The Withering Away of the Dentistry State', *The Review*, 2 (3)

Godelier, M. (1978) 'Infrastructures, Societies and History'. *New Left Review,* 112

Gramsci, A. (1934) *Prison Notebooks* (Selections). Lawrence and Wishart (1971)

Griffith, J.A.G. (1975) 'Judges and a Bill of Rights'. *New Statesman*, 10 January

—— (1977a) 'Judges, Politics and Social Class'. *New Statesman*, 21 October

—— (1977b) *The Politics of the Judiciary*. Fontana

Guyot, J. *et al.* (1978) *Migrant Women Speak*. Search Press

Hagan, J. *et al.* (1979) 'The Sexual Stratification of Social Control'. *British Journal of Sociology*, 30 (1)

Hall, S. (1971) 'Deviancy, Politics and the Media'. Paper to BSA Conference

—— (1978a) 'Reform and the Legitimation of Consent'. To appear in *Permissiveness and Control*. Macmillan (1979)

—— (1978b) 'Marxism and Culture'. *Radical History Review*, 18

—— (1978c) 'Some Paradigms in Cultural Studies'. *Annali di Instituto Orientale di Napoli*, 3

—— (1979) 'The Great Moving Right Show'. *Marxism Today*, 23 (1)

—— and others (1978) *Policing the Crisis*. Macmillan

Hammen, O.J. (1972) 'Marx and the Agrarian Question'. *American Historical Review*, 77

Harman, H. and Griffith, J.A.G. (1978) *Justice Deserted*. NCCL

Harrison, B. (1974) 'State Intervention and Moral Reform'. In *Pressure from Without*. Arnold

Harrison, R. and Mort, F. (1978) 'Patriarchal Aspects of Nineteenth Century State Formation'. Ch. 5 of P.R.D. Corrigan (ed.) (1979)

Hart, H.L.A. (1958) 'Positivism and the Separation of Law and Morality'. Ch. 1 of Dworkin (1977)

—— (1961) *The Concept of Law*. Oxford University Press

Hart, J. (1955) 'Reform of the Borough Police 1835-1856'. *English Historical Review*

—— (1956) 'The County and Borough Police Act 1856'. *Public Administration*, 34

Hay, D. *et al.* (1975) *Albion's Fatal Tree*. Allen Lane

Hill, C. (1978) 'Sex, Marriage and the Family in England'. *Economic History Review*, 31 (3)

Holloway, J. and Picciotto, S. (eds) (1978) *State and Capital: a Marxist Debate*. Arnold

Hume, D. (1777) *Enquiry Concerning Human Understanding and Concerning the Principles of Morals*. Clarendon Press (1975)

Humphries, J. (1977) 'Class Struggle and the Resistance of the Working Class Family'. *Cambridge Journal of Economics*, 1

Hunt, A. (1976) 'Law, State and Class Struggle'. *Marxism Today*, 20

—— (1977) 'Class Structure and Political Strategy'. *Marxism Today*, July

—— (1978) *The Sociological Movement in Law*. Macmillan

Jessop, D. (1977) 'Marx and Engels on the State'. In *Politics, Ideology and the State*. Lawrence and Wishart (1978)

Johnson, R. (1970) 'Educational Policy and Social Control in Early Victorian England'. *Past and Present*, 49

Jones, D.J.V. (1974) 'Crime, Protest and Community in Nineteenth Century Wales'. *Llafur*, 1 (3)

—— (1976a) 'Thomas Campbell Foster and the Rural Labourer . . . ' *Social History*, 1

—— (1976b) 'The Second Rebecca Riots: a Study of Poaching'. *Llafur*, 2 (1)

—— (1977) A 'Dead Loss to the Community': the Criminal Vagrant in mid Nineteenth Century Wales'. *Welsh Historical Review*, 8 (3)

—— and Bainbridge, A. (1979) 'The 'Conquering of China': Crime in an Industrial Community'. *Llafur*, 2 (4)

Jones, G.S. (1977) 'Class Expression Versus Social Control?' *History Workshop*, 4

Kettle, M. (1979) 'Trying to Make the Verdicts Fit the Evidence' *New Society*, 24 May; 'Several Stones Still Unturned'. Ibid., 30 May

Kiernan, V. (1965) 'State and Nation in Western Europe'. *Past and Present*, 31

King, M. (1978) 'Mad Dancers and Magistrates'. *New Society*, 14 September

Kuhn, A. (1978) 'Structures of Patriarchy and Capital in the Family'. Ch. 3 of Kuhn and Wolpe (1978)

Kuhn, A. and Wolpe, A.M. (1978) *Feminism and Materialism: Women and Modes of Production.* Routledge and Kegan Paul

Laski, H.J. (1930) *The Dangers of Obedience.* New York, Harper

Lazonick, W. (1974) 'Karl Marx and Enclosures in England'. *Review of Radical Political Economists*, 6 (2)

—— (1978) 'The Subjection of Labour to Capital'. *Review of Radical Political Economists*, 10 (1)

Linebaugh, P. (1976) 'Karl Marx, the Thefts of Wood, and Working Class Composition'. *Crime and Social Justice*

McDonald, L. (1976) *The Sociology of Law and Order.* Faber

MacFarlane, L.T. (1974) *Violence and the State*. Nelson

McIntosh, M. (1978) 'The State and the Oppression of Women'. Ch. 10 of Kuhn and Wolpe (1978)

Malcolmson, R.W. (1973) *Popular Recreations and English Society 1700-1850.* Cambridge University Press

Mao Tsetung (1941) 'Reform our Study' In his *Selected Works*, 3. Peking (1965)

—— (1977) *Selected Works*, 5. Peking

Marx, K. (1842a) 'Proceedings of the 6th Rhine Province Assembly'. 3rd article. *Debates on the Law of Thefts of Wood. CW*, 1

—— (1842b) *Justification of the Correspondent from the Mosel. CW*, 1

—— (1843) *On the Jewish Question. CW*, 3

—— (1846) With F. Engels. *The German Ideology. CW*, 5

—— (1847a) *The Poverty of Philosophy. CW*, 6

—— (1847b) *Moralising Criticism and Critical Morality. CW*, 6

—— (1848) With F. Engels. *Manifesto of the Communist Party. CW*, 6

—— (1852) *The Eighteenth Brumaire of Louis Bonaparte. CW*, 11

—— (1853a) 'The Duchess of Sutherland and Slavery' In *Articles on Britain*

—— (1853b) 'Irish Tenant Right'. Ibid.

—— (1857) 'General Introduction'. With *Grundrisse*

—— (1858) *Grundrisse.* Penguin (1973)

—— (1859) Preface to *A Contribution to the Critique of Political Economy.* Lawrence and Wishart (1971)

—— (1863) *Theories of Surplus Value*, 3 parts. Moscow (1963-71)

—— (1864) 'Inaugural Address of the Working Men's International Association'. In *Articles on Britain*

—— (1865) *Capital*, 3. Moscow (1971)

—— (1867a) *Capital*, 1. Penguin (1976)

—— (1867b) *Capital*, 1. Lawrence and Wishart (1967)

—— (1871a) *The Civil War in France.* Peking (1970)

—— (1871b, c) 1st and 2nd drafts cf *The Civil War in France*

—— (1872) With F. Engels. Preface to 2nd German edn of the *Manifesto* of 1848

—— (1874) 'Conspectus of Bakuninis's Statism and Anarchy'. In *The First International and After.* Penguin (1974)

—— (1875) *Critique of the Gotha Programme.* Peking (1972)

—— (1878) *Capital*, 2. Moscow (1967)

—— and Engels. F. *Collected Works*. London/New York/Moscow (1975 onwards). Cited as *CW*

—— *Selected Correspondence*. Moscow (1975)

—— *Articles on Britain*. Moscow (1971)

Mayer, H. (1959) 'Marx, Engels, and the Politics of the Peasantry'. *Etudes de Marxologie*, 3

Merriam, C.E. (1931) *The Making of Citizens*. Chicago University Press

Morris, T. (1976) *Deviance and Control: the Secular Heresy*. Hutchinson

Mosse, G.L. (ed.) (1975) *Police Forces in History*. Sage

Nicholson, G. (1973) 'Authority and the State'. In Roussopoulos (ed.) *The Political Economy of the State*. Montreal, Black Rose

Nozick, R. (1975) *Anarchy, State and Utopia*. Blackwell

Ollman, B. (1978) 'Marx's Vision of Communism'. *Critique*, 8

Pashukanis, E.V. (1929) *Law and Marxism: a General Theory* (3rd edn). Ink Links (1978)

Phillips, D. (1977) *Crime and Authority in Victorian England*. Croom Helm

Picciotto, S. (1979) 'The Theory of the State: Class Struggle and the Rule of Law'. Paper to BSA Conference

Pollard, S.C. (1963) 'Factory Discipline in the Industrial Revolution'. *Economic History Review*, 16

—— (1965) *Genesis of Modern Management*. Penguin (1968)

Poulantzas, N. (1974) *Classes in Contemporary Capitalism*. New Left Books (1975)

—— (1978) *State, Power, Socialism*. New Left Books

Powis, D. (1977) *The Signs of Crime: a Field Manual for Police*. McGraw-Hill

Rawls, J. (1972) *A Theory of Justice*. Oxford University Press

Redhead, S. (1978) 'The Discreet Charm of Bourgeois Law'. *Critique*; 9

Reiner, R. (1978) 'The Police, Class and Politics'. *Marxism Today*, 22 (3)

Renner, K. (1928) *The Institutions of Private Law and their Social Functions*. Revised edn, Routledge and Kegan Paul (1949)

Robertshaw, P. and Curtin, C.A.(1977) 'Legal Definition of the Family . . . ' *Sociological Review*, 25 (2)

Robins, D. and Cohen, P. (1978) *Knuckle Sandwich: Growing Up in the Working Class City*. Penguin

Rock, P. (1974) 'The Sociology of Deviance and Conceptions of Social Order'. *British Journal of Criminology*, 14

Roshier, R. (1976) 'Corrective Criminology'. Durham University, *Working Papers in Sociology*, 10

Sachs, A. and Wilson, J.H.(1978) *Sexism and the Law*. Robertson

Samaha, J. (1974) *Law and Order in Historical Perspective*. Academic Press

Sayer, D. (1975) 'Method and Dogma in Historical Materialism'. *Sociological Review*, 23 (4)

—— (1979a) *Marx's Method*. Harvester/Humanities Press

—— (1979b) 'Science as Critique: Marx *vs*. Althusser'. In *Issues in Marxist Philosophy*, vol. 3. Harvester

Schaar, J.H. (1970) 'Legitimacy in the Modern State'. In *Power and the Community*. New York, Pantheon

Silver, A. (1967) 'The Demand for Order in Civil Society'. In *The Police*. Wiley

Skillen, A. (1977) *Ruling Illusions*. Harvester

Slack, P.A. (1974) 'Vagrants and Vagrancy in England 1598-1664'. *Economic History Review*, 27

Smart, C. (1976) *Women, Crime and Criminology: a Feminist Critique*. Routledge and Kegan Paul

Spitzer, S. (1975) 'Towards a Marxian Theory of Deviance'. *Social Problems*,
    22 (5)
Storch, R.D. (1975) 'The Plague of Blue Locusts'. *International Review of Social
    History*
—— (1976) 'The Policeman as Domestic Missionary'. *Journal of Social History*,
    9
Sumner, C. (1979) *Reading Ideologies: an Investigation into the Marxist Theory
    of Ideology and Law.* Academic Press
Taylor, I., Walton,P. and Young, J. (1973) *The New Criminology.* Revised
    impression, Routledge and Kegan Paul (1975)
—— Walton, C. and Young, J. (1975) *Critical Criminology.* Routledge and
    Kegan Paul
Taylor, L., Morris, A. and Davies, B. (1976) *Signs of Trouble.* BBC
Thane, P. (1977) 'Women and the Poor Law in Victorian and Edwardian
    England'. *History Workshop*, 6 (1978)
Thompson, E.P. (1963) *Making of the English Working Class.* Penguin
—— (1964) 'Working Class Culture and the Transition to Industrialism'.
    Bulletin SSLH, 9
—— (1965) 'Peculiarities of the English'. Reprinted in *The Poverty of Theory
    and Other Essays* (1978)
—— (1967) 'Time, Work-discipline and Industrial Capitalism'. *Past and Present*,
    38
—— (1968) Postscript to Penguin edn of *Making of the English Working
    Class*
—— (1971) 'The Moral Economy of the English Crowd'. *Past and Present*, 50
—— (1974) 'Patrician Society, Plebian Culture'. *Journal of Social History*, 7
—— (1975) *Whigs and Hunters.* Allen Lane. (Revised impression, Penguin,
    1977)
—— (1976) Interview. *Radical History Review*, 34
—— (1977a) 'Eighteenth Century English Society'. *Social History*, 3 (2) (1978)
—— (1977b) 'Review essay on the Family'. *New Society*, 8 September
—— (1978a) 'The Poverty of Theory or an Orrery of Errors'. In *The Poverty of
    Theory and Other Essays* (1978)
—— (1978b) *The Poverty of Theory and Other Essays.* Merlin
—— (1978c) 'The State Versus its "Enemies"'. *New Society*, 19 October
    (Reprinted, Merlin Press)
—— (1978d) 'The Secret State Within the State'. *New Statesman,* 10
    November
—— (1978e) 'The Secret State'. Introduction to *State Research, Review of
    Security and the State 1978.* Julian Friedmann. Reprinted *Race and Class*,
    20 (3) (1979)
—— (1979) Interview. *Leveller,* January
Tigar, M. and Levy, M. (1977) *Law and the Rise of Capitalism.* Monthly Review
    Press
Tobias, J.J. (1967) *Crime and Industrial Society in the Nineteenth Century.*
    Penguin
—— (ed.) (1972) *Nineteenth Century Crime.* David and Charles
Vorspann, R. (1977) 'Vagrancy and the New Poor Law'. *English Historical
    Review*, 92
Wainright, H. (1978) 'Women and the Division of Labour'. Ch. 3 of Abrams
    (1978)
Watkins, C.K. (1975) *Social Control.* Longmans
Weber, M. (1918) 'Politics as a Vocation'. In *From Max Weber.* Routledge and
    Kegan Paul (1974)

—— (1920) *General Economic History.* Collier-Macmillan (1966)

Williams, R. (1956) 'Class and Classes'. *Highway*, 47

—— (1958) *Culture and Society.* Penguin (1963)

—— (1961) *The Long Revolution*. Penguin (1965)

—— (1973) *The Country and the City.* Paladin (1975)

—— (1976) 'Notes on Marxism in Britain since 1945'. *New Left Review,* 100

—— (1977a) Two Interviews. *Red Shift*, 3 and 4

—— (1977b) *Marxism and Literature.* Oxford University Press

—— (1979) *Politics and Letters.* New Left Books

Willis, P. (1976) 'The Class Significance of School Counter-culture'. In *The Process of Schooling.* Routledge and Kegan Paul/Oxford University Press

—— (1977) *Learning to Labour: How Working Class Kids Get Working Class Jobs.* Saxon House

—— (1978) *Profane Culture.* Routledge and Kegan Paul

—— (1979) 'Shop Floor Culture, Masculinity and the Wage-form'. In R. Johnson *et al.* (eds) *Working Class Culture.* Hutchinson

Yaney, G.K. (1966) 'Bureaucracy and Freedom'. *American Historical Review*, 71

3 THE DEVELOPMENT OF CAPITALISM AND THE FORMALISATION OF CONTRACT LAW

Roger Cotterrell

Introduction: Sociological Interpretation of Legal Doctrine

The object of this paper is to consider, in the particular context of the development of legal doctrines of contract, some aspects of the relationship between historical patterns of doctrinal legal development and changes in socio-economic structure. In this paper law is taken to mean, centrally and primarily, legal doctrine, that is, the concepts, rules, principles and patterns of reasoning which define legal discourse and are present in, and shape, lawyers' arguments, the style and reasoning of judicial decision making, and the terminology and conceptual structure of certain forms of legislation and of the legal theories and commentaries of jurists. The existence of legal forms does not, however, depend on the existence of all of these specific practices and institutions within which legal discourse finds its expression in various societies and historical periods since the conditions under which power is exercised through the medium of rules are historically extremely varied. The reason for focusing here on legal doctrine is to enable us to take seriously, and indicate ways of examining, the claim made by writers as different as Weber and Pashukanis that law is not merely synonymous with state coercion and that legal forms have a certain specific effectivity which justifies attempts to analyse law as a distinct social phenomenon. Treating such a claim seriously involves no denial of the fact that legal institutions and doctrines occupy an important part of the territory of political struggle and serve as instruments of political domination under definite historical conditions. Nevertheless the distinctive character of law is not to be found in these matters alone since the territory of political struggle is not *exclusively* occupied by law, and neither is law the only medium through which political power can be exercised.

The kinds of reductionist accounts of law which have been widely influential include those which reduce law to a more or less direct expression of class interests (as, for example, in Stuchka's early Soviet legal theory (Babb, 1951) heavily criticised by Pashukanis) or view it as a 'neutral', resource-allocating, interest-balancing mechanism of social integration passively reflecting the imperatives of the social system it serves (as in crude functionalism). Other approaches treat law merely as the state's technical apparatus of control or as a part of it identifi-

able as a set of functionally defined specific institutions. But, unless
legal form or legal reasoning is seen as having distinctive characteristics
which emerge with the historical development of legal institutions and
doctrine and which can be treated as raising sociological questions
about its possible independent effects on social and economic changes,
theoretical questions about law become merged into attempts to
construct general theories of the state and law as such ceases to be an
object of sociological interest. Accounts of historical changes in the
relationships of classes in the transition from feudalism to capitalism
in Western Europe often tend to see law in various territories and
historical periods as, on the one hand, a set of more or less formalised
customary practices and, on the other, a machinery of coercion the
controllers of which are of interest for historical and sociological
analysis but the internal mechanisms of which are regarded as raising
problems only for lawyers concerned with technical maintenance of a
machine which, in theory, is available to serve any master. By contrast,
following Marx's analysis of fetishised forms in *Capital*, Pashukanis and
some other Marxist writers have provided an analysis of law which
affirms the specificity of legal form as the distinctive form of the
relations of commodity exchange (Pashukanis, 1978). But the 'relative
autonomy' of the law is bought at a high price, the price of acceptance
of an 'ideological theory of ideology' (Hirst, 1972) which analyses
ideological forms as being in some way 'created by' the real. The
'autonomy' of the legal is thus an autonomy which frees it from reduction to an expression of 'the demands of powerful social actors' only
to reduce it to a necessary expression of 'the systematic requirements of
capitalism'. (Balbus, 1977). Law is thus an alien form in non-capitalist
systems, present to the extent that commodity exchange is present. To
the extent that law exists in, for example, feudalism, it can be analysed
only in relation to what it may become: an imperfect realisation of a
specific form which reaches full development – the realisation of its
essence – with capitalism. Law in pre-capitalist or non-capitalist
societies can thus be analysed only in relation to the legal essence
revealed in its fullness in capitalism alone, and the possibility of compre-
hensively analysing the patterns of legal ideas present in systems other
than those of capitalism, in all their variety and in the complexity of
their development, and of identifying important continuities in the
development of legal ideas which are not necessarily dependent on the
continuity of particular economic systems or patterns of social
relations, is effectively excluded. Further, in a theory of the autonomy
of legal form such as Pashukanis', the effectivity of law is limited to
expressing, fulfilling and guaranteeing the relationships of commodity
exchange, the 'social relationships between things' which are the
fetishised 'real' forms of social relationships under capitalism. Law can

have no other function or effects since the form and function of the law are reflections of each other. Legal form is determined by the logic of capital and, at the same time, expresses and guarantees the relationships of capital.

Such a view must be rejected. Legal forms and the characteristics of legal doctrine and discourse cannot be wholly explained by reference to matters external to legal process themselves.[1] Thus a recent radical critique of classical Marxist concepts accurately states:

> Capitalist relations of production presuppose a legal system which allows the formation of particular kinds of contractual relations and exchanges. The concept of the legal conditions of existence of capitalist relations of production therefore imposes definite constraints on the type of legal system compatible with the conditions of capitalist production. But it cannot tell us precisely how the necessary forms of contract will be provided for nor what other properties the legal system might possess. (Cutler, Hindess, Hirst and Hussain, 1977, p. 219)

Elsewhere, Hindess and Hirst have written that the transition from feudalism to capitalism involves a 'double transformation: in conditions of representation of the bourgeoisie and the landowning class at the political level; in the articulation of commodity relations in the structure of the economy as a whole' (1975, p. 307). They add that 'certain necessary transformations at the ideological level' are also required. The patterns of specific relations of production which are held to characterise capitalism have determinate conditions of existence which involve not only economic transformations but also political and ideological transformations which cannot be reduced to or wholly explained in terms of economic change or the internal logic of structures of economic relations. The coercive aspect of law obviously makes it a potent weapon in political struggle and in establishing and maintaining forms of political control. But strictly, if we are to treat seriously the hypothesis that law has an independent effectivity, the coercive power of the law must be treated primarily as the power of a political authority *guaranteeing* the law and, at the same time, directing and channelling its power *through* legal doctrine.

Law is thus, as Pashukanis correctly observed, not to be explained *merely* as coercion, although the effectiveness of law depends to a significant extent on coercion applied by political authorities. If law has any autonomy it is to be understood not merely as a device for the exercise of power but as a system of ideas at once legitimating and channelling the exercise of power. Analysis of the historical patterns of the development of legal doctrine is thus part of the field of study of the formation, modification and disintegration of ideologies. But it is a particularly important part because in legal doctrine major ideological supports of social order find expression and in legal practice and lawyers' rationalisations components of this ideological structure are elaborated in detail and often in remarkably explicit form. The impetus towards such elaboration derives largely from the more or less dramatic confrontation between these elements of ideology and everyday social experience which occurs in the specially constructed environment of the law court; a supposedly 'neutral' territory in which legal ideology battles against opposed ideologies, in which it struggles to impose its own meanings on, and therefore its exclusive control over, social and economic relationships of all kinds. Institutional legal history is primarily the record of the development of the conditions under which these ideological confrontations can take place and doctrinal legal history is, in its most important form, the record of the struggles themselves and their outcome.

At a humbler but still significant level doctrinal legal history is a record of the development of *techniques* by which power can be directed and applied through the medium of rules. Weber writes that

the absence of an economic need is by no means the only explanation of the lack of certain legal institutions in the past. Like the technological methods of industry, the rational patterns of legal technique to which the law is to give its guarantee must first be 'invented' before they can serve an existing economic interest. Hence the peculiar kinds of technique used in a legal system or, in other words, its modes of thought, are of far greater significance for the likelihood that a certain legal institution will be invented in its context than is ordinarily believed. Economic situations do not automatically give birth to new legal forms; they merely provide the opportunity for the actual spread of a legal technique if it is invented (1954, p. 131)

This is important but not to be exaggerated. Legal history shows the discovery, loss and rediscovery of specific ideas and techniques over time, the best-known example being the development, decline and medieval renaissance of the doctrines of Roman private law. It is extremely difficult to pick out clear lineal patterns of development of legal techniques so as to be able to relate them confidently and exactly to the existence or non-existence of particular forms of economic or social relationships and particular procedures and kinds of transactions at specific moments in history. As the history of commerce shows, legal techniques may be created in the course of development of particular spheres of economic activity while legal systems claiming

general territorial jurisdiction over areas in which such activities occur
have no place for such techniques within their body of legal doctrine.
The history of the development of doctrinal techniques in different
systems may thus tell us much about the nature of conflicts of jurisdiction between the several different kinds of legal orders which may
compete for dominance at particular moments in history and in relation
to particular territories or particular categories of legal claims and
relationships. These conflicts may, in turn, have a significance for
political developments, where various systems of courts controlling
different jurisdictions are themselves the legal instruments of different
political authorities.

If, therefore, law does have a degree of 'autonomy' and 'independence', it seems most likely that the key to an understanding of its
autonomous character will be found in the characteristics of its 'internal'
processes of doctrinal development, notwithstanding that in many,
probably most, cases of major developments in doctrine it is possible
to identify political or economic circumstances or developments which
provide the impetus towards doctrinal change.

Weber and the Development of the Legal Concept of Contract

Among the patterns of doctrinal development in legal history the evolution of contract is of major significance not only for an understanding
of the ideological transformations associated with the development of
capitalism but also as a unifying theme in the sociological interpretation
of legal history as a whole. At the most basic level contract is the legal
concept which most directly links law and economy because of the
significance of the numerous forms of exchange transactions for economic development. Further, contract in its developed form embodies
central ideas of modern Western law — the idea of legal obligations and
legal rights, the creation and modification of legal relationships through
agreement, the concept of the will and responsiblity of the legal
subject.

For these reasons contract provides a convenient doctrinal focus for
an attempt to assess the 'relative autonomy' of the law and the specific
effectivity of legal doctrine. But, at the same time, it cannot be
assumed that characteristics of one strand of legal doctrine, a roughly
severed segment from the complex of doctrinal legal history, can be
mechanically generalised as characteristics of a unified legal ideology or
of legal doctrine in its entirety.

Among social theorists of comparable stature, only Weber analyses
contract in relation to general concepts of a sociology of law in a
manner which genuinely seeks to take full account of the complexities

and ambiguities of doctrinal legal history and, for this reason, his work provides a useful basis for further analysis. The themes which run through Weber's convoluted treatment of the development of contract law are, of course, chosen in the context of a sociology of law concerned to relate developing patterns of legal rationality to an ideal type of capitalism formulated in terms of rational economic conduct orientated to the market. If we reject this typification of capitalism and replace it with a concept of capitalism distinguished by a dominance of specific social relations of economic production having definite legal and political conditions of existence, Weber's themes still remain relevant for an analysis of the emergence of certain technical prerequisites of economic development and of the cultural conditions of existence of capitalism. But his central concern with a single problem − that of 'rationality' − and his linking of law and capitalist development primarily in terms of the concepts of 'calculability' and 'predictability' limit and distort some of the important inferences he draws from doctrinal legal history.[2]

In his methodological essays Weber suggests that legal concepts can serve in appropriate cases as ideal types of social action (1949, p. 43 and *passim*). In his writings on contract, as elsewhere in his sociology of law, Weber frequently and implicitly does use legal ideas in this way, and here, as elsewhere in the descriptive passages of his sociological writings, there is a tendency for ideal type and 'concrete reality' to be confused. Doctrinal legal developments are, therefore often treated as though it can be assumed that they reflect or are reflected in actual changes in patterns of behaviour, actual economic changes, etc. Thus, for Weber, the relationship between the legal development of contract and expanding capitalism is relatively straightforward.

> There exists, of course, an intimate connection between the
> expansion of the market and the expanding measure of contractual
> freedom or, in other words, the scope of arrangements which are
> guaranteed as valid by the legal order or, in again different terms,
> the relative significance within the total legal order of those rules
> which authorize such transactional dispositions. (1954, p. 100)

But because of the limitations of the key linking concepts between law and economy on which his sociology of law is based he cannot systematically explore this 'obvious' relationship further. For this reason Weber's intricate account of the historical development of the concept of legal obligation arising from agreement is primarily an exercise in the writing of highly compressed 'pure' doctrinal history without any systematic explanation of the reasons for or sociological significance of particular doctrinal developments.

A few historical landmarks stand out. The development of money
provides the impetus for legal interpretation of bilateral transactions
dependent on rigid ceremonies and verbal formulae as in the Roman
law *stipulatio* dating from before the fifth century BC. Such legal
forms mark points of transition between major eras of legal history.
Economic demands give rise to new legal possibilities yet the new
forms preserve and are dependent on the irrational 'magic' sanctions of
what Weber calls the 'pre-contractual stage' of legal development
(1954, p. 115). It is the magic ceremonies which create legal bonds,
not the agreement of the parties nor their mutual reliance. Many
centuries later the spread of international Roman commerce gave rise
to legal recognition of informal consensual contracts. But the formal
contracts and those arising merely as a result of delivery of possession
continued to form part of the law so that Roman law never developed
a unified universally applicable contract form (Buckland, 1963,
pp. 412ff.).

Throughout his treatment of contract, Weber's object is to demonstrate long-term continuities of legal development which are not
reducible to mere reflections of patterns of economic development.
Contract in some form, Weber claims, existed in the earliest periods of
legal history. The development of market relations produced not a
wholly new form but a radical development and change of character
in an existing one. Yet the distinctions Weber makes between the
status contracts of early law and the purposive contracts peculiar to
market economies, are far more important legally and sociologically
than the continuities. Only with purposive contracts, 'neither affecting
the status of the parties nor giving rise to new qualities of comradeship
but aiming solely . . . at some specific (especially economic) performance or result' (1954, pp. 105-7), can the idea of limited, narrowly
defined reciprocal legal obligations, fundamental to the legal elaboration of the consequences of market transactions, arise. 'Fraternization'
contracts, the dominant form of status contracts, require that the
'person "become" something different in quality (or status) from
the quality he possesses before . . . Each party must thus make a new
"soul" enter his body' (1954, p. 106). The 'total legal situation' and
social status of the contracting parties are altered by their agreement.
The purposive contract with its potential for reducing all contracting
parties to identical legal units provides a prototypical framework for the
development of formal legal rationality. Implicit in Weber's rigid distinguishing of status contracts and purposive contracts is the attempt to
specify doctrinal landmarks in the historical emergence of the kind of
legal thought which Weber associates with the ideal type of formal legal
rationality.

The distinction between generalised, unspecific, 'fraternal' status relationships and limited, legally defined instrumental contractual relationships underlies Weber's discussion of the legal effects on 'third parties' of contractual ties and of the legal consequences of group membership – particularly in relation to the legal development of forms of incorporation. Since many of these group forms are created or developed to serve economic purposes, the elaboration of their consequences and characteristics is presumably significant in relation to economic development and it is in this area that Weber's linking of legal forms and capitalist development through the concepts of 'calculability' and 'predictability' and the emergence of formal legal rationality should receive its most direct test.

Yet he makes no serious and systematic attempt to specify the economic effects of various kinds of legal structure of groups or organisations in different historical periods. He stresses that the relations of the market are 'fundamentally alien to any type of fraternal relationship' such as that which characterises the internal membership relations within various kinds of group (1954, p. 193) and he discusses in very general terms the problems of representation of the group and fixing of liabilities which may be solved through the concept of corporate juristic personality. But this concept can be traced in various forms to ancient and, in Weber's terms, presumably 'irrational' sources (see Lobingier) and it is not easy to see how Weber's arguments about the legal forms of groups are directly related to his thesis concerning the significance of formal legal rationality. In fact, he notes that '[m]any of our specifically capitalistic legal institutions are of mediaeval rather than Roman origin, although Roman law was much more rationalized in a logical sense than mediaeval law' (1954, p. 131) and he recognises powerful *irrational* forces at work in their development. For example, the development of negotiable instruments (pp. 124-5), solidary group responsibility towards outsiders and the recognition of many different kinds of special funds (p. 131) were all favoured by irrational modes of thought. The 'backwardness' and illogicality of legal thought prevented the establishment of rigid conceptual systems in mediaeval law and hence promoted 'a far greater wealth of practically useful devices than had been available under the more logical and highly rationalized Roman law' (p. 131).

What Weber's analysis of contract shows is that elements which he understands as rational *and* irrational enter into the construction and elaboration of legal ideas in highly complex combinations when legal development is viewed in a broad historical perspective. He shows, in relation to contract, that there are striking continuities in the development of legal doctrine over long periods and that the processes and consequences of doctrinal change cannot be *wholly* explained by economic developments. All this is of value. But, as Albrow remarks, by

Weber's 'own historical analysis it is difficult to show any clear relationship between formal law and the modern economy'. (Albrow, 1974, p. 29). The development of formal legal rationality does not underpin key phases in the development of capitalist enterprise, as Weber understands this development, in the direct manner which the use of his concepts of calculability and predictablity in relation to both law and economic action suggests. Furthermore, the distinction between purposive and status contracts, so important to him because of its implications for his classification of modes of legal thought, is much less clearcut than his ideal types of contract encourage us to believe.

This is only a symptom of the more fundamental problem that Weber's analytic distinctions of rational/irrational and formal/substantive legal thought are not adequate for the tasks to which they are applied. The development of contract shows a blending of rational and irrational elements and formal and substantive concerns sufficiently complex to cast doubt on the utility of his classification even as an admittedly ideal typical formulation. Formal rationality is defined in such a way as to exclude consideration of the values of the law and the way they are developed and generalised throughout legal doctrine (cf. Albrow, 1974, p. 21). So Weber does not see the processes of development of legal doctrine as processes by which political ideology can be developed and elaborated in forms which make it applicable for the official definition and control of all socially significant relationships. And the typification of formal and substantive legal rationality allows him to present these types as excluding each other; as different *kinds* of legal thought rather than as different *facets* of legal thought. The complex character of legal reasoning and its ideological significance are thus obscured.

The Legal Ideology of Contract

The primary ideological significance of legal contract form is twofold. Firstly, it lies in the idea of legal *equivalence*, the exact legal balancing of reciprocal rights and obligations of formally equal contracting parties assumed to be acting freely. In this way the law systematically interprets actual relations and conditions of inequality and substantial unfreedom as relations of equality and free choice, and attaches legal consequences accordingly.[3] Secondly, the ideological significance of legal contract form lies in the idea of its *universality*. It is, in its developed form in capitalism, capable not only of being applied to the interpretation of economic relations of distribution and production but to other relations not directly concerned with economic production and it lends itself to generalisation and further abstraction as a major political ideology, supported and elaborated in the detail of legal rules.[4] In the hands of a practically minded legal profession, legal doctrine may be developed through creative modification deriving its impetus from many sources including the need to compete with rival legal jurisdictions (e.g. in England the powerful competition of ecclesiastical, commercial and other court systems, at various times, encouraged doctrinal innovations in the common law applied by the royal courts). Such developments may involve and rely on *irrational* as well as rational tendencies in legal thought. But, at the same time, unified professional 'guardianship' of a legal system seeking, and, by virtue of the political authority supporting it, capable of eventually acquiring jurisdiction over all legally significant social relations, fosters tendencies towards the application of broadly consistent modes of thought throughout *all* areas of developing legal doctrine within such a legal order. The importance of legal contract to capitalism is thus not primarily in the provision of technical devices to support the developing complexity of economic relations. Although such devices must be developed they often emerge in the internal norms of economic groups or institutions and are only later reflected in formal law recognised by courts of general jurisdiction not controlled by commercial authorities themselves. And while the developing rationality of the law is an element contributing in various ways to the achievement of the ideological functions of legal doctrine it is not necessarily of pre-eminent importance in all phases of social and economic development. The pervasive legal ideology of contract, slowly created over a long period of history, promotes the breakdown of all major status differentials unconnected with the needs of an economy based on market exchanges and confirms and defines the particular form of individualism in terms of which capitalist social relations are conceptualised.[5]

What then are the historical conditions which contribute towards the creation of this ideology and its progressive legal elaboration? The most basic legally relevant needs of commerce are, firstly, the guarantee of peace and order within its area of operations. This involves the *internal* guarantee of security of transactions through enforcement procedures and the *external* guarantee protecting commercial arrangements and relationships from 'outside' attack, for example from those outside the commercial community or hostile to its activities. Secondly, commerce requires conceptual devices for the construction of forms of transaction and structures of business organisation suitable to its operations. But the satisfaction of these needs as they exist at various stages of the development of commerce does not necessarily demand reliance on legal resources external to the commercial community itself. Private courts of commercial communities play an important role in the development of enforceable norms of commercial conduct and the

political authority of the autonomous community may be adequate
to secure enforcement. Hence the stability of the autonomous structures of the German medieval sodalities. As regards the development of
transactional techniques and concepts, for example in relation to
credit, agency and negotiable instruments, much more flexibility may
be possible in the elaboration of techniques within the commercial
community than could be possible within an evolving system of legal
doctrine of courts of general territorial jurisdiction not merely
concerned with commercial affairs. A major restraining influence in
the development of legal doctrine, and one important cause of resort to
legal fictions (Fuller, 1967, pp. 60-2; Pound, 1921, pp. 166ff.), is the
problem of unforeseen and perhaps undesired consequences, in various
and possibly disparate areas of law, arising as a result of doctrinal
development in a seemingly narrow area.

Development beyond the stage of legal development of contract-
based transactions centred on commercial enclaves towards a 'contract-
ualisation' of societies seems to depend on such situations as the
following:

1. A situation in which further economic development requires a
system of norms and enforcement procedures beyond those which
commercial communities can create for themselves. For example, the
development of multiple group membership breaks down the system of
personality of laws, the system under which legal jurisdiction over
individuals is determined by their group membership which determines
status. Because of the complexities of determining which law is to be
applied to a person who is a member of several groups the need for
certain common legal principles, a *ius gentium* co-existing with the
norms of particular groups, is required (Weber, 1954, pp. 142-3).

2. The establishment of the dominance of a single system of law within
a territory which can support an integrated market economy as the
basis of its economic structure. This development depends, in turn, on
political factors, particularly on the establishment of centralised political
authority and the emergence of a legal profession centred on the courts
controlled by that authority. England provides the obvious example
with the development of such authority from the time of the Norman
Conquest and, much later, the victory of the common law enforced by
the King's courts over other competing systems (see e.g. Milsom, 1969,
pp. 1-25).

3. The existence of conditions under which those who control the
creation of legal doctrine of such a dominant legal system are prepared
to provide a system of rules and doctrines to support and guarantee the

expansion of market activity. Thus, well-known accounts of the alliance of royal power and bourgeois interests in particular historical periods, particularly in England, and the alliance of bourgeoisie and common lawyers in the English Revolution, are of obvious relevance (see e.g. Tigar and Levy, 1977, Hill, 1965; cf. Malament, 1977).

4. The availability of doctrinal legal techniques to transform the existing doctrine of the dominant legal system so as to secure economic needs in a manner sufficiently compatible with existing political and cultural conditions (cf. Pound, 1921, p. 11). In this context the *fief-rente*, a legal device of the twilight of Western European feudalism, seems to provide a good example of a long-lasting and significant transitional legal form reflecting the ties of personal loyalty of the disappearing feudal bond of tenure as well as emerging contractual relations to be developed with the returning money economy. Involving the grant of an annuity to secure military service, it arose at a time when legal relations of service were inconceivable except in relation to feudal ties of homage and fealty and, surviving from the twelfth to the early fifteenth century, the legal relationship of *fief-rente* is said to have 'paradoxically enabled feudalism to survive . . . far beyond the time when based solely on land it would have ceased to exist' (Lyon, 1957, p. 273). Just as the Roman law *stipulatio* and other formal contracts established legal relations relevant to a money economy but in commercially inconvenient forms (Watson, 1977, pp. 12ff.) reflecting the impossibility of breaking with inherited modes of legal thought circumscribed by magic, so transitional legal devices involved in the movement from feudal relations to the contract relations of a money economy show the complex processes of modification of legal thought; processes which have, themselves, social and economic effects.

Indeed, legally, there are significant continuities between the legal conceptualisation of relations of lord and tenant in the feudalism of Western Europe and some important characteristics of contract as it features in the legal ideology of capitalism. The feudal bond is patently a relationship of unequals which eventually forms the focus of a class struggle more important for the break-up of feudalism than the struggle between bourgeoisie and feudal lords focused on the growth of commerce (see e.g. Dobb, 1963). Yet it is interpreted legally as a structure of reciprocal obligations (Milson, 1976, pp. 38ff.) and the oath of fealty becomes 'a detailed contract, carefully drawn up' (Bloch, 1962, p. 219). The feudal 'contract' is not even *legally* a relationship of equals, yet in this bond, affecting virtually all levels of society throughout Western Europe (cf. Poggi, 1978, pp. 23, 27-8), is a germ of the socially pervasive legal ideology of contract with its systematic obscuring of factual inequalities which makes the notion of free agreement creating reciprocal obligations a legal construction of major ideological significance.

The development of a pervasive legal ideology of contract as a centrally significant component of the cultural conditions within which capitalist social relations develop is thus, it may be suggested, partly the consequence of certain important legal doctrinal continuities traceable through pre-capitalist phases of social development — and particularly within Western European feudalism — which furnish ideological 'residues' influencing, and being modified in, further legal development. It is also partly the result of the gradual universalisation of legal ideas originally developed in specific commercial contexts (and themselves traceable at least to some extent to historical origins in modes of thought developed in spheres unconnected with specifically economic transactions). The creation of the historical conditions for this universalisation in particular societies depends on a variety of determinate political, economic and cultural developments which cannot be explained theoretically as the necessary consequence of any single unifying historical process.

This is not, it must be stressed, a claim that developed ideas of contract are wholly the result of legal development and legal processes. But their modern systematisation into an elaborate complex of generalised reciprocal obligations capable of abstract and exact interpretation irrespective of the realities of economic relationships or power relationships is primarily the result of legal doctrinal development. Partly on these foundations, ideological edifices are built (Nenner, 1977; Hill, 1965, pp. 268-9) to extend their consequences far beyond the confines of the law court while remaining grounded in the developing detail of legal interpretation of specific social and economic relationships. It has been argued that

> during the sixteenth and seventeenth centuries . . . many European nations obtained knowledge of their history by reflecting . . . upon the character of their law; that the historical outlook which arose in each nation was in part the product of its law, and therefore, in turn, of its history . . . (Pocock, 1957, pp. vii-viii)

In so far as patterns of legal doctrine have been interpreted in particular societies in particular historical periods to shape images of history, the forms in which social relations are conceived and the terrain of political controversy, their ideological significance is clear and where long historical continuities in the development of legal doctrine can be demonstrated law's ideological significance can be substantially enhanced.

The 'relative autonomy' of the law thus appears as the significant effects of the processes of reasoning promoting continuities in the development of legal doctrine. 'Legal ideas have their own strength' (Milsom, 1969, p. xi) and the patterns of their development are not always predictable. One can understand fears such as those of Frederick William II of Prussia which impelled him, in the decree introducing his 1794 General Land Law for the Prussian States, to forbid the judges 'to indulge in any arbitrary deviation, however slight, from the clear and express terms of the laws, whether on the ground of some allegedly logical reasoning or under the pretext of an interpretation based on the supposed aim and purpose of the statute' and to threaten severe sanctions on any judicial miscreant (cf. Zweigert and Kötz, 1977, p. 81). In 1790 in France, in an attempt to protect the supposed consequences of the Revolution, a statute required that judges must seek the advice of the *corps législatif* 'whenever they believe it necessary either to interpret a law or make a new one' (ibid.). But such attempts at control invariably fail unless political authorities have the power, the will and the skill to exercise total and permanent control over all aspects of the creation and application of legal doctrine. These conditions have frequently not been satisfied through the historical development of legal ideas. For this and other reasons law has been able to develop 'autonomous' characteristics through its 'internal' processes of development in various ways, to varying extents, in various societies and historical periods. The gradual construction of the legal ideology of contract, as a particular product of legal development in certain societies,demonstrates one particularly important form in which the specific effectivity of law as regards social and economic change can manifest itself in the development of ideology to channel and legitimise the exercise of state power in a manner supportive of the patterns of social relations constitutive of capitalism.

Notes

1. I.e. the processes of the institutions concerned with the application and interpretation of rules through which political power is channelled.
2. Hunt (1978, pp. 128ff.) considers the treatment of contract in Weber's sociology of law to be set apart from and perhaps merely incidental to the major themes of his sociological analysis of law. Yet, in a sense, it is one of the central testing grounds of his theories because modern contract, as Weber interprets it, embodies directly in legal form, and thereby guarantees, the central characteristics of economic nationality upon which his conception of capitalism is constructed.
3. Modern contract law is the classic legal embodiment and support of the notion that 'in the modern state "vertical", power-focused, and power-activated relations could obtain only between the state itself and private individuals; among

the latter, all relations were supposed to be "horizontal", contractual, and power-free' (Poggi, 1978, p. 94). Furthermore, legal notions of contract have a potential for development into an ideological interpretation of the relationship of state and individual (or state and 'people' or, specifically, the state and a particular class or classes) in 'horizontal' terms (Nenner, 1977; cf. Hill, 1965, pp. 268-9).

4. On the importance of private law concepts in the formulation of major political controversies in seventeenth-century England see Nenner '[R]elationships between King and Parliament and King and people were consistently reduced to analyses based upon the lawyer's understanding of property, contracts, and trusts' (1977, p. 198). Nenner makes clear that it was the developing legal doctrine of contract which was the ideological herald of the new age while nevertheless retaining certain continuities with an earlier medieval order (see pp. 39ff.).

5. To say this is to speak only of a particular area of legal doctrine — a particular component of legal ideology — and it is not to be assumed that the characteristics of the legal ideology of contract are the only characteristics of legal ideology as a whole, nor that characteristics of other aspects of legal ideology are necessarily compatible with those of legal contract ideology.

References

Albrow, M. (1974) 'Legal Positivism and Bourgeois Materialism: Max Weber's View of the Sociology of Law'. *British Journal of Law and Society*, 1, p. 14.

Babb, H.W. (1951) *Soviet Legal Philosophy* (translated). Harvard University Press

Balbus, I.D. (1977) 'Commodity Form and Legal Form: An Essay on the "Relative Autonomy" of the Law'. *Law and Society Review*, 11, p. 571

Bloch, M. (1962) *Feudal Society* (translated by L.A. Manyon, vol. 1). Second edn, Routledge and Kegan Paul

Buckland, W.W. (1963) *Textbook of Roman Law*. Third edn, Cambridge University Press

Cutler, A., Hindess, B. Hirst P. and Hussain, A. (1977) *Marx's 'Capital' and Capitalism Today*, vol. 1. Routledge and Kegan Paul

Dobb, M. (1963) *Studies in the Development of Capitalism*. Revised edn, Routledge and Kegan Paul

Fuller, L.L. (1967) *Legal Fictions*. Stanford University Press

Hill, C. (1965) *Intellectual Origins of the English Revolution*. Oxford University Press

Hindess, B. and Hirst, P.Q. (1975) *Pre-Capitalist Modes of Production*. Routledge and Kegan Paul

Hirst, P.Q. (1972) 'A Critique of Rancière's and Althusser's Theories of Ideology'. Unpublished mimeo

Hunt, A. (1978) *The Sociological Movement in Law*. Macmillan

Jolowicz, H.F. (1978) *Historical Introduction to Roman Law*. Third edn, Cambridge University Press

Lobingier, C.S. (1938-39) 'The Natural History of the Private Artificial Person: A Comparative Study in Corporate Origins'. *Tulane Law Review*, 13, p. 41

Lyon, B.D. (1957) *From Fief to Indenture*. Harvard University Press

Malament, B. (1977) 'The "Economic Liberalism" of Sir Edward Coke'. *Yale Law Journal*, 76, p. 1321

Milsom, S.F.C. (1969) *Historical Foundations of the Common Law*. Butterworth
—— (1976) *The Legal Framework of English Feudalism*. Cambridge University Press

Nenner, H. (1977) *By Colour of Law*. University of Chicago Press

Pashukanis, E.B. (1978) *Law and Marxism: A General Theory* (translated by B. Einhorn). Ink Links

Pocock, J.G.A. (1957) *The Ancient Constitution and the Feudal Law*. Cambridge University Press

Poggi, G. (1978) *The Development of the Modern State*. Hutchinson

Pound, R. (1921) *The Spirit of the Common Law*. Marshall Jones

Tigar, M.E. and Levy, M.R. (1977) *Law and the Rise of Capitalism*. Monthly Review Press

Watson, A. (1977) *Society and Legal Change*. Scottish Academic Press

Weber, M. (1949) *The Methodology of the Social Sciences* (translated by E. Shils). Free Press

—— (1954) *On Law in Economy and Society* (translated by E. Shils and M. Rheinstein). Harvard University Press

Zweigert, K. and Kötz, H. (1977) *An Introduction to Comparative Law* (translated by T. Weir), vol. 1. North Holland

4 THEORY AND PRACTICE IN LAW AND HISTORY: A PROLOGUE TO THE STUDY OF THE RELATIONSHIP BETWEEN LAW AND ECONOMY FROM A SOCIO-HISTORICAL PERSPECTIVE

David Sugarman

Introduction

In the history of British intellectual thought there are few more unfortunate paradoxes than the fact that, whilst the work of two of the founding figures of modern sociology, Marx[1] and Weber, reflects a commitment to the inseparability of theory and history, the relationship between history and sociology in Britain has tended towards suspicion and rivalry.[2]

For some time the literature at least from the sociological side of the border has recognised the importance of history to sociology. Indeed, C. Wright Mills went so far as to say that 'history is and must be the very shank of social science'.[3] However, whilst it is possible to point to sociologists whose work embodies an historical focus, it is significant that almost all such work has in the past been done in the United States or Continental Europe. As David Matza opined in 1971, 'anyone with half an ounce of sense has always said that a main defect of sociology and criminology is that they are not historical. We've always admitted it, but we have not done anything about it.'[4] Only a thorough-going history of British sociology can elicit the reasons for its failure to develop a tradition of sociological history.[5] It is something of a commonplace, however, to explain the gulf between sociology and history by referring to the dichotomy between 'empiricism' and 'theory'. Put crudely, some sociologists regard history as irretrievably tainted by empiricism, i.e., an atomistic inclination 'to account for social events in terms of a total of individual actions'[6] rather than in economic, structural or class terms. The fact that the history of British sociology, especially during its early days, reflects a close connection between political and methodological individualism,[7] and that much of history is apparently bereft of epistemological and methodological concerns, has reinforced this aversion to history. British historians have until recently been reluctant to utilise the tools of sociological theory, in part because of sociology's association with dogma, evolutionary theories and reductionism.

One consequence of the artificial separation of theory and history

is that the relationship between law, economy and society from a
historical perspective has tended to be ignored or, alternatively, viewed
as unproblematic by both sociologists and historians. This deficit has
been accentuated by the fact that legal history in Britain has, with the
possible exception of its treatment of the Middle Ages, added little to
our knowledge of the interaction between law and economy. Typically,
that small amount of the total output of legal history devoted to
eighteenth- and nineteenth-century Britain is exclusively preoccupied
with explaining the development of legal phenomena by reference to
other legal phenomena or intellectual forces, notably Benthamism.[8]
As a result, it elevates the procedure of doctrinal reclassification over
the substance of the changes effected by that reclassification. Thus
much of legal history is characterised by a Whiggish 'emphasis on
continuity and a corresponding de-emphasis on change'. It has been
argued that the failure of legal history to concern itself with economic,
social and political desiderata has resulted in it advancing

> a profoundly conservative interpretation of the role of law in . . .
> society. [Its] basic categories contain fundamentally conservative
> political preferences dressed up in the neutral garb of expert and
> objective legal history . . . The main thrust of lawyers' legal history,
> then, is to pervert the real function of history by reducing it to the
> pathetic role of justifying the world as it is.[9]

In recent years, whilst the barriers dividing history and sociology have
by no means dissolved, there are signs that both sociologists and
historians are beginning to borrow from one another. Social historians,
for instance, have been utilising concepts such as social control to
examine some of the ways in which the instruments of law and order
contributed to the maintenance of social order in nineteenth-century
Britain.[10] In particular, Marxist historians have made a significant contribution to our understanding of the relationship between law and
economy in eighteenth- and nineteenth-century Britain and America,
in part, by drawing upon the theoretical constructs of Gramsci.[11]
Those concerned with the development of criminology and socio-
legal studies, in their efforts to circumvent traditional academic
boundaries, have begun to focus attention on the historical emergence
of legislation.[12] In the United States, part of the attack on formalism
that began at the turn of this century generated a history of law
centrally concerned with the influence of economic doctrine on legal
development.[13] Indeed, especially since the 1950s, there has been a
significant movement towards realising Boorstin's call for a legal history
that would be 'more concerned with the relationship at any time
between legal institutions and the rest of society, and less concerned

with the embryology of the professional vocabulary'.[14]

It is clear from what has been said already that law and legal institutions have served as a focal point in at least the more recent work which consciously or unconsciously marries historical and theoretical concerns. The reasons at this point in time for this attention to things legal would require the kind of detailed consideration out of place in this essay. In any such explanation, however, an important role would have to be attributed to the current preoccupation with the formation and role of the state under capitalism which itself is part of a wider re-examination of 'superstructure' and its relationship with the 'sub-structure' of industrial capitalism.

What follows in this paper is a preliminary and highly selective attempt to make available to a wider audience some of the more important recent historical work illuminating the relationship between law and economy in Britain and the United States during that crucial period when industrial capitalism came of age, i.e. *circa* 1700-1900. In addition, it seeks to illustrate the contribution which work of this nature can make, not only to such academic disciplines as 'law', 'sociology', 'criminology' and 'history', but also at the more general level of theory and practice.

Law as an Instrumentality of Industrial Capitalism

To what extent did law shape economy? In other words, to what extent was law an instrumentality or determinant of industrial capitalism? Most economic historians have taken the view that in the long run law is a 'dependent variable, symptom rather than determinant of the means and ends of the economic process'.[15] Mathias, for instance, says that there is overwhelming evidence to suggest that the formal restrictions in law associated with the eighteenth and early nineteenth century 'were very largely ineffective in the long run in economic terms; and their removal did not immediately produce any noticeable changes of trend. On all these issues other, non-legal, criteria were the prime determinants of change.'[16]

This conclusion is clearly consistent with an analysis of law in terms of the base-superstructure metaphor. At first blush, however, it does appear to contradict the view normally attributed to Weber that law played an indispensable role in guaranteeing the security and certainty that capitalism required. Upon further investigation, Weber's views turn out to be more complex and subtle. In answer to the question, 'Can it be said that a stable private economic system of the modern type would be "unthinkable" without legal guarantees?'[17] Weber insightfully set out what he saw as the significant limits on legal coercion in economic life.

His position seems to have been that, whilst the theoretical implications of the law's coercive power to guarantee certainty and predictability would lead one to assume that the law was essential to market capitalism, in practice this was not always the case.[18] 'As a matter of fact we see that in most business transactions it never occurs to anyone even to think of taking legal action. Agreements on the stock exchange, for example' are unenforceable at law.

> Nevertheless, a dispute practically never occurs. Likewise, there are corporate groups pursuing purely economic ends the rules of which nonetheless dispense entirely, or almost entirely, with legal protection from the state. Certain types of 'cartels' were illustrative of this class of organization.[19]

Having enumerated a number of other such instances in the economic and political sphere,[20] Weber contended that whilst today 'economic exchange is quite overwhelmingly guaranteed by the threat of legal coercion', from 'the purely theoretical point of view legal guarantee by the state is not indispensable to any basic economic phenomenon'.[21] Only 'case studies',[22] he concluded, will indicate the extent to which the law has moulded and facilitated economic behaviour.

Weber's recognition that the relationship between law and economy is problematic, that law may affect economy and that only case studies can provide us with the much-needed data we lack has recently been echoed by two economic historians: David Landes and Max Hartwell. Landes has written:

> The history of commercial and civil law in the West is in large measure the story of the progressive adaptation of the usages of an agrarian, community-centred, tradition-bound society to the requirements of an industrial, individualistic and rational — hence mobile — capitalism. The full story remains to be told; . . . lack of data and analysis does make it difficult to integrate legal considerations into the complex of factors shaping economic growth. Clearly, many of these changes are simply surface manifestations of a deeper transformation; the law is the reflection — frequently the belated reflection — of man's values and material needs. But the fact that it is often belated is evidence that it is not simply a dependent variable in the service of economic development. Not only do economic interests conflict and pull both legislation and administration in different directions; non-economic considerations have their say, and questions of morality and social prejudices intervene. Finally the law has a rationale of its own — a conservatism built on precedent and the niggling complexity of institutionalized justice.[23]

Hartwell has similarly opined that the relationship between law and economy is a two-directional one, that it is a complex relationship and that 'legal institutions have some autonomy of their own which, in varying degrees makes them exogenous variables in any process of economic change'.[24] In what represents a significant departure from the mainstream of economic history, he has argued that law and legal institutions played an important role in facilitating industrial capitalism; and that the supposed differences between a more flexible judge-made English law and an allegedly more rigid code-bound continental law partly explain Britain's initial leadership in industrialisation. Before and during the Industrial Revolution, he claims, individual and economic freedoms were enlarged and strengthened.[25] The

> outcome was, by the early nineteenth century, that in the organization of economy as much free play as possible was given to 'the spontaneous forces in society' and as little resort as possible was made to 'the coercive forces in society', especially those of government.[26]

So far we have been concerned primarily with the influence of law on economy.[27] It is now time to confront more directly the influence of economy on law. Much of the historical work on this subject has been produced in the United States, pioneered by the work of Willard Hurst at Wisconsin.[28] The most outstanding general study of the relationship between law and economy in recent years is undoubtedly Morton Horwitz's *The Transformation of American Law, 1780-1860*.[29] The importance of this work is such that it merits detailed consideration. Central to Horwitz's thesis is the notion that a radical break with pre-capitalist society and its law occurred after 1790; and that in the period 1790-1860 the American common law courts engineered the facilitation and legitimation of industrial capitalism. Law is attributed a central role in this metamorphosis principally because the judges moulded the law so as to promote emergent mercantile interests at the expense of other weaker groups within the community, thereby resulting in a profound redistribution of power and wealth. In order to support this thesis Horwitz draws upon an astonishing range of legal subject-matter. He argues that in the period 1790-1850 the very conception and function of law changed. Eighteenth-century law was conceived of as a static set of principles reflecting customary ideas of justice and practice derived from natural law. After 1790 this was supplanted by a more functional, 'instrumental' conception of the common law. Judges 'came to think of the common law as equally responsible with legislation for governing society and promoting socially desirable conduct.[30] The instrumental approach adopted by the

judiciary soon led to the transformation of private law. In one of his
most impressive essays Horwitz describes the transformation of the idea
of property

> from the eighteenth century view that dominion over land above all
> conferred the power to prevent others from interfering with one's
> enjoyment of property to the nineteenth century assumption that
> the essential attribute of property ownership was the power to
> develop one's property regardless of the injurious consequences to
> others.[31]

Common law rules which obstructed the demands of economic growth
were repudiated or suitably amended. Eighteenth-century law which
imposed liability for interfering with the enjoyment of property or
with another's livelihood irrespective of fault was replaced by a lower
level of duty (and, thus, a considerably restricted liability) in
negligence. Whereas under eighteenth-century law juries traditionally
had a wide power to award damages on the basis of their own sense of
fairness and equity, in the nineteenth century the courts shaped the
new legal rules to restrict or eliminate that discretion. The judiciary
were seeking to accommodate 'the new insistence of entrepreneurial
groups that certainty and predictability of legal consequences were
essential for economic planning'.[32]

A major facet of the transformation of private law after 1790 was
'the extent to which common law doctrines were transformed to create
immunities from legal liability and thereby to provide substantial
subsidies for those who undertook schemes of economic development'.[33]
Examining the consequences of legal subsidisation, Horwitz argues that
the courts imposed a disproportionate share of the cost of economic
development 'on the weakest and least organized groups in American
society'.[34] Furthermore, subsidisation through technical legal doctrine
mystified the underlying political choices. It avoided spreading the
cost over a wider segment of society and the more open public
discussion and scrutiny that would have resulted if development had
been encouraged by direct taxation.

Nowhere is his analysis of the relationship between law, economy
and society in nineteenth-century America more striking than in his
masterly essay on the transformation of contract law.[35] Eighteenth-
century law required that contracts be 'fair' and generally permitted
courts to set aside transactions that were unfair to one of the parties. In
part, these principles mirrored a pre-capitalist economy characterised by
local markets, relatively stable prices, a community sense of the 'just
price' and the virtual absence of complex executory bargains. With the
development of national markets after 1815, the increasing use of

'futures' contracts (either to insure against fluctuations in the market
or simply to speculate) and the needs of business for certainty and
uniformity induced the courts to discard their judicial review of contracts where equity so demanded it and to substitute in its place a body
of doctrine embodying the philosophy of 'buyer beware'. The shift
from basing contract upon communitarian notions of fairness and
value to that more suited to the needs of market capitalism was brought
about in two stages. In the early part of the nineteenth century,
contract law doctrine increasingly adopted the position that all value
was subjective and that the only basis of legal obligation was that the
parties' minds 'met' on this issue. By mid-century, legal doctrine was
further transformed to accommodate the needs of trade and industry
by grounding contractual obligations 'objectively' in the light of
commercial practice. This embodied the fiction of freedom of contract:
that equal bargaining power must normally be assumed to exist in all
commercial transactions. In effect 'class legislation'[36] had been
disguised. The new law favoured the 'commercially sophisticated
insiders' at the expense of labour and consumers.[37] The doctrine of
freedom of contract facilitated the incorporation of wide exemption
clauses and in the context of employment contracts led to drastically
reduced limits being imposed on the employees' rights to sue their
employer.

> Thus, the contractarian ideology above all expressed a market con-
> ception of legal relations. Wages were the carefully calibrated
> instrument by which supposedly equal parties would bargain to arrive
> at the proper mix of risk and wages. In such a world the old ideal of
> legal relations shaped by a normative standard of substantive justice
> could scarcely coexist. Since the only measure of justice was the
> parties' own agreement, all pre-existing legal duties were inevitably
> subordinated to the contract relation ... The circle was completed,
> the law had come simply to ratify those forms of inequality that the
> market system produced.[38]

By 1850 this process of transformation was more or less complete.
    At the very heart of the metamorphosis of American law in the
period 1780-1860 was, argues Horwitz, an alliance between the legal
profession and mercantile and entrepreneurial interests. Prior to 1790
lawyers and judges chiefly served the interests of the landed and were
unsympathetic to the needs of commerce. After 1790 as it became clear
where the future lucrative legal practice lay, the courts began to
promote the emerging interests of trade and industry. As a result of this
and other factors these groups increasingly looked to the courts for the
facilitation and legitimation of their interests.

Although a number of strands of his argument are not unfamiliar, the breadth and scholarship of his work is prodigious. His emphasis on the transformation of American law primarily as a result of the pressures of economic interests is a conscious challenge to consensus legal historiography which regarded law as almost wholly autonomous from society and economy. By emphasising that this metamorphosis occurred in the face of resistance and disquiet his study constitutes an important counter to earlier Whiggish studies which have treated economic growth and industrialisation as unproblematic, simply reflecting a solid consensus of almost *volksgeist* proportions. As a result he reflects conventional historical wisdom which would take modernisation, uniformity and certainty to be inevitable and unqualified goods involving no underlying political or economic assumptions.[39] Repeatedly he asks the question which often other historians have eschewed: in whose interest were laws forged?[40] This is closely related to one of Horwitz's prime objectives: to challenge the tendency in orthodox historiography (and indeed legal scholarship generally) to treat law as morally and politically value free.[41] Law, for Horwitz, was inevitably an active participant in the process of economic growth, the distribution of wealth and political power. In this sense, his study is a monumental effort of demystification. The role of law in the process of capital accumulation has in the past been barely considered.[42] Horwitz's analysis directs attention as to how the legal system encouraged the transition from community rights to a reified conception of property ownership which defined labour as a 'marketable commodity' and placed large property owners in a more advantageous position relative to small property owners. His study confirms the view that the modern law of contract and its ideology is historically closely related to classical economic theory; and that it dominated private law and practice during much of the nineteenth century. As in the work of Willard Hurst and Lawrence Friedman,[43] Horwitz's study represents a significant reorientation in the sense that historians, sociologists and criminologists have tended to concentrate on public law, i.e., constitutional and criminal law. As he contends, private law (tort, contract, property and commercial law) constitutes 'an infinitely more typical pattern of the use of law . . . By thus focusing on private law we can study the more regular instances in which law, economy and society interacted'.[44] In the research that is required on the relationship between law and economy in eighteenth- and nineteenth-century Britain, Horwitz's study is likely to serve as a major focal point.

Whilst the work of Hartwell and Horwitz testifies to the promise of the 'new legal history', it also highlights the problem of method which confronts not only the 'new legal history' but, in one sense, all research which seeks to explain law by reference to non-legal phenomena.

Obviously the study of the relationship between law and economy requires the investigation of the influence of law on economy and economy on law. Whilst they are concerned to relate legal development to extra-legal phenomena, Horwitz and (to a lesser extent) Hartwell concentrate their research energies almost exclusively on case law and legislation. In other words, law reports and legislation supply much of their data. The work of both, when it transcends the discussion of particular cases or legislative enactments, tends to be characterised by a generality and abstraction that is not apparently grounded in primary or even secondary sources. As a result of their lack of data on 'economy', much of what they say about economy — as both a determinant of law and as something influenced by law — can, until further empirical work has emerged, be little more than hypothesis.[45] For example, Horwitz asserts that pre-revolution legal doctrine imposed greater economic costs on industrial development than the new legal rules which supplanted them. However, he provides no evidence of their comparative costs.[46] Similarly, Hartwell's assertion that the needs of trade and industry were better served by the common law than by the civil law is problematic in that the historical evidence of Brtish merchant opinon (to which Hartwell does not allude) also supports the view that they preferred the civil law courts of England to their common law counterparts.[47] Indeed, as far as Weber was concerned, the civil law system was of its nature more 'formal' and 'rational' and therefore more conducive to the needs of capitalism than was the common law.[48]

Furthermore, because the bulk of their data derives from case reports and legislation the definition of 'law' implicitly underlying their work is artificially circumscribed. One of the most important contributions of the American legal realists was to stress that any real understanding of the operation of law in practice required that the focus of study shift from court decisions to the actual practices and norms of regulatory bodies, companies and individuals. Thus, it has been stressed that other public agencies or private institutions perform the same functions in society as courts; and that for much of business these are more significant than courts or the letter of the law. Moreover, all the recent empirical evidence suggests that businessmen pay little or no attention to the rules of commercial law in planning their relationships.[49] If this is even partly true then the emphasis placed on the history of case law and legislation rather than business activity and extra-legal institutions may be misleading. The resources of business archives, company records, contemporary literature, the myriad of documents and advices stored within the legal profession and the published state papers are just some of the obvious sources that require investigation. Only when *all* these different dimensions have been investigated historically will we have a more accurate picture of the relationship between law and economy. Clearly this is a colossal, not to say daunting, proposition; but it cannot be shirked.

Nor is this simply a call for a mindless Baconian empiricism.[50]

> It would seem high time that common sociological questions were introduced into economic and legal history, the tools of micro-sociology brought to macro-sociological problems, and the abstractions of society, law and economy brought down to their day to day reality for empirical analysis.[51]

This is merely to recognise that language and theory determine what we can observe. We cannot take 'data' as given. As Maureen Cain put it, data are

> constituted ideologically at their moment of recording; they should be re-constituted theoretically at their moment of use. Nor is the social historian or sociologist confronted with a choice between a painstaking analysis of specific and concrete people and groups engaged in political action and simplistic generalisation. The researcher's theory should enable her to recreate her research materials in their use, and as an intrinsic part of the same process to refine and develop the elements of her theory in the light of, and to take account of, these specificities. . . . Thus what at first presents itself as scholarly care, on closer inspection emerges as a *lack* of theoretical work; what presents itself as a stylistic repetitiousness and inability to change pace, turns out to be a tedious function of insufficiently differentiated raw materials.[52]

It is the combination of wide-ranging empirical research on law and economy harnessed to a sufficiently sensitive theoretical framework that is likely to produce the most insightful research on the relationship between law and economy from a historical perspective.

Neither Hartwell nor Horwitz ideologically decode their data in an acceptable way. Hartwell accepts and reinforces the ideological framework within which his data are impregnated. His consensus-value framework is, thus, wholly insensitive to the conflict, tensions, contradictions and clash between and within classes which accompanied the rise of industrial capitalism. His is unashamedly 'history from above'; from this vantage point *laissez-faire* and the common law were major facilitators of individual freedom. From 'below', however, things may have looked very different. 'The law might not appear as a "bulwark" but as a bully.'[53] Unlike Horwitz's careful analysis of the law of contract, Hartwell's tools are too blunt to detect the coercion and ideology which pervades 'freedom of contract'. Even in the eyes of the law it was not

until 1875 that a manual worker and an employer were theoretically
on an equal footing. Until the enactment of the Conspiracy and Protection of Property Act 1875 it was a criminal offence for an employee,
but not an employer, to act in breach of his contract of employment.[54]
To explain the development of private law in terms of 'commercial
uniformity' and 'legal certainty and predictability', 'conceals a whole
set of political and economic values which were, in fact, resisted from
the beginning of the century.[55] Similarly, it is more profitable to ask:
whose freedom — and at whose cost? In his laudable desire to escape
the conservatism of consensus historiography and the blandness of
pluralism, Horwitz resorts to an instrumentalist framework which
exaggerates the nature and extent of the break between colonial and
post-revolutionary America and their law, and the communitarian
nature of colonial as contrasted with the materialistic nature of early
post-revolutionary America.[56] His instrumentalism comes close to
explaining the relationship between American law and industrial capitalism in what Rock, in a criticism of Quinney, termed 'anthropomor-
phic conspiracy theory'. Rock argued that

> The perspective offers no understanding of law as a complex and
> variegated rule-system whose origins are frequently as mysterious to
> elites as to governed. It offers no vision of a legal system as a series
> of constraints upon law-giver and ruled alike. It does not refer to
> legitimacy and authority other than in the context of manipulation
> and mystification. It does not provide for the elaborate patterns of
> accommodation that characterise many situations of social control.
> The law-giver is an Olympian figure endowed with a rationality, an
> innocence of unintended consequences and a clear self-interested-
> ness.[57]

In effect, Horwitz's instrumentalism casts the relationship between
economy and law in terms of the base-superstructure metaphor.[58]
Unlike Hartwell and others, he seems to dismiss the relative autonomy
of law as merely an instance of a self-interested legal profession's desire
to create the appearance of a neutral legal system.[59] Considerations of
this kind, to a large extent, explain the abstraction and reification that
is apparent in their otherwise markedly different studies.

What conclusions can be drawn about the extent to which economy
shaped law and vice versa in Britain and the United States during the
eighteenth and nineteenth centuries? We have seen that historians have
differed considerably in their assessment of the role played by law in
shaping economy. We have also seen that there is general agreement
that law is largely determined by economy. If and when the necessary
empirical case studies have been undertaken it is likely that they will

deduce that the kind of central role allotted to law in shaping economy as posited in the work of Hartwell and others is overstated. For example, it is reasonably certain that some legal checks to the growth of industrial capitalism in Britain (such as the Bubble Act of 1720 and the laws against usury) were for a considerable period relatively easy to circumvent and not unattractive at an ideological or cultural level to a significant range of those who represented the dominant economic interests. When the instrumental, ideological and cultural dimensions of this legislation gradually came to antagonise such interests the pressure to change the law began to mount. 'In both Britain and Germany', says Landes,

> business and buinessmen have always found ways of evading or transcending legalistic limitations . . . when the rewards were sufficient. With time they built a code of company law to suit their requirements. And once they had attained their objective, their use of this freedom was conditioned by the particular possibilities and activities of their respective economies.[60]

This, of course, comes perilously close to treating the relationship between law and economy as, after all, a relationship of base determining superstructure. However, the recent work of 'experiential' historians has confirmed that, especially once the ideological facts of law are considered, the relationship between law and economy becomes altogether more 'complex and contradictory'.[61]

Law, Ideology and Hegemony

According to orthodox Marxism the most important generator of society is the sheer force of economic relations: the economic base determines the political, social and cultural superstructure erected thereon. In a class society, therefore, law has been characterised in orthodox Marxism (particularly in the writings of Lenin) as nothing more than the direct embodiment of the interests of the dominant economic classes in society. However, the work of Marx and Engels as a whole does not subscribe to essentialism, that is, to the view that all social phenomena can be reduced or derived from the economic. In fact there has been increasing recognition that the nature of the relationship between base and superstructure is problematical; delimiting that relationship has become the central question in modern Marxist theory.[62] In this section I consider the contribution of recent legal histories in illuminating those dimensions of law that are not directly coercive. This work constitutes an important complement to the bulk of materialist analyses of law (whether in criminology, sociology, law or history) which in the past have tended to emphasise the directly coercive nature of law as part of their efforts to unmask the hypocritical character of law's claim to neutrality. Important as demystification is, it, of itself, cannot provide a sufficient basis for understanding the nature and functions of law in economy and society. Inevitably, I have had to be highly selective. I have concentrated on those 'experiential' histories that have eschewed the base-superstructure metaphor and have in its place substituted an analysis strongly influenced by Gramsci's notion of 'hegemony'.

Law is much more than a directly coercive behavioural injunction. 'Among other things it includes educational efforts, rewards and other incentives, symbolic deployment of legal forms, publicity (favourable or adverse), continuous supervision, public signs and signals, recognised statutes and entities, grants with strings attached, and on and on and on'.[63] Whilst in recent years conventional jurisprudence has focused on undermining those definitions of law that treat it exclusively as orders backed by threats,[64] it has given little attention to its non-directly coercive facets. Here the recent work of some 'experiential' historians on law can be seen as advancing a number of insights already distilled within mainstream and critical sociological theory.

In addition to emphasising the coercive nature of law Marx and (in more detail) Weber also pointed to the role of legal institutions in legitimating the power structure of capitalist society. Weber noted that it was not only in the sphere of production that domination took place. The 'rational-legal' domination associated with formal justice, legalism, bureaucracy, professionalisation, impersonal relations and so on had impregnated all spheres of society, economic *and* cultural.[65] In terms of understanding the role of these phenomena as mechanisms for institutionalising popular consent the work of Antonio Gramsci is particularly suggestive.[66] Gramsci's concepts 'cut across the simple topographical model of base and superstructure'.[67]

> breaks with the conception of ideology as a simple reflection of relations at the economic level, and as the uniform expression of the ruling class. Whilst the dominant ideology . . . presents itself as universal, it does not spring automatically from the ruling class, but is usually the result of the relation of forces between the fractions of the ruling bloc. Hence Gramsci conceives of the differential appropriation of the dominant ideas within the ruling bloc itself and within the dominated class . . . The concept of hegemony is produced by Gramsci to analyse these relations within classes and between classes. It involves the organisation of 'spontaneous' consent which can be won, for example, by the ruling bloc making economic

concessions . . . combined with other measures that foster forms of
consciousness which accept a position of subordination . . . Gramsci
writes of the 'positive educative' influence of the schools and the
'repressive and negative educative' influence of the courts . . .
Ideology is not a 'trick' imposed by a ruling class in order eternally
to deceive the workers . . . Ideologies have their ground in material
realities and are themselves material forces.[68]

As Gramsci recognised,

> The process is more complex than the dissemination downwards in
> society of a single, dominant 'class world view' . . . It is thus
> important to emphasize . . . that hegemony should not be seen on a
> static and omnipotent system, but rather as an ongoing and problem-
> atic historical process[69] . . . Hegemony then, refers more to a *mode
> of organizing* beliefs and values, than to any particular set of beliefs
> and values; and the concept directs attention to the institutions
> and practices that carry and reproduce ideology within a particular
> social formation.[70]

The law then is not merely coercive. It is an instrument also (together
with the school system, religions and other institutions and activities)
by which certain attitudes are eliminated whilst others are dissemin-
ated.[71]

It is the law's 'educational', 'symbolic' and related ideological
dimensions which have in recent years been stressed in a number of
historical studies touching upon the relationship between law and
economy. For instance, in his history of the culture and world of the
American slaves, Eugene Genovese devoted a section to 'the hegemonic
function of law'.[72]

> One of the primary functions of the law concerns the means by
> which command of the gun becomes ethically sanctioned. But if we
> left it at that we could never account . . . for the undeniable influ-
> ence of the law in shaping the class relations of which it is an
> instrument of domination. Thus, the fashionable relegation of law to
> the rank of superstructural and derivative phenomena obscures the
> degree of autonomy it creates for itself. In modern societies, at least,
> the theoretical and moral foundations of the legal order and the
> actual, specific history of its ideas and institutions influence, step
> by step, the wider social order and system of class rule, for no class
> in the modern Western world could rule for long without some
> ability to present itself as the guardian of the interests and senti-
> ments of those being ruled . . . In southern slave society, as in

other societies, . . . the law cannot be viewed as something passive
and reflective, but must be viewed as an active, partially autonomous
force, which mediated among the several classes and compelled the
rulers to bend to the demands of the ruled . . . Only possession of
public power can discipline a class as a whole, and through it, the
other classes of society. The juridical system may become, then, not
merely an expression of class interest, nor even merely an expression
of the willingness of the rulers to mediate with the ruled; it may
become an instrument by which the advanced section of the ruling
class imposes its viewpoint upon the class as a whole and the wider
society. To accomplish these tasks it must manifest a degree of even-
handedness sufficient to compel social conformity; it must, that is,
validate itself ethically in the eyes of the several classes, not just the
ruling class.[73]

A year after the publication of these remarks followed two studies on
crime and society in eighteenth-century England which echo the
hegemony-based analysis akin to that of Genevese's above, and the
impact of which has far transcended the world of English 'experiential'
history: *Albion's Fatal Tree*[74] and *Whigs and Hunters.*[75]

In his remarkable history of *The Making of the English Working
Class,*[76] E.P. Thompson observed that,

the conviction that the rule of law was the distinguishing inheritance of the 'free-born Englishman' and was his defence against
arbitrary power, was upheld even by the Jacobins . . . Hence the
paradox . . . of a bloody penal code alongside a *liberal* and, at times,
meticulous administration and interpretation of the laws . . . This
question of the *limits* beyond which the Englishman was not
prepared to be 'pushed around' and the limits beyond which
authority did not dare to go is crucial.[77]

In his essay, 'Property, Authority and the Criminal Law,[78] Douglas Hay
attempts to explain how and why the 'moral consensus' and paradox
pin-pointed by Thompson characterised eighteenth-century England.
'The English ruling class', Hay argues, 'entered the eighteenth century
with some of its strongest ideological weapons greatly weakened'.[79]
The Crown had lost much of its potency as a source of authority as had
religion once the notion of Divine Right of Kings was jettisoned.
'Equally important, a return to the severities of the Tudors and early
Stuarts probably would not have been tolerated by the people.' Thus,
'from the later seventeenth century the importance of managing
opinion had made nuance, discretion and less obvious coercion a
necessary part of the art of ruling'.[80] Allowing for the simplifications

necessitated by summary, Hay's thesis is that by combining the *terror* which accompanied the enormous increase in capital offences with a legal ideology that combined 'majesty', 'justice', 'mercy' and therefore *discretion* to pardon, eighteenth-century criminal law moulded, 'the consciousness by which the many submitted to the few'.[81] The criminal law, he contends, 'more than any other social institution, made it possible to govern eighteenth-century England without a police force and without a large army. The ideology of the law was crucial in sustaining the hegemony of the English ruling class'.[82]

How did the law sustain this hegemony? Hay distinguishes three aspects of the criminal law as ideology which facilitated and legitimated that hegemony: 'majesty', 'justice' and 'mercy'. The majesty of the criminal law, that is, the spectacle and elaborate ritual surrounding the visits of judges 'had considerable psychic force'.[83] The court was a stage from which 'the multitude' were addressed.

> The aim was . . . to impress the onlookers by word and gesture, to fuse terror and argument into the amalgam of legitimate power in their hands . . . In its ritual, its judgments and its channelling of emotion the criminal law echoed many of the most powerful psychic components of religion.[84] . . . The secular mysteries of the courts had burned deep into the popular consciousness, and perhaps the labouring poor knew more of the terrors of the law than those of religion.[85]

The ideological dimension of 'justice' stemmed from the theory that once in court 'all men were equal' and therefore even the poorest was assured justice:

> The punctilious attention to forms, the dispassionate and legalistic exchanges between counsel and the judge, argued that those administering and using the laws submitted to its rules. The law thereby became something more than the creature of a ruling class — it became a power with its own claims, higher than those of prosecutor, lawyers and even the great scarlet-robed assize judge himself. To them, too, of course, the law was 'The Law.' The fact that they reified it, that they shut their eyes to its daily enactment in Parliament by men of their own class, heightened the illusion. When the ruling class acquitted men on technicalities they helped instil a belief in the disembodied justice of the law in the minds of all who watched. In short, its very inefficiency, its absurd formalism, was part of its strength as ideology.[86]

'Ideologies do not rest on realities, however, but on appearances.'[87]

Of course social class did preserve some from the rigours of the criminal law. However, the execution of a man of position or property and the occasional success of a labouring man 'probably helped sustain the belief that the integrity of the law was a reality and not merely the rhetoric of judges and gentlemen'.[88] The law was held to be their guardian. 'Gentlemen held this as an unquestionable belief: that belief, too, gave the ideology of justice an integrity which no self-conscious manipulation could alone sustain.'[89] The local power of the gentry was reinforced by a form of legal administration which permitted a great deal of discretion. Beyond London, society was made up of 'close and persisting personal relationships'[90] within which an economic and cultural nexus of fear and gratitude coexisted simultaneously. The ideological dimensions of 'mercy' in such communities did much to cement that nexus of dependency, loyalty, paternalism, trust and deference. Character witnesses were of crucial importance and this gave enormous discretion to men of property other than the prosecution. 'A labourer accused of a serious crime learned again his enormous dependence on the power of property to help him, or abandon him, as it chose.'[91] Since pardons were common and the word of a man of property had the greatest weight, 'mercy was part of the currency of patronage'.[92] The manner in which pardons were thus obtained — by resort to personal ties which 'bridged great vertical distances in the social order'[93] and the weight attached to 'respectability' and 'connections' in pardons meant that claims of class and respectability were much more influential than the claims of humanity. Because the law like society was organised hierarchically, it also served to increase the solidarity of the ruling class. If a local person of property could not obtain a pardon for a convict, he could ask someone with more influence. Although the

> convolutions of the patronage system were known at the lowest level to every man . . . pardon-dealing went on at the highest levels only, well concealed from the eyes of the poor. Therefore the royal prerogative of mercy could be presented as something altogether more mysterious, more sacred and more absolute in its determinations. Pardons were presented as acts of grace rather than as favours to interests.[94]

In short, the majesty, justice and mercy of the criminal law 'helped to create the spirit of consent and submission, the 'mind-forged manacles', which Blake saw binding the English poor'.[95] Eighteenth-century criminal law was important as coercion. It was equally important as ideology as an 'instrument of authority', and as a 'breeder of values'.[96]

Taken together *Albion's Fatal Tree* and *Whigs and Hunters* reconstruct 'from the ground upwards' the nearest we have to a three-dimensional view of the social, economic and political significance of eighteenth-century criminal law. More generally, the essence of a social formation in transition has been crystallised. These studies vividly record the process by which the law and brute force were used to facilitate and legitimate the redefinition of non-monetary use-rights and traditional expectations and forms of dignity to crimes such as poaching, theft and trespass. In this way, the law mediated and reinforced a reified conception of absolute property ownership the sacredness of which was declared 'in terms hitherto reserved for human life'.[97] To this and much else — which is recovered through the masterly deployment of rich and varied empirical detail — it is impossible to do justice in the space available.

To what extent does the work of Hay, Thompson *et al.* offer a more convincing interpretative framework of the relationship between law, economy and society than that of consensus and instrumentalist historiography? Clearly, the suitability or otherwise of their interpretative framework can only be judged in the light of the extent to which they affect the central concerns to which they are addressed. Here at its most succinct it is assumed that the central concerns of socio-historical studies of the relationship between law and economy in England since *circa* 1750 are the extent to which the law and legal institutions facilitated and legitimated the development of industrial capitalism; the relationship between economy, society and the construction, conceptualisation and form of law and legal institutions; and the relationship between economy, society, dominant ideologies and legal ideologies. In terms of addressing these concerns, *Albion's Fatal Tree* and *Whigs and Hunters* do hint at a problematic which offers a more authentic and inclusive interpretative framework of the relationship between law, economy and society than that of consensus and instrumentalist historiography. In part, this is because at its best their implicit appropriation of Gramsci's concept of hegemony contributes to a history not merely of individuals from 'below' or 'above' but the whole complex set of relations in which they live and within which they make themselves and are made social beings.[98] Unfortunately, 'experiential' historians tend to seem reluctant fully to theorise the results of their researches and acknowledge theoretical borrowings.[99] In this sense, Hay's paper outlined above and the conclusion of Thompson's *Whigs and Hunters* are exceptional in their overt concern to chart the implications of their work in theoretical terms. As a result the task of pinpointing and elaborating the problematic within which they operate is decidedly more difficult. The problem is compounded by the fact that, conceptually, Thompson's work has not remained static, and that any assessment of the interpretative framework within which he operates must recognise these changes — especially those embodied in his most recent work. Furthermore, there are problems in treating the work of Hay, Thompson *et al.* as one undifferentiated whole, i.e., 'experiential history'. At one level it is true that they represent a particular *genre*. However, on an individual level, some aspects of their work are more subject to criticism at a methodological level than others. Indeed, a more simplistic reductionist analysis may be found to coexist alongside a more complex and informed analysis in the same text. The force of these objections, however, is not, I believe, such as to render such an exercise futile. What follows is a preliminary attempt to focus upon the strengths and weaknesses of the problematics imbibed by Hay and Thompson. In fact, I shall be almost exclusively concerned with one facet of their problematic, albeit an important one: namely, their efforts to avoid 'determinism' whilst maintaining some meaningful degree of 'determination' in their work on the relationship between law, economy and society. Is it possible to develop an analytical framework which is holistic, that accounts for the complexity and fragmentation of modern sociey, that eschews those reductionisms that treat social, political, legal and ideological phenomena as merely the exegesis of 'economy' without succumbing to an organic 'safe, colourless, "multiple-factor" view of causation'?[100] Whilst the dilemma posed by this question is of direct significance to Marxist thought, the issues it raises — the nature of the relationship between law, economy and society — are clearly of direct relevance to non-Marxists too.

If we return to Hay's essay, 'Property, Authority and the Criminal Law',[101] we can locate absences and elements which, taken in isolation, do add up to a portrayal of the ideological hegemony of eighteenth-century criminal law which is tinged with reductionisms. The ideological hegemony of the criminal law that he describes is a well-nigh all-embracing, smothering, 'world-view'.[102] It is not 'a realized complex of experiences, relationships and activities with specific and changing pressures and limits'.[103] In Hay's piece 'the limits beyond which authority did not dare to go' turn out to conceal a well-hidden ruling-cass conspiracy (within the strict legal definition of the term!);[104] the 'limits' themselves are in fact not real but illusory. There is no account whatsoever of resistance and opposition within plebeian culture to the increasing deification of property and the draconian nature of eighteenth-century criminal law.[105] Yet the reality of hegemony requires consideration of the manner and extent to which hegemony is resisted, limited, altered and challenged by pressures not at all its own. His use of hegemony fails to embrace the counter-hegemonic and alternative hegemony which, as other accounts of eighteenth-century plebeian culture testify, were real and persistent elements of historical practice. As a result, the sense of loss and deprivation felt by plebeian culture are seemingly ignored.[106] There is no sense in which alternative forms of property and culture coexisted at the same time that absolute conceptions of property ownership were becoming pre-eminent, during the long transition between modes of production portrayed by Dobb and Thompson.[107] 'For of course in transitional phases and especially in the transition to industrial capitalism, emergent and residual social classes [and definitions of property] co-exist. History is unlikely to be determined wholly by the classes of landed society or those of modern industry.'[108] Hay's essay gives the impression that the penetration of legal ideology within plebeian culture was almost complete throughout the country with the exception of London. Otherwise geographical, local, factional and cultural differences and the effect these might have on the production of dominant ideology and the extent of their penetration are barely considered.[109] Similarly, there is no recognition that the ideology of the dominant class is modified through their inevitable adaptation to the varied conditions of existence. In sum, much of Hay's essay portrays the legal hegemony of eighteenth-century England in terms resembling familiar models of 'one-dimensional control in which all sense of struggle or contradiction is lost'.[110] However, to stop there would be grossly unfair to Hay. In an all-too-brief but important 'methodological' interlude, Hay does seem to put the brakes on, recognising that he is veering perilously close to a deterministic account of legal hegemony.[111] He begins by pointing to a danger,

> which perhaps this [Hay's] essay has not avoided, of giving the impression that a system of authority is *something* rather than the actions of living men . . . [Much] of the ideological structure surrounding the criminal law was the product of countless short-term decisions . . . [and] not a plot worked out by eighteenth-century experts in public relations for a fee.[112]

Does this imply that Hay is withdrawing the confident assertion of a few sentences earlier that legal hegemony amounted to a 'ruling-class conspiracy'? No — Hay attempts to maintain his position. He seeks to do this by defining conspiracy in such a way that it is both accurate and meaningful as a historic description *and* not a reified, deterministic epithet. 'The course of history', he argues, 'is the result of a complex of human actions — purposive, accidental, sometimes determined — and it cannot be reduced to one transcendent purpose'.[113] Whilst the course of history generally cannot be so subsumed, the historian must make explicit unspoken convictions if we are to understand the actions of those who held them and, if the evidence warrants it, deduce a conspiracy therefrom. This, he contends, is not the same as reifying and abstracting the course of history. Similarly, to make explicit the assumptions and actions of the ruling class and draw conclusions about the relationship between those assumptions and actions and the nature of the legal system does not succumb to imposing a 'world-view' on history. This is because, unlike the course of history, the ruling class is 'a more substantial concept' of men

> agreed on ultimate ends. However much they believed in justice (and they did); however sacred they held property (and they worshipped it); however merciful they were to the poor (and many were); the gentlemen of England knew that their duty was, above all, to rule. On that depended everything. They acted accordingly.[114]

In other words, in the administration of justice the ruling classes' 'duty to rule' determined in the sense of 'setting bounds' or 'setting limits'[115] their assumptions and actions. What Hay seems to be arguing (and this is his strength) is that the histories of eighteenth-century criminal law have been flawed because they lack a notion of *power*, in the sense of explaining the mobilisation of popular support behind particular beliefs about the proper ordering of society. The 'moral consensus' Thompson had detected is on closer inspection an ideological matrix which justified the domination of the landed class in eighteenth-century England. What Hay seems to be arguing is that the history of the criminal law reforms, in its emphasis on the relative morality of its participants (as judged by the standards of today), is unhistorical because it ignores the class nature of society and class struggle, and the ultimate desire of the rulers to maintain their rule. In these ways Hay seeks to steer a course between determinism and organic, pluralistic or consensus-value frameworks. Irrespective of his success, it is a thoughtful and illuminating effort.

As in the 'experiential' histories of E.P. Thompson, class and class struggle are *the* master categories,[116] i.e., they are the principal structures through which economic determination occurs.[117] It has been argued that this overloads the Marxist conception of 'class struggle' and results in a view which omits to take account of the objective determinant economic conditions

> which set limits to what it is possible for any group of men or women to do . . . [In 'experiential' histories] Class . . . supplies a kind of structure that sits on the surface of things, is there to be seen by anyone who looks (or listens). The problem, in general, with such sociologies, is that they abandon the ground of 'determinations' or of explanations of *why* things (or relations) appear as they do.[118]

This later omission can be illustrated in the light of the reasons why the late eighteenth and early nineteenth centuries witnessed the rise and eventual success of a movement which liberalised English criminal law. 'After all, if the interests of the British ruling class lay so firmly on the side of the *status quo ante*, as Hay appears to affirm in his concluding pages, why did the reforms take place at all?'[119] Class struggle and the power of the law as ideology cannot of themselves explain the defeat of the conservative opposition to reform — though it does make sense of the delay in introducing the reforms. Only by reference to changes in the mode of production, in the economic focus of the dominant class (i.e., of the power relations between the landed and the rising middle classes), can we begin to explain the reform movement and its eventual success as well as trace the corresponding adjustment in the ideological hegemony of the law which justified the new set of relations. As Hay himself notes, albeit schematically, the gentry were relatively unconcerned with the effectiveness of the criminal law as a mechanism for reducing the theft of property because their immense personal wealth was grounded in land which was secure and their goods could be protected without the need of public intervention.[120]

Theft for the gentry was more a political affront than an economic threat. Middling-men of trade and industry, on the other hand, had a much greater economic stake in the liberalisation of the criminal law especially since, as a result of the expansion of trade and urbanisation, theft had become increasingly prevalent. With the gradual rise to power of the middle classes and changes in political economy the gentry's powers of social control increasingly became undermined. The inadequacies of the old bloody code, economically and as a social control, became impossible to defend. Arguably, changes in economic structure set both the limits of the increase in crime and also the changes in the balance of political power necessary to bring about the reform of the criminal law. In the 'experiential' problematic which Hay and Thompson imbibe, however, economic relations tend to be assumed; changes in economic relations are understood almost exclusively *through* their ideological, social or political manifestation rather than in themselves.[121]

However, Thompson's most recent work does possess a number of strengths it is important not to overlook. *Whigs and Hunters* marks an important advance over his early work such as *The Making of the English Working Class*. Their respective titles attest to the change in perspective. Whilst the latter is not simply the history of a particular class it is *primarily* focused upon the experience, culture and aspirations of working people. In *Whigs and Hunters*, on the other hand, he charts some of the critical social and economic tensions that spanned vertically across the supposedly harmonious society of eighteenth-century England. It is not a history in the sense of providing a comprehensive survey of eighteenth-century English society. As in Thompson's earlier work, only more so, certain specific individual occurrences serve as the quintessence of a social formation. The perspective is holistic. It is a history constructed 'from below' in that he opens with the foresters whose customary rights were being invaded and their opposition thereto and closes with the Whig oligarchy whose measures, ideology and law suppressed that opposition. Another change evidenced in *Whigs and Hunters* – and more explicitly in his recent essays on eighteenth-century plebeian culture[122] – is that his earlier ambivalance towards 'hegemony' as a tool of historical analysis has given way to its incorporation as a major category in his work.[123] It is Genovese rather than Gramsci whose dissection of hegemony and reciprocity is acknowledged as of 'great relevance'[124] and whose 'significance . . . cannot be overstated'.[125] Perhaps this is a symptom of Thompson's intense efforts to distance himself politically and methodologically from those appropriations of Gramsci's conception of hegemony which impose

> an all-embracing domination upon the ruled . . . reaching down to the very threshold of their experience, and implanting within their minds at birth categories of subordination which they are powerless to shed and which their experience is powerless to correct. This may perhaps have happened here and there, but not in England, not in the eighteenth century.[126]

In order to convey the flavour of Thompson's usage of hegemony and reciprocity I shall briefly recount the thesis he first elaborated in his paper on Patrician society, plebeian culture in 1974.[127] Here Thompson 'directed attention to the actual erosion of paternalist forms of control through the expansion of "free" masterless labour'.[128] English cultural and social life were, as a result, significantly changed. It did not, however, generate any 'crisis' in the old order. The cultural hegemony of the gentry was maintained because change was contained within the pre-existing structures of power. The maintenance of the gentry's cultural hegemony was contingent upon the gentry performing certain roles and accepting a certain degree of plebeian self-assertion and identity. Thompson concluded, then, that as regards

> the special case of the eighteenth century . . . I find the notion of gentry-crowd reciprocity, of the paternalism – deference equilibrium in which both parties to the equation were, in some degree, the prisoners of each other, more helpful than notions of a 'one-class society' or of consensus.[129]

As a consequence of his insistence that the hegemony of the gentry in

eighteenth-century England was not all-embracing, Thompson's view of
the degree to which legal ideology penetrated the world and consciousness of rural plebeian life is more equivocal than that of Hay.[130] As
Thompson explains,

> we have the paradox of a customary [plebeian] culture which is not
> subject in its daily operations to the ideological domination of the
> rulers. The gentry's hegemony may define the limits . . . within
> which the plebeian culture is free to act and grow, but since this
> hegemony is secular rather than religious or magical it can do little
> to determine the character of this plebeian culture . . . The law may
> punctuate the limits of behaviour tolerated by the rulers; it does not,
> in the eighteenth century, enter into the cottages, find mention in
> the housewife's prayers, decorate the chimney-piece with icons, or
> inform a view of life.[131]

In contrast to Hay's 'hypothesis' that the criminal law of eighteenth-
century England was more important than any other social institution
in maintaining the hegemony of the ruling class, Thompson does not
seem to regard the law (both criminal *and* civil) as the pre-eminent
constituent of gentry hegemony; rather for him it is but one of the
major ingredients. Thus, Thompson describes the ingredients of the
particular equilibrium of social relations of eighteenth-century England
as 'a structured set of relations, in which the State, the Law, the liber-
tarian ideology, the ebullitions and direct actions of the crowd' were
paramount.[132] Of these, Thompson concludes that it was as much the
form of state power established by the Settlement of 1688 (which fixed
the form of rule for an agrarian bourgeoisie) as it was the mode of production, which determined the politics and culture of most of the
eighteenth century.[133] The state, he contends

> weak as it was in its bureaucratic and rationalizing functions, was
> immensely strong and effective as an auxiliary instrument of produc-
> tion in its own right: in breaking open the paths for commercial
> imperialism, in imposing enclosure upon the countryside, and in
> facilitating the accumulation and movement of capital, both
> through its banking and funding functions and, more bluntly,
> through the parasitic extraction of its own officers. It is this
> specific combination of weakness and of strength which provides
> the 'general illumination' in which all colours of that century are
> plunged; which assigned to the judges and the magistracy their roles;
> which made necessary the theatre of cultural hegemony and which
> wrote its paternalistic and libertarian script; which afforded to the
> crowd its opportunity for protest and for pressures; which laid

down the terms of negotiation between authority and plebs, and
which established the limits beyond which negotiation might not
go.[134]

Perhaps as an exegesis of his conception of eighteenth-century English
society and the kind of hegemony he there locates, Thompson's latest
work stresses the vast range of differences, regional, chronological and
social, which make it impossible to talk of the plebeian culture without
exceptions. It would surely follow that the nature and extent to which
legal ideology penetrated plebeian culture would similarly have to be
prefaced by such qualifications. His efforts to transcend the reductionism of an all-embracing conception of hegemony and penetrate the
complexity and fragmentation of power relations in class society can
also be seen in his recent emphasis on the symbolism and theatre of
political life with its contests for symbolic authority.[135] He goes
further, however, for

> it is not sufficient merely to *describe* popular symbolic protests . . .
> it is necessary also to recover the significance of these symbols with
> reference to a wider symbolic universe and hence to locate their
> force, both as affronts to the rulers' hegemony and as expressions of
> the expectations of the crowd . . . [136] Everything transmitted to us
> through the polite culture has to be scrutinized upside-down[137]

i.e., 'decoded' in the sense advanced by Cain above. In the case of the
riots for possession of the bodies of the hanged at Tyburn, for instance,
what appeared 'conduct' premised upon 'popular ignorance' and
'archaic customs' to some distanced paternalistic gentry is 'decoded' by
Peter Linebaugh[138] to show us the rioter as being motivated by solidarity with the sufferer, class solidarities, notions of the respect due to
the integrity of the corpse and to the ritual of burial, and hostility 'to
the marketing of primary values'.[139]

If Thompson's more recent work on law and society suggests a
number of important methodological insights which avoid many of the
reductive tendencies noted earlier, this work also brings to the fore the
dilemma confronting contemporary Marxist analyses of law and
economy previously noted. Thompson's aversion to all-embracing
conceptions of cultural hegemony is also reflected in a long-standing
characteristic of his work: his criticism of the base-superstructure metaphor as an accurate illusion to the relationship between class and
economy in history. The tensions generated within an avowedly
'Marxist' analysis of the relationship between law and economy by
Thompson's strictures, will now be considered in the light of
Thompson's critique of the base-superstructure metaphor.

The Base-Superstructure Metaphor

E.P. Thompson's rejection of an economistic interpretation of the
relationship between economy and society is long standing. For
Thompson 'class is a cultural as much as an economic formation'.[140]
Human agency and ideas match economy — are 'two sides of a coin' —
and the one is not reducible to the other.[141] It is this problematic, and
the historical conjuncture which it emanates from (the emergence of a
new kind of English socialist and humanist history after the mid-1950s)
which explains Thompson's aversion to the base-superstructure
metaphor. That his recent work has stressed that historically speaking
law does not simply mirror the necessities of an economic infrastructure is therefore hardly surprising. Nor does he treat law as a wholly
autonomous institution distinct from an economic infrastructure.[142]
In fact, his analysis of the relationship between law, economy and
society is highly suggestive. The essence of his view is that law is 'deeply
imbricated within the very basis of productive relations, which would
have been inoperable without this law'.[143] He elaborates this insight
in a number of ways so as to cast doubt upon the simple equation of
law as 'superstructure' or 'class power'; and, more recently, as part
of his polemic against Althusser's conception of superstructure as
relatively autonomous 'levels' (political, legal, aesthetic, etc.).[144]

'I found', writes Thompson,

> that law did not keep politely to a 'level' but was at *every* bloody
> level; it was imbricated within the mode of production and produc-
> tive relations themselves (as property-rights, definitions of agrarian
> practice) and it was simultaneously present in the philosophy of
> Locke; it intruded brusquely within alien categories, reappearing
> bewigged and gowned in the guise of ideology; it danced a cotillion
> with religion, moralising over the theatre of Tyburn; it was an arm
> of politics and politics was one of its arms; it was an academic
> discipline, subjected to the rigour of its own autonomous logic; it
> contributed to the definition of self-identity both of rulers and of
> ruled; above all, it afforded an arena for class struggle, within which
> alternative notions of law were fought out.[145]

This not simply reaffirms that law is sometimes relatively autonomous
— a warning against collapsing law back into 'economy' or 'class'. He
also emphasises law's diverse functions and forms, and that if its
ideology is to facilitate and legitimate hegemony it must impose certain
constraints upon the rulers themselves. 'The essential precondition for
the effectiveness of law, in its function as ideology, is that it shall . . .

seem to be just. It cannot seem to be so without . . . on occasion actually *being* just.'[146] The Rule of Law may actually limit the exercise of the law as a weapon of class rule.

Despite the insights afforded by Thompson's 'problematic', it is not without its problems. In a paper which has generated a flurry of indignant correspondence, Richard Johnson[147] (echoing Hindess and Hirst's criticism of Genovese[148]) has claimed that Thompson tends to collapse the economic structure and political and cultural superstructure. In fact, as Johnson would probably admit, this criticism has considerably less force when applied to Thompson's most recent work; and, indeed, some of his earlier work too.[149] Of course, the novelty and, in one sense, the strength of Thompson's most recent analysis of law and economy is precisely his emphasis on the way in which economy and superstructure do coalesce in practice. But how is it possible within a problematic of 'dialectic interaction' to maintain a notion of determination in the Marxist sense, i.e., of the objective *economic* relations of a society setting the bounds of class conduct? It is difficult not to disagree with Johnson that historical outcomes in Thompson's work (as in Hay's) are the product of class struggles; that it is the dynamic of 'class struggle' at the experiential level which in Thompson's work determines the nature of society rather than economic relations.[150] As a result, claims Johnson, Thompson's methodology 'suppresses Marx's major substantive achievements – the analysis of the forms, tendencies and laws of the capitalist mode of production'.[151] As we have seen, it is also an invariable problem for analyses, such as those of Thompson,that seek to transcend determinism and emphasise the heterogeneous, complex nature of society and economy.[152]

Thompson's discusson of the relative autonomy of law does shed a little new light on this notoriously elusive concept. However, many questions still abound: autonomous of what? how relatively? why only relative? The few historical studies touching upon the relationship between law and economy offer wildly differing conclusions. Some such as those of Watson, Simpson, Ferguson and Hirst[153] emphasise the fact that law developed almost autonomous of economy. Others such as those of Renner, Danzig and Friedman[154] emphasise the close relationship between the needs of industrial capitalism and the development of law. Others, such as Tushnet, White and Klare,[155] in different ways emphasise the relative autonomy of the law. Balbus, on the other hand, has contended that, at the level of theory, the conventional conception of the relative autonomy of law is untenable in a Marxist analysis of law in terms of a commodity/exchange analysis.[156] But if, as Thompson claims, law even shapes (in part) relations of production, then the emphasis in the work of Balbus and others on the relationship between law and commodity-form is at best but a fragmented view of

law and economy.[157] What is clear is that an advance in our understanding of the relative autonomy of the law is unlikely to occur at a
high level of abstraction. Broad generalisation is likely to prove
difficult. Only diverse historical case studies will provide us with the
data we so far lack. If we assume that, at least in the short term, some
area of business law is out-of-tune with economy, and if this is the case
over decades, will it not have a direct effect on at least the conduct of
business? In the long run how influential, if at all, is short-run relative
autonomy on the economy?[158]

Conclusion

In the historical work of Hartwell, Horwitz, Hay and Thompson on law
and economy we can identify at least three approaches or problematics:
a consensus-value approach (Hartwell); an instrumentalist approach
(Horwitz); and various kinds of 'experiental' or 'imbricationist' ways of
thinking about law and economy (Hay and Thompson). I have
suggested that each is, of itself, in some way inadequate. However, the
problematic imbibed by Thompson and Hay does offer important hints,
for example, on how to begin to overcome the reductionism of class
ideology as well as law and economy and (as in Horwitz's work) escape
the conservatism of traditional consensus historiography. In particular,
the recent work of Hay and Thompson points to some of the building
blocks necessary to construct a better historical practice. The task of
formulating an appropriate problematic remains a major task in the
development of a new history of the relationship between law and
economy. Questions of theory and method cannot be left unarticu-
lated or blithely disregarded. Conceptual or epistemological issues
should play a more important role than in the past in formulating the
ways in which the new legal history frames its questions, forms its
arguments and draws its inferences.[159] This is not to stress conceptual
refinement as an end in itself; nor to regard history as secondary to
theory. As a recent *History Workshop* editorial put it:

> The starting point . . . , that theoretical propositions can't be
> derived from empirical evidence is, to some of us at least, a correct
> one. But it by no means follows that the inverse of this is true, i.e.,
> that the construction of new theoretical concepts can proceed by a
> purely deductive process of reasoning without reference to empirical
> work . . . Theory-building cannot be an alternative to the attempt
> to explain real phenomena, but is, rather, a way of self-consciously
> defining the field of enquiry, clarifying and exposing to self-criticism
> the explanatory concepts used and marking the limits of empirical

investigation.[160]

Empirically grounded work of the kind being undertaken by historians on the relationship between law and economy has an important role to play in the development and criticism of theory. The recent work of Thompson and Hirst,[161] for instance, raises questions as to what it is that makes something distinctively 'Marxist'. Thompson's view that the rule of law is 'an unqualified human good',[162] and the controversy it has engendered, has posed important political questions such as the desirability or otherwise of regarding law as a focus of political struggle. 'History' is too important to be left only to historians; and, 'theory' is too important to be left only to sociologists. As I have attempted to demonstrate, in practice they really are inseparable.

I believe that a significant proportion of the most exciting and provocative work on the relationship between law and economy at the present time is to be found in the realm of history.

> It would, however, be a great pity if any of that vigour became lost in pursuing sectional academic claims, or, on the other hand, if the greater theoretical and logical rigour of sociology was not appreciated and incorporated into historical analysis. It is pertinent for us all to remember that the sub-divisions of academic disciplines do not relate to any *real* differences of interest or ability, but reflect only another division of labour, one which those of us who wish to explain society and, perhaps, to change it, would do well to struggle against.[163]

Notes

1. See for instance, T.B. Bottomore and M. Rubel, *Karl Marx: Selected Writings in Sociology and Social Philosophy* (1963), pp. 17-43.
2. See, for instance, A. Briggs, 'Sociology and History' in A.T. Welford *et al.* (eds), *Society* (1967), pp. 94-101; P. Abrams, 'Sociology and History', *Past and Present*, 52 (1971), pp. 118-25; and G.S. Jones, 'From Historical Sociology to Theoretical History', *British Journal of Sociology*, 27 (1976), pp. 295-305.
3. Quoted in Briggs, 'Sociology and History', p. 95.
4. J.G.Weis, 'Dialogue with David Matza', *Issues in Criminology*, 6 (1971), pp. 33-53, see p. 53.
5. However, a number of useful insights can be gleaned from S. Collini, 'Sociology and Idealism in Britain 1880-1920' *Archives of European Sociology*, 19 (1978), pp. 3-50; and see now S. Collini, *Liberalism and Sociology: L.T. Hobhouse and Political Argument in England 1880-1914* (1979).
6. C. Taylor, 'Marxism and Empiricism' in B. Williams (ed.) *British Analytical Philosophy* (1966), pp. 227-46, see p. 236.
7. Collini, 'Sociology and Idealism', pp. 43-4.
8. This is a more general phenomenon of English legal education; see

Z. Bankowski and G. Mungham, *Images of Law* (1976), pp. 32-48.

9. M.J. Horwitz, 'The Conservative Tradition in the Writing of American Legal History', *American Journal of Legal History*, 7 (1973), pp. 275-94, see p. 276.

10. See, for instance, A.P. Donajgrodzki (ed.), *Social Control in Nineteenth Century Britain* (1977), and R. Johnson, 'Educational Policy and Social Control in Early Victorian England' *Past and Present*, (1970), XLIV Cf. G.S. Jones, 'Class Expression Versus Social Control', *History Workshop*, 4 (1977), pp. 162-70.

11. See, for instance, E. Genovese, *Roll, Jordan, Roll: The World the Slaves Made* (1974); D. Hay (ed.), *Albion's Fatal Tree* (1975); E.P. Thompson, *Whigs and Hunters: The Origin of the Black Act* (1975).

12. See, for example, the excellent work of W.R. Carson, 'Symbolic and Instrumental Dimensions of Early Factory Legislation: A Case Study in the Social Origins of Criminal Law' in R. Hood (ed.), *Crime, Criminology and Public Policy* (1974), pp. 107-38 and 'The Conventionalization of Early Factory Crime' *IJSL*, 7 (1979), pp. 37-60.

13. See, for instance, C.A. Beard, *An Economic Interpretation of the Constitution* (1913) and J.R. Commons, *Legal Foundations of Capitalism* (1923).

14. D.J. Boorstin, 'Tradition and Method in Legal History', *Harvard Law Review*, 54 (1941), pp. 424-36, see p. 434.

15. D.S. Landes, 'The Structure of the Enterprise in the Nineteenth Century: The Cases of Britain and Germany', *Comité International des Sciences Historiques, Rapports*, vol. V (1960), pp. 107-128, see p. 122.

16. P. Mathias, *The First Industrial Nation* (1969), pp. 36-7.

17. M. Rheinstein (ed.), *Max Weber on Law in Economy and Society* (1954), pp. 29-30.

18. Ibid., p. 31. For an interesting case study which bears out Weber's position see R.B. Ferguson, 'Commercial Expectations and the Guarantee of the Law: Sales Transactions in Mid-19th Century England' in G.R. Rubin and D. Sugarman (eds), *Law and Economy: Essays in the History of English Law, 1700-1920* (Macmillan, forthcoming).

19. Rheinstein (ed.), *Max Weber*, p. 30.

20. Ibid., pp. 29-40.

21. Ibid., p. 39.

22. Ibid., p. 38.

23. D. Landes, *The Unbound Prometheus: Technological Change and Industrial Development in Western Europe from 1750 to the Present* (1969), p. 199 but cf. note 15 above.

24. M. Hartwell, *The Industrial Revolution and Economic Growth* (1971), p. 256.

25. Ibid., pp. 244-61 and M. Hartwell, 'Legal Change, Legal Reform and Economic Growth in England Before and During the Industrial Revolution', International Economic History Congress (1978), pp. 216-22. For a detailed critique of the views there espoused see D. Sugarman, 'Max Hartwell on Law and Economy During England's Industrial Revolution' (forthcoming).

26. Hartwell, 'Legal Change, Legal Reform and Economic Growth', p. 216. Hartwell is here attempting to apply F.A. Hayek's concept of a 'spontaneous order' as elaborated, for instance, in his *The Constitution of Liberty* (1960). For a more thoroughgoing application of Hayek's concept to the realms of modern legal history see R. Bridwell and R.U. Whitten, *The Constitution and the Common Law: Decline of the Doctrines of Separation of Powers and Federalism* (1977).

27. Space does not permit consideration of the role of the legal profession in shaping economy. During the eighteenth century and well into the nineteenth century, lawyers were almost universally satirised as pettifoggers and quacks.

Their 'professional' respectability is a relatively recent phenomenon. The attorney was perhaps an important figure in eighteenth-century provincial society; and he played an important role in the negotiation of loans, the formation of capital (as a middle-man, putting clients' money on mortgage) and, of course, in matters concerning landed property. In truth, we know far too little about the work of lawyers, their clients and their involvement in economy and society. Here, prosopographical research could prove extremely useful. See, generally, R. Robson, *The Attorney in Eighteenth Century England* (1959); L. Namier, *The Structure of Politics at the Accession of George III* (1963), pp. 42-4; and B.L. Anderson, 'Law, Finance and Economic Growth in England: Some Long-Term Influences' in B.M. Ratcliffe (ed.), *Great Britain and Her World 1750-1914* (1975), pp. 99-118.

M. Bloomfield's *American Lawyers in a Changing Society 1776-1876* (1976) is rather disappointing. Cf. M.S. Larson's suggestive socio-historical work, *The Rise of Professionalism* (1977), discussed by R.L. Abel in 'The Rise of Professionalism', *British Journal of Law and Society*, 6 (1979), pp. 82-98.

28. See, for instance, W. Hurst, *Law and the Conditions of Freedom in the Nineteenth Century United States* (1956) and *Law and Economic Growth: The Legal History of the Lumber Industry in Wisconsin 1836-1915* (1964). See also R.W. Gordon's excellent 'J. Willard Hurst and the Common Law Tradition in American Legal Historiography', *Law and Society Review*, 10 (1975), pp. 9-55.

29. M. Horwitz, *The Transformation of American Law, 1780-1860* (1977).

30. Ibid., p. 30.

31. Ibid., p. 99.

32. Ibid., p. 81.

33. Ibid., pp. 99-100.

34. Ibid., p. 101.

35. Ibid., pp. 160-210. Cf. A.W.B. Simpson, 'Innovation in Nineteenth Century Contract Law' *Law Quarterly Review*, 91 (1975), pp. 247-78, see, p. 277 n43.

36. Horwitz, *Transformation of American Law*, p. 192.

37. Ibid., p. 200.

38. Ibid., pp. 209, 210.

39. Ibid., pp. 211-12.

40. Ibid., p. xiv.

41. Ibid., pp. xii-xiii and 266.

42. For a rare example, see B.L. Anderson, 'The Attorney and the Early Capital Market in Lancashire' in F. Crouzet (ed.), *Capital Formation in the Industrial Revolution* (1972), pp. 223-55.

43. On Hurst see note 28; on Friedman see, for instance, L.M. Friedman, *Contract Law in America: A Social and Economic Case Study* (1965) and *A History of American Law* (1973).

44. Horwitz, *Transformation of American Law*, p. xii. On this theme see D. McBarnet and H.F. Moorhouse, 'Business Law and Bourgeois Ideology – A Prologue to a Research Project', unpublished mimeo (1977), p. 5.

45. Contrast the rich variety of material incorporated in the work of 'experiential' historians. Cf. J.W. Hurst, 'Old and New Dimensions of Research in United States Legal History', *American Journal of Legal History*, 23 (1979) pp. 1-20 and W.R. Cornish, 'Criminal Justice and Punishment' in W.R. Cornish *et al.*, *Crime and Law in Nineteenth Century Britain* (1978), pp. 7-62, see p. 13.

46. See M. Tushnet, 'A Marxist Analysis of American Law', *Marxist Perspectives* (1978).

47. I.e., that courts of civil law such as the High Court of Admiralty were generally preferred by merchants to the common law courts. See G.F. Steckley,

'Merchants and the Admiralty Court During the English Revolution', *American Journal of Legal History* 22 (1978), pp. 137-75, esp. pp. 137-9, 174-5; D.E.C. Yale, 'A View of the Admiral Jurisdiction: Sir Matthew Hale and the Civilians' in D. Jenkins (ed.), *Legal History Studies* (1975), pp. 87-109; and P. Anderson, *Lineages of the Absolutist State* (1974), pp. 24-9 and 425-6.

48. Rheinstein (ed.), *Max Weber* Chs 7, 11 and 14.

49. S. Macaulay, 'Non-Contractual Relations in Business: A Preliminary Study', *American Sociological Review*, 28 (1963), pp. 55-69; Friedman, *Contract Law in America;* H. Beale and T. Dugdale, 'Contracts Between Businessmen: Planning and the Use of Contractual Remedies', *British Journal of Law and Society*, 2 (1975), pp. 45-60; and for an anthropological perspective, S.F. Moore, 'Law and Social Change: The Semi-Autonomous Social Field as an Appropriate Subject of Study', *Law and Society Review*, 7 (1973), pp. 719-30, esp. pp. 723-9.

50. Not a call to reduce theoretical inquiry to empirical questions which has in the past been a tendency common to legal realism, legal anthropology, and consensus through to 'experiential' histories.

51. McBarnet and Moorhouse, 'Business Law and Bourgeois Ideology', p. 2.

52. M. Cain, Book Review *British Journal of Criminology*, 18 (1977), pp. 93-4, see p. 93. Similarly, see E.P. Thompson's notion of 'decoding' in Eighteenth Century English Society: Class Struggle Without Class?' *Social History*, 3 (1978), pp. 133-65, see pp. 150-65, 150-1, 155 and n43, 157.

53. Thompson, 'Eighteenth Century English Society', p. 136.

54. See, for instance, D. Simon, 'Master and Servant' in J. Saville (ed.), *Democracy and the Labour Movement* (1954), pp. 160-73 and 190-200.

55. Horwitz, *Transformation of American Law*, p. 212.

56. On the materialistic attitudes and practices of pre-industrial society see H.E. Hallam, 'The Medieval Social Picture' in E. Kamenka and R.S. Neale (eds), *Feudalism, Capitalism and Beyond* (1975), pp. 28-49, and A. Macfarlane, *The Origins of English Individualism* (1978).

B. Bailyn, *The New England Merchants in the 17th Century* (1955), J. Lockridge, 'Social Change and the Meaning of the American Revolution', *Journal of Social History*, 6 (1973), pp. 402-13, and S.N. Katz, 'Looking Backward: The Early History of American Law', *University of Chicago Law Review*, 33 (1966), pp. 867-84, esp. pp. 882-4, highlight the materialistic, divided and transitional nature of pre-revolutionary America respectively.

57. P. Rock, 'The Sociology of Deviancy and Conceptions of Moral Order', *British Journal of Criminology*, 14 (1974), pp. 139-47, see pp. 144-5.

58. For a more detailed critical evaluation of Horwitz's methodology and findings see D. Sugarman, 'Morton Horwitz and the Relation Between Economy and Law in America, 1780-1860' (forthcoming). For an extended attack on Horwitz's thesis which, although not without interest, fails substantially to detract from its undoubted worth see Bridwell and Whitten, *The Constitution and the Common Law*.

59. Horwitz, *Transformation of American Law*, p. xiii.

60. D. Landes, 'Structure of the Enterprise in the Nineteenth Century', pp. 107-28, see p. 122.

61. Thompson, *Whigs and Hunters*, p. 264. Cf. D. Trubek, 'Complexity and Contradiction in the Legal Order', *Law and Society Review*, 11 (1977), pp. 529-69.

62. See, for example, G.A. Cohen, *Karl Marx's Theory of History: A Defense* (1978), esp. Ch. VIII; E.O. Wright, *Class, Crisis and the State* (1978); S. Hall, 'Re-thinking the "Base-and-Superstructure" Metaphor' in J. Bloomfield (ed.), *Class, Hegemony and Party* (1977), pp. 43-71; R Williams, *Marxism and Literature* (1977), pp. 75-89 and E.P. Thompson, 'Folklore, Anthropology, and Social

History', *Indian History Review*, 3 (1977), pp. 247-66, esp. pp. 261-6.

   63. R.S. Summers, 'Naive Instrumentalism and the Law' in P.M.S. Hacker and J. Raz (eds), *Law, Morality and Society: Essays in Honour of H.L.A. Hart* (1977), pp. 119-31, see p. 126.

   64. See H.L.A. Hart, *The Concept of Law* (1961), pp. 18-119.

   65. See Rheinstein, *Max Weber* pp. 322-7.

   66. See, generally, C. Bogg, *Gramsci's Marxism* (1976), pp. 36-55; S. Hall *et al.*, 'Politics and Ideology: Gramsci' in *On Ideology* (1977), pp. 45-76; and P. Anderson, 'The Antinomes of Antonio Gramsci', *New Left Review*, 100 (1976-77), pp. 5-78. For an analysis of some potentialities of Gramsci's 'hegemony' as applied to law see A. Hunt, 'Perspectives in the Sociology of Law' in P. Carlen (ed.), *The Sociology of Law* (1976), pp. 22-44, see pp. 33-43.

   67. Hall *et al.*, 'Gramsci', p. 47.

   68. Ibid., pp. 48-53.

   69. R.Q. Gray, *The Labour Aristocracy in Victorian Edinburgh* (1976), p. 5.

   70. Ibid., pp. 5-6.

   71. See A. Gramsci, *Selections from Prison Notebooks* (ed. Q. Hoare and G.N. Smith, 1971), pp. 246-7 and 258-9.

   72. Genovese, *Roll, Jordan, Roll*, pp. 25-49.

   73. Ibid., pp.26-7.

   74. Hay, *Albion's Fatal Tree* (1975).

   75. Thompson, *Whigs and Hunters* (1975).

   76. Thompson, *The Making of the English Working Class* (Pelican edn, 1968).

   77. Ibid., pp. 90 and 87.

   78. See Hay, *Albion's Fatal Tree*, pp. 17-63. Cf. G.R. Elton's less than enthusiastic reception of Hay's essay, in J.S. Cockburn (ed.), *Crime in England 1550-1800* (1977), pp. 1-14, see pp. 7, 11-13 and n10.

   79. Hay, *Albion's Fatal Tree*, p. 58.

   80. Ibid., p. 57.

   81. This is how Hay explains the seeming paradox of a 'bloody penal code' which, however, did not result in an increase of the number of those actually hanged. See also M. Foucault, *Discipline and Punish: The Birth of the Prison* (1977, Penguin edn), pp. 3-69.

   82. Hay, *Albion's Fatal Tree*, p. 56.

   83. Ibid., p. 27.

   84. Ibid., p. 29.

   85. Ibid., p. 30.

   86. Ibid., p. 33.

   87. Ibid., p. 36.

   88. Ibid., p. 34.

   89. Ibid., p. 35. Cf. Gramsci's conception of 'hegemony' as discussed in the text above, pp. 17-18.

   90. Hay, *Albion's Fatal Tree*, p. 55.

   91. Ibid., p. 42.

   92. Ibid., p. 45. See also Foucault, *Discipline and Punish*.

   93. Hay, *Albion's Fatal Tree*, p. 42.

   94. Ibid., p. 47.

   95. Ibid., p. 49.

   96. Ibid., p. 58.

   97. Ibid., p. 17. Cf. C.B. MacPherson, *The Theory of Possessive Individualism: Hobbes to Locke* (1962); E.P. Thompson, 'The Grid of Inheritance: A Comment' in J. Goody *et al.*, *Family and Inheritance: Rural Society in Western Europe 1200-1800*, pp. 328-60; and V.G. Kiernan, 'Private Property in History' in Goody, *et al.*, *Family and Inheritance*, pp. 361-98.

98. This is also true of the work of Eugene Genovese. In part, their breadth stems from their unspoken commitment to a holistic analysis.

99. See R. Johnson, 'Thompson, Genovese and Socialist-Humanist History', *History Workshop*, 6 (1978), pp. 79-101, see pp. 87-9; 'Culture and the Historians' in J. Clarke *et al.*, *Working Class Culture: Studies in History and Theory* (1979) pp. 41-71, see pp. 66 and 70; and 'Three Problematics: Elements of a Theory of Working Class Culture' in Clarke *et al.*, *Working Class Culture*, pp. 201-37, see p. 216. These papers have much influenced this and the ensuing section of this essay.

100. C. Wright Mills, 'The Professional Ideology of Social Pathologists' in I.L. Horowitz (ed.), *Power, Politics and People* (1963), pp. 525-52, see p. 537.

101. Hay, *Albion's Fatal Tree*, pp. 17-63.

102. Cf. Williams, *Marxism and Literature* pp. 112-13. My point is that Hay's tendency to portray the ideological hegemony of the law as monolithic (save in his discussion on pp. 52-6) is both a misappropriation of hegemony as Gramsci perceived it, and is historically too simplistic. As a result he exaggerates the importance of the ideological force of the law. In this respect, and in others, Hay's other essay in *Albion's Fatal Tree*, 'Poaching and the Game Laws on Cannock Chase', pp. 189-253, is more satisfactory. This *caveat* apart, it remains a highly suggestive and important essay.

103. Williams, *Marxism and Literature*, 112.

104. Hay, *Albion's Fatal Tree*, p. 52 and n3: the latter is no doubt somewhat tongue-in-cheek.

105. This strongly contrasts with much of E.P. Thompson's work.

106. Ibid.

107. See M. Dobb, *Studies in the Development of Capitalism* (1946) on which see R. Johnson *et al.*, *Economy, Culture and Concept*, pp. 3-27; and E.P. Thompson, for instance, 'The Moral Economy of the English Crowd in the Eighteenth Century', *Past and Present*, 50 (1971), pp. 76-136, 'The Grid of Inheritance' and *Whigs and Hunters*.

108. R. Johnson, *Peculiarities of the English Route: Barrington Moore, Perry Anderson and English Social Development* (1975), p. 5.

109. On which see the other essays in *Albion's Fatal Tree*.

110. Johnson, 'Three Problematics' p. 230 (as a criticism of Althusser).

111. Hay, *Albion's Fatal Tree*, pp. 52-6. Particularly important is his contrast of London with rural England; and his admission that legal hegemony 'was never complete and unbroken': p. 55.

112. Ibid., p. 53.

113. Ibid.

114. Ibid.

115. See Williams, *Marxism and Literature*, p. 84.

116. See E.P. Thompson, 'Eighteenth Century English Society' pp. 147-8, 156-8, and generally, 'The Poverty of Theory' in E.P. Thompson, *The Poverty of Theory and Other Essays* (1978), pp. 193-397, see pp. 322-69.

117. See Johnson, 'Thompson, Genovese and Socialist-Humanist History', pp. 92 and 98; and 'Three Problematics', pp. 215 and 221 — a criticism prefigured in T. Tholfsen, *Working Class Radicalism in Mid-Victorian England* (1976), pp. 19-20.

118. Johnson, 'Thompson, Genovese and Socialist-Humanist History' p. 92. Cf. Thompson's rejection of this kind of criticism in 'Eighteenth Century English Society', pp. 149-50, 'Folklore, Anthropology and Social History' esp. pp. 261-6 and 'The Poverty of Theory'.

119. J.N.J. Palmer, 'Evils Merely Prohibited', *British Journal of Law and Society*, 3 (1976), pp. 1-16. The discussion in the remainder of this paragraph and

the following paragraph draws heavily upon this essay.

120. Hay, *Albion's Fatal Tree*, pp. 20 and 60.

121. See generally the essays of Johnson quoted in note 99 above.

122. See Thompson, 'Eighteenth Century English Society'.

123. See E.P. Thompson, 'The Peculiarities of the English' (1965) in *The Poverty of Theory and Other Essays*, pp. 35-91, see pp. 72-4.

124. Thompson, 'Eighteenth Century English Society', pp. 138 n7.

125. Ibid., p. 137 n7.

126. Ibid., p. 164.

127. Thompson, *Journal of Economic History*, 7 (1974), pp. 382-405.

128. Thompson, 'Eighteenth Century English Society', p. 144.

129. Ibid., p. 150.

130. Cf. 'And the law did nòt enforce uniform obedience, did not seek total control': Hay, *Albion's Fatal Tree*, p. 55.

131. Thompson, 'Eighteenth Century English Society', p. 154.

132. Ibid., p. 161.

133. Ibid., p. 162.

134. Ibid.

135. Ibid., p. 158. See also E.P. Thompson, 'Anthropology and the Discipline of Historical Context' *Midland History*, 1 (1972), pp. 41-55. Obviusly this emphasis on the 'symbolic' is by no means unique to Thompson.

136. Thompson, 'Eighteenth Century English Society', p. 155 n43, and pp. 155-7.

137. Ibid., p. 157.

138. See P. Linebaugh, 'The Tyburn Riot Against the Surgeons' in Hay, *Albion's Fatal Tree*, pp. 65-117.

139.Thompson, 'Eighteenth Century English Society', p. 157.

140. Thompson, *The Making of the English Working Class*, p. 10.

141. See Johnson, 'Thompson, Genovese and Socialist-Humanist History', p. 87.

142. See Thompson, *Whigs and Hunters* pp. 266-7. Nor does he deny the class-bound and mystifying functions of law: p. 260.

143. Ibid., p. 261.

144. See, generally, Thompson, 'The Poverty of Theory'. See also R. Kinsey, 'Marxism and the Law' *British Journal of Law and Society*, 5 (1978), pp. 202-27, see pp. 204 and 206-10; Thompson, 'The Grid of Inheritance' and 'Folklore, Anthropology and Social History', pp. 261-6.

145. Thompson, 'The Poverty of Theory', p. 288.

146. Thompson, *Whigs and Hunters*, p. 263. Cf. M. Cain and A. Hunt, *Marx and Engels on Law* (1979), pp. 145-7.

147. See Johnson, 'Thompson, Genovese and Socialist-Humanist History', p. 91. Cf. K. McClelland, 'Some Comments on Richard Johnson', *History Workshop*, 7 (1979), pp. 101-15; G. Williams, 'In Defence of History', *History Workshop*, 7 (1979), pp. 116-24; and the 'Readers' Letters', *History Workshop*, 7 (1979), pp. 220-5.

148. B. Hindess and P.Q. Hirst, *Pre-Capitalist Modes of Production* (1975), pp. 150-77.

149. See, for example, E.P. Thompson, 'Time, Work-Discipline and Industrial Capitalism' *Past and Present*, 38 (1967), pp. 56-97.

150. Johnson, 'Thompson, Genovese and Socialist-Humanist History', pp. 92 and 98 and 'Three Problematics', pp. 221-4.

151. Johnson, 'Thompson, Genovese and Socialist-Humanist History', p. 97.

152. For Thompson the dichotomy between 'economy' and 'class culture' is fallacious; it embodies an over-narrow definition of 'economy' which is incompat-

ible with Marx's own work. On this, and Thompson's detailed efforts to refute the kind of arguments Johnson poses, see for example Thompson, 'The Poverty of Theory' and 'Folklore, Anthropology and Social History', pp. 261-6.

153. See A. Watson, *Society and Legal Change* (1977); Simpson, 'Innovation in Nineteenth Century Contract Law'; R.B. Ferguson, 'Legal Ideology and Commercial Interests', *British Journal of Law and Society*, 4 (1977), pp. 18-38; and P. Hirst, *On Law and Ideology* (1979), pp. 127-52 but cf. D. Sugarman, 'The Instrumental and Ideological Dimensions of the Companies Acts, 1825-1862' in G.R. Rubin and D. Sugarman (eds), *Law and Economy: Essays in the History of English Law 1700-1920* (Macmillan, forthcoming).

154. See K. Renner, *The Institutions of Private Property and their Social Functions* (1949); R. Danzig, 'Hadley v. Baxendale: A Study in the Industrialization of the Law', *Journal of Legal Studies*, 4 (1975), pp. 249-84; and Friedman, *A History of American Law*. See also M.E. Tigar and M.R. Levy, *Law and the Rise of Capitalism* (1977); J. Hall, *Theft, Law and Society* (2nd edn, 1952); R. Gregory, 'Trespass to Negligence to Absolute Liability', *Virginia Law Review*, 37 (1951), pp. 358-81; and R. Brenner, 'Nuisance Law and the Industrial Revolution', *Journal of Legal Studies*, 3 (1974), pp. 403-32.

155. See. M. Tushnet, 'The American Law of Slavery, 1810-1860: A Study in the Persistence of Legal Autonomy', *Law and Society Review* (1975), pp. 119-84, esp. pp. 177-80; G.E. White, 'The Intellectual Origins of Torts in America', *Yale Law Journal*, 86 (1977), pp. 671-93 and 'The Impact of Legal Science on Tort Law, 1880-1910', *Columbia Law Review*, 78 (1978), pp. 213-40; and K.E. Klare, 'Judicial Deradicalisation of the Wagner Act and the Origin of Modern Legal Consciousness, 1937-1941', *Minnesota Law Review*, 62 (1978), pp. 265-310. On the relative autonomy of the ideology of the legal profession, see P. Miller's pioneering (but flawed) study, *The Life of the Mind in America: From the Revolution to the Civil War* (1965), pp. 99-265; and M. Tushnet, 'Perspectives on the Development of American Law: A Critical Review of Friedman's "A History of American Law" ', *Wisconsin Law Review*, (1977), pp. 81-109, see pp. 87-94.

156. Balbus, 'Commodity Form and Legal Form: An Essay on the "Relative Autonomy" of the Law', *Law and Society Review*, 11 (1977), pp. 571-8.

157. See R.A. Warrington, 'The Necessity of Law – The Rise, Orthodoxy and Withering Away of Pashukanis' (1979), unpublished mimeo, p. 23.

158. See Landes, 'The Structure of the Enterprise in the Nineteenth Century', pp. 122-3.

159. The following represent important attempts to illuminate the theoretical concerns raised by the historical study of law and economy: McBarnet and Moorhouse, 'Business Law and Bourgeois Ideology', Tushnet, 'Perspectives on the Development of American Law'; and P. Young, 'A Sociological Analysis of the Early History of Probation', *British Journal of Law and Society*, 3 (1976), pp. 44-58.

160. 'History and Theory' *History Workshop*, 6 (1978), pp. 1-6, see p. 4.

161. See, for instance, Thompson 'The Poverty of Theory' and Hirst, *On Law and Ideology*.

162. Thompson, *Whigs and Hunters*. For an important elaboration of this viewpoint see E.P. Thompson, 'The Rule of Law in English History', *Bulletin of Haldane Society of Socialist Lawyers*, no. 2 (1979), pp. 7-10. For a critical assessment of Thompson's views see D. Sugarman, 'E.P. Thompson and the Relationship between Law and Economy from an Historical Perspective' (forthcoming).

163. H.F. Moorhouse, 'History, Sociology and the Quiescence of the British Working Class', *Social History*, 4 (1979), pp. 481-90, see p. 490.

In the United States there are real signs that the borderline between legal and economic history is beginning to give way to a new inter-disciplinary history. See, for example, the papers contained in a recent special issue of *Business History Review* devoted to the interaction between law and business in American economic development: *Business History Review*, no. 3, L111 (1979) — these fascinating papers appeared too late to be considered here.

Acknowledgements

I am grateful to Léonie Sugarman and Ronnie Warrington for their encouragement and criticisms.

P.S. Atiyah, *The Rise and Fall of Freedom of Contract* (1979) and R. Stevens, *Law and Politics: The House of Lords as a Judicial Body, 1800-1976* (1979) and A.W.B. Simpson, 'The Horwitz Thesis and the History of Contracts', *University of Chicago Legal Review*, 46 (1979), pp. 533-601 appeared too late for me to consider them.

SOCIOLOGY IN JURISPRUDENCE: THE
PROBLEM OF 'LAW' AS OBJECT OF
KNOWLEDGE

Iain Stewart

The Looking-Glass Problem

'Law', to a sociologist,[2] seems evidently real, and yet chimerical. It is
plainly real both as social action and as meaning. But the meanings tend
to bundle themselves off into a realm of their own which turns to confront the sociologist as a rival reality, embracing even a rival version of
the social action through which those meanings have been discovered.
The sociologist — and also the jurist who attempts to take up a sociological standpoint — are baffled by this resistance of the object of
knowledge. Although, as academic disciplines, sociology of law is the
same age as general sociology — Durkheim proposing a sociology of law,
specifically to get away from the study of law by 'pure exegesis', in his
introductory lecture of 1887[3] — Llewellyn and Hoebel could still say
in 1941 that modern law

> becomes a world of its own. It is a world like Alice's Looking-Glass
> — both difficult to break into, and difficult, once one has become
> acclimated to it, to break out of. [...] Even the specialists of the
> social disciplines find the self-contained world of authoritative legal
> doctrine a sort of unchartable fourth-dimensional space. Effort after
> effort at synthesis of the social disciplines over the past ten years
> has made worth-while headway in all phases, except that of inte-
> grating law-stuff[4] with the rest.
> [...] The obstacle is the acceptance of the realm of Law as
> being of a different order; for if of a different order, then it sets its
> own premises and becomes impenetrable on any premises except its
> own.[5]

Since then, sociology of law has developed the study of legal norms.
Yet, while designating these norms as specially important because
'legal', sociologists of law have made relatively little headway into
theorising their specific 'lawness'. This task has remained largely in the
hands of jurists — hands which reach from beyond the looking-glass,
from a world in which law is presupposed simultaneously both as object
of knowledge and as frame in which to think, and even when offered in
assistance tend to pull the sociologist through the looking-glass and

away from sociological bearings.[6]

Somehow, the very act of taking law as an object of sociological knowledge seems to commit the sociologist to a path from one world, one reality, into another. If so, then a sociological theorisation of lawness requires a thorough epistemological relativism, which raises sore problems at the level of philosophy. Otherwise the sociologist must be content with just the identification of a louring 'legal absolutism'.[7] Faced with these difficulties, the sociologist might decide to confide the task after all to jurisprudence. But through the looking-glass the sociologist can glimpse the carcasses of the attempts that since the Renaissance have repeatedly been made, then one after another abandoned, to enrich jurisprudence itself with a specific study of society.

This looking-glass problem calls in question the possibility of 'law' as a sociological object of knowledge. One promising line of inquiry into that question is to investigate the failed and current sociological movements within jurisprudence. To pursue such a line one must be able to scan through the looking-glass without succumbing to its effect. This requires foundations, at the level of philosophy, of a thorough epistemological relativism.

Foundations

What is required, to put it shortly, is a theory of the immediate, that is, of the apparently unmediated.[8] There is space here to present such a theory only in outline.[9]

It may be asserted that the whole of determinate reality is constructed and that that construction is social and historical.[10]

It may then be said that, while much of accepted construction of reality is taken for granted in the sense that it is accepted provisionally, leaving open the possibility of future redetermination and of the social negotiation of that redetermination,[11] sometimes elements of accepted reality are held to lie beyond question, are taken as absolutely[12] given. Contradictorily, they are constructed as being unconstructed, as being transsocial and transhistorical. This contradictory construction of an entity may be called its *alienation*. In being alien, the entity appears as a pregiven reality confronting the subject, to which the subject's construction ought to conform. The alien is the apparently immediate. Divorced from the subject, the apparent alien object of knowledge confronts the subject as something from which, in a secondary sense of the word, the subject is alienated. This alienation of the subject is the more acute when the alien object of knowledge is itself a subject. Anything at all, it seems, can be alienated in the primary sense — such alienation, with its contradiction, is found in both idealism and empiricism.[13]

In the face of the alien object of knowledge, all else comes to be understood in its light — as refracting, instantiating, its essence. Even the knowing subject, seeking to overcome its separation from the alien object, 'subjects' itself to that object by coming to understand itself as an instance of the object's essence. The alien entity, in its supposed absoluteness, grounds an imperialist frame of thought which may be called an *ideology*.[14]

If A alienates some entity, taking it as absolutely given for himself, he will also take it as absolutely given for B. Should B not agree, considering that construct to be false or only provisional, A is liable to maintain that B is 'under an illusion', 'insane', 'primitive', or the like.[15] A will not be prepared to admit any possibility that the entity in question does not exist, nor even that it is not absolute. This can happen, whether B takes anything as absolute or not, hence whether B's frame of thought, or problematic,[16] is an ideology or not. A and his problematic, which will be an ideology, will be closed to B, admitting no possibility of a justifiable contrary reply by him. Thus A and his problematic *nihilate*[17] B and his problematic.

In terms of this constellation of concepts — alienation, ideology and nihilation — an entity or construct has three principal possible forms: an unalien form, in which it can appear simply as itself; an independently alien form, in which it is alienated alone and may not appear as itself; and a dependently alien form, in which it may appear as itself yet as an instantiation of the independently alien form of another entity or even of itself. For example: the subject as itself, as independently alien in the form of 'God',[18] and as a 'soul' instantiating 'God'. Some entities are exclusively alien forms, e.g. 'God'.

Also in terms of this constellation, the category 'mediation' must itself be mediated. When the divorce of object from subject through alienation is overcome, there remains for the subject neither a pristine positive entity to be originally negated nor a transcendent rule of reason to govern negation of negation. One may then establish, beneath and comprehending negation of negation, a deeper dialectic of positing and annulling, of position and annulment. It can then be said, for example, that in alienation the unalien form of the entity or construct is annulled in favour of a newly posited alien form and that in nihilation the positions of another subject are annulled in favour of positions posited by the nihilating subject.

Jurisprudence

Introduction

In order to come, under that constellation, at the sociological movements within jurisprudence, it is necessary first to consider jurisprudence, generally, in the same light.

Jurists commonly classify 'law' into three main types: 'natural', 'positive' and 'customary'. 'Natural law' is said to consist of norms that are taken as natural because considered implicit in the 'order of things', and often as having been laid down by a divine creator of that order. 'Positive law' is said to consist of norms 'posited' by 'God' or (more usually) by a human ruler.[19] 'Customary law' is said to consist of norms that arise by way of 'custom'. These classes overlap more than is ordinarily acknowledged by modern jurists. I will deal for the time being only with natural and positive law.

Alleged Absoluteness of 'Law'

Both natural and positive law are held to be absolute, in at least three ways. Practically: it is claimed that law can provide absolute justifications – above all, for killing someone. Rationally: it is claimed that the norms applied in a legal system (the 'legal order') form a completely coherent set capable of yieding an absolutely valid answer to a practical question. This answer would be an absolutely valid conclusion, presupposing the availability of both absolute premises and an absolutely secure mode of reasoning. The claim to rational absoluteness is vital to the claim to practical absoluteness. Conceptually: everything tends to get presented as either legal norms or their contents.[20] This follows from the allegations of absolute premises and an absolutely secure mode of reasoning.

For both natural and positive law, these claims to absoluteness have been grounded in ascribing the norms to an alleged absolute subject as their author. For natural law, this subject has been 'God' or a personified 'Nature'; for positive law, it has been 'the sovereign', 'the state' personified, a somewhat personified Supreme Court, even a personification of positive law itself.[21]

The Exegetical Tradition in Jurisprudence

Through this attribution to an alleged absolute subject, legal norms come to be presented as refractions or instantiations of the essence of that subject and secondarily of objectively ideal essences located in the supposed mind of that subject. Accordingly, the method of jurisprudence (as also of the more particular legal disciplines) has been objective-idealistic.[22] The particular legal norm is understood as an existent instantiating an objectively ideal essence which is its true being, within the alleged absolute subject and which itself is immanently deontic (normative).[23] Inquiry is therefore *exegetical*: a querying of the existent to hand in order to uncover the essence that it is assumed to refract.

To the medieval Christian, reality consisted of immanently deontic essences located in the mind of 'God' and the refraction of those essences in the world understood as the contents of the divine norms. These norms were conceived as a divine natural law which was not yet firmly differentiated into moral, aesthetic or natural-scientific 'laws' nor a narrower notion of 'law' that excluded these. Inquiry of any kind, juristic or other, proceeded through a unified exegetical method.[24]

With the rise — or restoration — of capitalist commodity relations on a large scale, beginning in northern Italy around the end of the eleventh or beginning of the twelfth century, local rulers (who may also have been entrepreneurs) found it necessary to issue trade regulations that, if they did not run counter to the divine natural law, did not evidently rest on it as source of authority, were not obviously 'good' refractions of it. To get these regulations unquestioningly obeyed, the ruler had to extend his claim to discretion allowed by divine law, under which he claimed to have been appointed. This commenced a secularisation of legal authority, toward 'the sovereign' or 'the state' as sufficient authority for its laws.

Legal authority was translated from the religious alleged absolute subject, 'God', not, however, to human beings but to 'the sovereign', 'the state', and so on, as secular alleged absolute subject.[25] Along with this went the separation off of a secular idea of 'law', together with the segregation from theology of the study of such law. But, since this secular law was still ascribed to an alleged absolute subject as its author, the study of it retained an objective-idealist, exegetical method.[26]

The alleged absolute subject, in its confrontation of the relative knowing subject, appears as absolutely objective. So, consequently, do the objective ideals located in its supposed mind. The norms ascribed to that subject as their author and understood to instantiate it and those ideals therefore partake of that objectivity. That objectivity is both indicative and deontic. Indicatively, it is thus that legal norms appear as possible objects of knowledge. This being the mode of their objectivity, the only proper approach to them is apodictic and exegetical. Deontically, they ought absolutely to be obeyed. In the objective-idealist unity of indicative and deontic, therefore, knowledge of the legal norm ineluctably comports a duty to conform to it. At the level of the alleged absolute subject, such unity further comports a duty to defend the norms ascribed to that subject. Accordingly, exegetical juris-prudence — that is, jurisprudence as it has existed — is committed *a priori* to obedience and apology. In addition, there is an *a priori* commitment to reform, in so far as lesser legal norms remain to be posited by actual human beings (although ultimately they are under-stood to be posited by the alleged absolute subject, whence their lawness derives).

In pursuing these commitments, the jurist assumes the threefold claim to absoluteness. It is in this intrinsically antisociological and antihistorical matrix that the sociological movements in jurisprudence have arisen and met their fate − to understand which it is necessary to consider also the primarily historical movements out of which the sociological movements developed.

Sociology in Jurisprudence

Historical and Proto-sociological Movements

The medieval resumption of large-scale commodity relations was not a local but a regional and later a continental process. *Ad hoc* local regulation thus led to a legal diversity inconvenient to the merchant and, to overcome this, the sixth-century codification of Roman civil law, the *Corpus iuris civilis*, was given a new lease of life, either as a source of inspiration or, in some areas, as applicable law.[27]

By the fifteenth century the exegetical method, scholastically refined, had closed legal studies off from all that could not be shown to proceed from the *Corpus* (excepting the Bible) and had turned the exegesis of the *Corpus* into a veritable spaghetti of split hairs.[28] In this and the following century the humanist movement reacted against such closure, insisting, at least for the benefit of professional lawyers having to relate the provisions of the *Corpus* to contemporary life, that those provisions be seen with specific reference to the historical and social circumstances of their origin and application. But these tendencies became nihilated by the exegetical tradition: law tended to be seen as a summary of history and society.[29]

When the humanist historical and proto-sociological lean was renewed in the early nineteenth century by Savigny, a similar nihilation occurred.[30] Hegel places more emphasis on the state but, like the humanists and Savigny, his historising tendency is in any case nihilated by the Christian ideology. Maine, less polemical than Savigny and less philosophical than Hegel, founded a largely independent historical and comparative movement in the 1860s.[31] Although Maine insists that the science of history is in principle no different from natural science,[32] a similar nihilation occurs again. For, though Maine's scientism is part of his evolutionism, that evolutionism is still cast in terms of a fundamentally idealist problematic.[33] Thus, notwithstanding that he thinks of particular legal norms as transient,[34] Maine is still able to work from an ideal essence of law, tending to understand history and society as content of legal norms which instantiate that essence and therefore themselves instantiating it. Marx − Hegel's heir, Savigny's student and Darwin's admirer − adopts on the philosophical plane a radically antialienatory outlook, placing special emphasis on historicity. But, though he sees that this relativises the idea of 'the state',[35] he does not notice that it also challenges the objectivity of law.

Later historically inclined writers have seen contradiction between exegesis and historicity, but have not found a way out.[36]

Pragmatist Jurisprudence

In the United States the socialisation of production that everywhere gave rise to general sociology and to sociology of law combined with a historistic emphasis on practice to form pragmatist philosophy and its offshoot pragmatist jurisprudence.

Holmes — judge, legal theorist and one of the founders of pragmatist philosophy[37] — is a watershed figure in American jurisprudence. He straddles the ridge between a minor nineteenth-century historistic reaction against dogmatism of the doctrinaire blackstonian type and the supersession of that reaction, at the turn of the century, by a socially oriented pragmatist jurisprudence. On neither side of that ridge, however, did he seriously contemplate a breach with the exegetical tradition. The way to 'gain a liberal view' of the law, he told students,

> is not to read something else, but to get to the bottom of the subject itself. The means of doing that are, in the first place, to follow the existing body of dogma into its highest generalizations by the help of jurisprudence; next, to discover from history how it has come to be what it is; and, finally, so far as you can, to consider the ends which the several rules seek to accomplish, the reasons why those ends are desired, what is given up to gain them, and whether they are worth the price.[38]

Social considerations appear in this scheme only as contents of actual and potential legal norms. Pragmatism, with its teleological orientation indebted to Christianity and to Hegel, slides comfortably into the embrace of juristic objective idealism. Holmes's theorisation of social considerations remains 'in the law'.[39] Indeed, he locates his very life 'in the law'.[40] He regards 'theory' as 'the most important part of the dogma of the law'[41] and jurisprudence as 'simply law in its most generalized part'.[42] Like his Renaissance predecessors, he sees history as summarised, even embodied, in the contents of legal norms[43] and the study of history as useful, at best, 'in the explanation of dogma'.[44] He conceives the study of law entirely as the education and informing of the legal profession and the 'means' for that study almost exclusively as 'a body of reports, of treatises, and of statutes'.[45] Overreacting against iusnaturalism, he wishes to banish from the law 'every word of moral significance' and to adopt other words 'which should convey

legal ideas uncolored by anything outside the law'.[46] Consistently with
locating his life 'in the law', Holmes declares his 'devotion' to and
'veneration' of the law, denying that he criticised any of it except to
improve it.[47]

This inauspicious beginning was enriched, yet not opened up, by the
'sociological jurisprudence' of Pound. 'Sociology of law', Pound wrote,
'proceeds from sociology toward law', while 'sociological jurisprudence'
proceeds 'from historical and philosophical jurisprudence to utilization
of the social sciences, and particularly of sociology, toward a broader
and more effective science of law. It begins with Holmes [...] '.[48]
The 'science of law', to Pound, is unashamedly not a descriptive so
much as a practical science, merely making use of description for
practical projects that sociology of law, as primarily descriptive science,
can be made to serve but is not meant to fulfil.[49] The practical aim of
'sociological jurisprudence' is also limited to servicing the three classic
branches of government — legislature, executive and judiciary.[50]
Pound conceives this task technocratically, cheerfully employing
Dewey's expression, heavy with consensualism, 'social engineering'.[51]
He can write, like Holmes, of 'our revered common law'[52] and, though
he criticises the tendency of lawyers (he has practitioners mainly in
mind) to accept the prevailing supposedly human positive legal order as
'natural',[53] his eye is not on alienation but only on fixity as against
progressive reform. Although he thought of himself as finally rescuing
jurisprudence from the exegetical tradition,[54] he was actually only
enriching that tradition by, still within it, transcending merely doctrinal
dogmatism.[55]

The impetus given by Holmes and Pound received a mediation from
behaviouristic sociology, giving rise to the movement known as
American 'legal realism'.[56] Contemporary with the European 'free law'
movement, legal realism may have had political reasons for playing up
judicial discretion at the expense of legislature and executive. One
realist went so far as to hold that law existed only in judicial
pronouncements.[57] Since a 'judge' or a 'court' is so only according to
legal norms, this view shows how far the realists, despite tending to
challenge the claim to rational absoluteness, still accepted legal
concepts as furnishing a natural framework of thought. However, the
influence of social science led some realists further. Llewellyn, simply
as jurist, is not much perturbed by the exclusivity of legal thought, its
purporting to be 'final and conclusive',[58] and is content to think of
law as less a delimited entity than a focus, a point of reference, 'with
the bearings and boundaries outward unlimited', so that it is 'as broad
as life'.[59] But, in confronting the exegetical tradition with social
science, he experiences a kind of looking-glass effect.

When one turns his eyes from law outward, the first effect is to make law shrink into seeming insignificance. There is so much outside. And it so obviously bears in upon and changes and remodels law itself. After a further while — so to speak as the eyes grow adjusted to the glare — one attains a truer picture. One perceives an interplay of causation between law and the world outside. One begins to suspect something of the nature of the interplay.[60]

Passing from 'inside' to 'outside', what had seemed everything recedes into 'seeming insignificance'. It is from this 'external' standpoint that Llewellyn (even before his extensive anthropological fieldwork[61]) comes to see law as constituting (to use his own phrase) an impregnable 'world of its own'. Another realist, Arnold, was (crudely) inspired by psychiatry and concluded — although, like many of the pragmatist jurists, a judge[62] — that law was eyewash, a 'logical heaven' in which all conflicts could be resolved neatly, objectively and with impeccable equity.[63] However, he recanted, holding this very unreality of the legal to be a social necessity, providing ideals for people to strive after.[64]

'Law and Society'

The pragmatist jurists, for all their social-scientific inspiration, did not transcend the exegetical tradition but amplified it.

One descendant of American legal realism, 'jurimetrics', has cleaved more closely to the mediation with behaviouristic sociology.[65] But in doing so it intensifies the contradiction between the behaviourist tendency to deny the deontic, and the unity of deontic and indicative in the fundamental legal concepts. Although those concepts are employed as if they were empirical generalisations and the task of jurimetrics is seen as prediction,[66] those concepts retain their deontic constitution and prediction is seen as dedicated to assisting the trial lawyer.

A broader view has been taken by the many American and British exponents of the 'law and society' tendency. A leader of this tendency (it is too diffuse to be called a movement) in Britain has been Twining, a pupil of Llewellyn. He and his colleagues at Warwick have pursued an educational policy of rejecting the 'expository orthodoxy' (meaning doctrinal dogmatism) and 'broadening the study of law from within'.[67] But Twining does not follow Llewellyn in asking definitely what it means to be 'within' and how one has got there. Jurisprudence has been characterised by Stone as 'the examination of the law in the light of other disciplines', in short 'the lawyer's extraversion'.[68] Twining comments: 'the essential nature of the process is for someone to venture forth from the intellectual milieu of the law and to come back with spoils from elsewhere and to present them in assimilable form.'[69]

But, if 'the law' is 'a world of its own', such 'assimilation' looks like nihilation.

Such a 'magpie' conception of jurisprudence[70] is the typical concept of the 'and society' element in the 'law and society' tendency. Thus this tendency, like its predecessors, departs from doctrinal dogmatism without transcending the exegetical tradition as such. It appears that exegetical jurisprudence can embrace any amount of reference to society and history so long as such reference presents social and historical phenomena as contents of actual or potential legal norms.

The ideologically restricted unity of indicative and deontic in the objective idealism which is the matrix of this nihilation binds description to specifically legal aims. At the same time, on the side of the subject, the jurist conceives himself as 'in the law' and the apparently objective aims of the legal order to which he subscribes as his own aims. Thus, one is told, the 'proper activity' of the jurist is simply 'to discover the gaps or imperfections in the legal system in force and to suggest solutions that may usefully supply these deficiencies'.[71] And neither on the side of the object nor on that of the subject does reference to society and history necessarily overcome, or even seriously challenge, the restrictions of that orientation. We have seen that to be so in the work of the pragmatist jurists. More recently Willock, introducing the *British Journal of Law and Society*, characterises himself as 'one speaking from within the law' and, with approval, distinguishes 'lawyer' and sociologist as the one tethered to servicing the machinery of the state and the other a free-ranging theorising observer. 'Lawyers are involved in the law' as 'doers', not 'watchers' or even all that much 'thinkers'. 'They are in business, supplying those who manage the great society that is the state with legal rules, the most effective weapons of social control, and applying these rules.' For the 'lawyer', law 'is not a mere pressure to be identified, but an instrument to be wielded'. 'The contrast with sociologists is complete.' The jurist is to take, from sociology, for teaching purposes, 'what will best illuminate the law'. The study of 'law in society' is best undertaken by persons who have studied law first and sociology afterwards.[72]

The legal nihilation of the sociological extends into the apologetical role of jurisprudence. Lloyd links reform and apology when he states, without argument, that law is 'one of the institutions which are central to the social nature of man and without which he would be a very different creature', and advocates later that

the enormous importance of the idea of law as a factor in human culture only serves to emphasize how great is the duty upon those who are concerned with its exposition, as well as with its application in practice, to strive continuously to refurbish th[e] image [of law] , to keep it bright, and to subject it to constant re-analysis so as to keep it in touch with the social realities of the period.[73]

Dworkin writes that, if a theory of law

> is to provide a basis for judicial duty, then the principles it sets out must try to *justify* the settled rules by identifying the political or moral concerns and traditions of the community which, in the opinion of the lawyer whose theory it is, do in fact support the rules.

This may involve 'deciding which of two different justifications of our political institutions is superior'. Legal theory constitutes 'the elaborate scheme of justification required to justify the body of laws'.[74] By 'principles' Dworkin means those moral and political principles which are incorporated in the legal order through their influence on the formulation and application of legal rules. By this path, social considerations are subsumed within the task of legal apologetic.

These nihilations seem to stem not from mere unimaginative legal-professionalism but from sharing the legal professional's 'allegiance'[75] to the law. And what Willock, Lloyd and Dworkin are saying — perturbing though it be to a social-scientific eye — is not bad jurisprudence but perfectly good jurisprudence. I am not praising theoretical considerations over practical: a practical orientation is never objectionable as such. What is objectionable in the undefeated exegetical tradition is the *a priori* restricted practical commitment of theory. The similarities that some have noted, between jurisprudence and theology,[76] are accidental neither historically nor logically. The *a priori* commitment nihilates not only the possibility of practice that is committed against the legal order in question[77] but even the possibility of theory that could ground a *choice* whether to commit oneself *for or* against that order. Yet this restriction follows from the objective-idealistic premisses of exegetical jurisprudence. It may be a defect *of* exegetical jurisprudence, but it is not a defect *in* it.

This restricted practical commitment extends to the definition of 'law'[78] and furnishes the *raison d'être* of exegetical jurisprudence so much that jurisprudence is seen as a part of the legal order.[79] Consequently the sociological movements in jurisprudence are on a different plane from sociology of law.[80] On one hand, it has been said, lie 'socio-legal studies' and, on the other, 'sociology of law' — the former somehow 'inside' and committed to immanent adjustment of the legal order, the latter somehow an attempt to describe the legal system from 'outside'.[81] It is a question of the two sides of the looking-glass. A sociology of law which is not going constantly to get dragged through the looking-glass, or alternatively remain baffled by lawness as such, is going to have to *overcome* the looking-glass. Merely to negate the exegetical tradition will not be enough: the negation will remain dependent on the negated and one will find oneself in a limbo[82] which wheeling some other basis into the negation[83] will not by itself alleviate. The current 'law and society' tendency is likely to suffer the fate of its predecessors unless it can fully accept a sociological standpoint. And that means withdrawing from and theorising the looking-glass effect as such.

Jurisprudence as Ideology

It appears that the ascription of legal norms to an alleged absolute subject as their author is what constitutes their specific lawness. 'Customary law' is a limiting case to prove this rule: precisely the lack of such ascription has given rise to severe doubts whether 'customary law' is really law and some writers have denied that it is.[84]

If, then, the alleged absolute subject is an independently alien form of the self, the legal norm may be seen as an alien form of a suggestion or demand made by that self. This will be a dependently alien form, since it depends on the alleged absolute subject. On this view, just as the alien form of the self can be distinguished from the unalien form of the self, so the alien form can be distinguished from the unalien form of that self's suggestion or demand.

If this analysis of the exegetical-juristic concept of 'law' may be assumed to hold for actual law (and that assumption must be tentative), 'law' will appear initially as not a single but a double object of knowledge. There will be, on the one hand, the suggestion or demand in its unalien form, ascribed to the self in its unalien form as its author, and on the other the suggestion or demand in its alien form as a legal norm, ascribed to the alien form of the self, the alleged absolute subject, as its author. But an unalien and an alien form are not separate: the first is the truth of the second and, under the constellation of concepts I have proposed at the level of philosophy, the second may be expressed in terms of the first, as the alien form *of* the first.

It would follow that each actual legal order is an ideology, grounded in an allegation of an absolute subject and having as its principal elements legal norms in a constitutive as well as a regulative role.[85]

It would follow, further, that a person wishing to study that order and taking as object of knowledge legal norms as such (that is, the alien form) could have such objects of knowledge only at the price of performing the alienation (of the self) on which their existence depends. And, in performing that alienation, the knower will enter into the legal ideology which is that legal order. The knower will then have become, in the ways I have outlined, an exegetical jurist. Exegetical jurisprudence, therefore, is in this sense ideological. It is as a part of the legal order as an ideology that jurisprudence presents the legal order as absolute. That is to say, jurisprudence is the legal order's self-representation — although this is not to say that it is its main self-representation.

To this it may be objected that, in that case, there would be a separate jurisprudence for each legal order and that, consequently, in legal positivism (the view that only norms posited by a secular absolute subject are law) there can be no general theory of law, since either there is a plurality of secular absolute subjects (and there cannot be a plurality of absolutes) or a single secular absolute subject is alone the author of genuine legal norms and the patron of a genuinely general jurisprudence (which is empirically false); therefore the existence of legal-positivist general theory of law and even of a common forum of legal-positivist debate disproves the whole picture I have drawn of law. This objection may be countered by the denial, for which I think there is evidence,[86] that legal-positivist theory of law is ever genuinely general and that the legal-positivist forum of debate is genuinely common.

If what I have said be accepted, jurisprudence as ideology is an aspect of *legal* ideology, of actual legal orders as ideologies. It follows that, if one's understanding of the sociological movements within jurisprudence is not to be legal-ideological, one must understand first actual legal orders — in their constitutive aspect as well as in their regulative aspect — and then the jurisprudence that they contain, and only then the sociological movements within that jurisprudence.

It also follows that the opposition between exegetical jurisprudence and sociology is not an opposition between practical and theoretical but a confrontation first of all between incommensurable senses of being — on the plane of language, meanings of 'is'. In legal ideology, therefore in exegetical jurisprudence, being is thought of as objectively ideal. In sociology it is thought of as material or *ideell* (like the propositions of pure mathematics). The senses of being as material or *ideell* are incommensurable with the sense of being as objectively ideal: each pertains to a different problematic. There is a confrontation of 'is' and 'is', and only afterwards perhaps of 'is' and 'ought'.

It follows, further, that the enforcement of legal norms is first of all the enforcement of a particular, legal-ideological construction of reality and that exegetical jurisprudence, including the sociological movements within it, as a factor in that construction is also a factor in the enforcement. Above all, the presentation of law as authored by an absolute subject and therefore itself absolute renders legal norms 'binding' in the sense that the possibility of a justifiable contrary reply is nihilated.[87]

It is in these ways, it would seem, that law, and within it jurisprudence, constitutes 'a world of its own' — which the inquirer who takes legal norms, as such, as object of knowledge cannot but inhabit and desire to serve.

The Persistence of Legal Ideology

The foregoing argument, however, may remain unconvincing, or at least notably incomplete, unless it can be explained how such objective idealism can have persisted, and with such strength, into a materialist and nominalist age. I will try to sketch the response that the capitalist mode of production gives rise, simultaneously, to two contradictory types of ideology: evolutionism and legal positivism.[88]

The capitalist universalisation of commodity production presupposes the isolation of producers and appropriators, who come as strangers to a market that no one of them controls and that readily appears to each to be controlled by none — an absolutely objective process transcending their subjectivity and reducing them and all else to its supposedly objective terms. This market consists principally of those social relations which are exchange-values composing capital. Hence the objectivation, i.e. the alienation, of the market is essentially an *alienation of capital.*[89]

These exchange-values, subsuming labour, instruments and raw materials as means for the valorisation of capital, which is the principal aim of capitalist production, are quantified in terms of productive labour-time, represented in money. This quantification particularly serves the task of prediction, on which capitalist production depends to an exceptional degree. The production process, and consequently the whole of life, thus undergo — in the frame of homogeneous, endless and essentially empty dimensions of time and space — a reduction to calculability, a *calculative reduction.*[90]

In the 'last instance' of material production, which is physical labour, the basic form of object is physical. But what is last for theoretical reflection is first in practice. The theoretical predication of the exchange-value of a commodity upon its physicality expresses the practical production of that value first of all by physical labour. This practice, calculatively reduced, finds analogy in causal laws. (Such analogisation is assisted by the emphasis on time and practice of historisation, to which I will come in a moment.) In addition capital, being intrinsically a social relation, cannot have an independently alien form in which it continues to appear as itself. Accordingly, it seems, the analogy becomes a reduction and capital is alienated in the form of a comic physical process. The concept of this process grounds an ideology and the determination of all else as instances of that process constitutes *reification.*[91]

Practical questions, accordingly, come to be conceived first of all as questions of intervention in causal processes according to objective criteria established with the detachment of natural science. A calculative reduction in practical reasoning constitutes *instrumentalisation*, most evident in utilitarianism.

Persons, isolated in the competitive division of labour and of possession which is a precondition for capitalist market relations, have that situation confirmed as objective and 'natural' by the apparently objective terms of the market, which first divorce them and then link them with an apparently objective bond. This naturalness of segregation and competition fosters, as apparent fact and apparent norm, bourgeois *individuality and individualism.* Moreover, these elements are projected into the cosmic process itself and appear as a natural cosmic situation and law of 'survival of the fittest'.[92]

At the same time, the evident social changes wrought by the rise of capitalist production foster a structural consciousness of historicity. There is a *historisation* of the world — the physical as well as the social.[93] This tendency, becoming reified, confirms the cosmic physical process as a diversifying and ethically progressive *evolution.*

Finally there is a *comparatist* tendency, engendered by the spread of the market across cultures. Like historical events, however, the comparata become understood as instances of the cosmic evolution.

If, then, evolutionism, composed of these elements, is the specific ideology of capitalism, one might expect to find legal ideology succumbing to a behaviouristic nihilation of the deontic or at least of the rationality of the deontic. There are a number of reasons why this has not happened.

First: the very comprehensiveness of that nihilation renders it unconvincing — consequently, rather than defeating legal ideology and exegetical jurisprudence, behaviourism appears as inadequate to the juristic task.

Second: a new ideology does not spring fully armed out of the mode of production that engenders it but arises through that mode of production's mediation of existing ideology and thus one finds evolutionism slow to shed a religiose, objective-idealistic component.[94]

Third: the capitalist mode of production, while giving rise to evolutionist ideology, also, in a different mediation of the Christian ideology, gives rise to legal-positivist ideology. The legal guarantee of private appropriation, as also of notional equality in disputes between private appropriators, requires an actual detachment of legal apparatus from individual appropriators and, in order to succeed regularly, a legitimation of that apparatus as a paradigm of impartial justice. This legitimation — to repeat an earlier point from a different angle — perpetuates the alienation of the authorship of positive legal norms. In addition, these norms are understood as products of volition. That volition, if alien, will appear as absolute and hence must be understood as unique and unified. Consequently positive legal norms are ascribed to a personified state apparatus as their author.

The threefold claim to absoluteness of law follows from the very presupposition of an absolute subject. But — even though no such subject can be admitted in terms of the philosophical positivism which characterises the evolutionist ideology[95] — the capitalist mode of production, with its universalisation of commodity production, lends plausibility to that claim. As to the practical absoluteness, the increased division of labour and socialisation of production mean that for the state to 'organize war, police and justice is no longer adequate. The state must see to it that a whole series of industrial functions are in organised operation. It must prevent their interruption for a single moment.'[96] As to the rational absoluteness, the legal order is required to be increasingly coherent.[97] The conceptual absoluteness receives particular emphasis. According to Marx, the typical commodity has three aspects: a physical, a use-value and an exchange-value aspect.[98] But one can also find a fourth, *legal* aspect. On one hand, in societies (capitalist and other) where commodity production has been extensive, the private appropriation of the product has been made possible on a wide scale through legal protection. On the other, there has been legal regulation of the conditions of sale of articles and labour-power, of the prices at which these are sold, of the quality and quantity of the money-supply, and of conditions of production (e.g. statutory safety measures) in such a way that the cost of compliance is added into the price. Also, taxation has ever been a legal affair, and the taxpayer who is also a seller tries to recoup the tax payment by an addition to the price.[99] Thus law has not only contributed vitally to the creation and maintenance of commodity relations but has entered crucially into the constitution of value and price. Those suggestions and demands that have been alienated as legal norms have entered in a practical way into the constitution of the commodity, giving it a specifically legal aspect.[100] At the same time the individual in the market, acting continually with reference to those suggestions and demands, acquires a legal aspect of individual personality. With the universalisation of commodity production almost every object becomes an actual or potential commodity and almost every subject an actual or potential commodity dealer. This practically constituted legal *aspect* of object and subject is readily confused with and hence makes more plausible[101]

the theoretically constituted legal *determination* of object and subject
— above all as contents of legal norms of possession and ownership
(norms which with respect to the person are included in the idea of
'legal personality'[102]). And the plausibility of legal determination is that
of legal ideology, hence also of the alienation in which that ideology is
grounded.

Fourth: legal and evolutionist ideology find certain areas of mutual
accommodation. In general it would seem that, at least to a considerable extent, the elements of each can be manipulated together
precisely because they are constituted in an alienatory sense of being;
they share, especially, a supposedly absolute objectivity. More
particularly, and in each case exemplifying this general point, legal
ideology is able, to a considerable extent, to assimilate the tendencies
that compose evolutionist ideology. The sense of individuality and its
accompanying individualism are accommodated without difficulty, for
example in the individualistic versions of iusnaturalism. An instrumentalisation of the legal 'ought', athough difficult for iusnaturalists,
is readily achieved by legal positivists.[103] In each case evolutionist-
ideological elements are *glossed onto* legal-ideological elements. This
is especially so with reification. There is no direct reification of legal
norms. The behaviouristic attempt at this falls short. Rather, a
scientistic approach to cognition of legal norms is glossed onto a basic
exegetical approach.[104] The historising and comparatist tendencies are
assimilated partly directly into legal ideology and partly through
scientism: directly or indirectly, historical events and comparata come
to be understood as instantiating legal objective ideals (as we have seen
in the case of the historical movements in jurisprudence).

The Supersession of Legal Ideology

The evolutionist ideology, in its historising and comparatist tendencies,
contains the seeds of a general relativisation which promises the supersession of ideology as such. The pioneer of this relativisation, with
whom at the level of philosophy we are still catching up, has been
Marx. The proposals offered in the second part of this paper move in
the same direction.

In jurisprudence, from as early as the twelfth century the historising
tendency forces a distinction between the eternal principles of Christian
natural law and mutable norms of both natural and positive law.[105]
This tendency is supported by a comparatism that can be found even in
Roman law.[106] That historisation of legal ideology continues in both
iusnaturalism and legal positivism to the point at which it is now difficult
to state anything eternal and what is claimed to be universal can be

revealed as a projection of the local.[107] At the present time the comparatist tendency is becoming even more relativistic with the self-assertion of some of the comparata against ethnocentrism and intellectual colonialism: this forces one toward epistemological relativism.[108] In this cultural situation there also arise more relativistic interpretations of the physical world,which through scientism and more generally have a reciprocal enhancing effect on the cultural relativisation. Moreover, the instrumentalistic horrors of the capitalist world wars and other wars have called established authority and morality increasingly into question. Finally, the very opposition, within the superstructure of capitalist society, between evolutionist and legal ideology tends to the relativisation and hence the supersession of both.

An exceptional concurrence of these factors in Austria-Hungary during the early part of this century can be associated with what I would like to contend is the beginning of a disintegration of exegetical jurisprudence and, by implication, generally of legal ideology. The argument for this contention must be presented elsewhere, but the key texts are the penultimate chapter of Kafka's *The Trial*[109] and the first and last major works by Hans Kelsen.[110]

So long as the historising and comparatist tendencies, as well as sociology as a discipline, challenged legal ideology only on planes of the relatively particular, legal ideology, including exegetical jurisprudence, was able to nihilate their challenge — usually by some express or tacit distinction between form and content, allowing content to be relativised while form remained universal. In this it was abetted by philosophy, which was reacting in the same way. But, once those challenges began to succeed in philosophy, the relativising tendency was able to challenge legal ideology from the level of philosophy — and by an attack at that level it could be, and I believe is being, defeated. This paper is intended to further that attack.

This is also to say that the supersession of legal ideology is part and parcel of a supersession of ideology as such, hence of ideology generally. It follows that exegetical jurisprudence cannot be superseded by a sociology of law, or any other approach to law, which is itself ideological in any way. Such a sociology does not yet exist — but the transcendental-phenomenological and Marxist tendencies in sociology offer such a promise.

'Law' as Object of Knowledge

The reason why 'law' appears to a sociologist to be both evidently real and yet chimerical, partly graspable in sociological terms and partly resistant to them, seems to be that the sociologist is trying to take as object of knowledge something that really is not on offer to sociology. Two forms of appearance[111] have been distinguished. There is the alien form of a suggestion or demand, which is the legal norm as such. This is what the jurist takes, exegetically, as object of knowledge. It is an object only in an objective-idealist sense of being. It appears to the jurist as a unity: that is, the suggestion or demand appears to the jurist 'always already'[112] in its alien form. Secondly, there is the unalien form of the suggestion or demand, in which it appears as itself: this is what a sociologist can take as object of knowledge. It is an object in a sense of *ideell* being. So far as sociologists have concentrated on this form, in (uncomfortable) abstraction from the question of its lawness, they have been relatively successful. But that question remains to be answered.

To answer it, the sociologist has to make a choice whether the concept of law is true or false. To accept it as true, it can now be seen, the sociologist must perform the alienation in which legal ideology is grounded. This means that either sociology succumbs entirely to jurisprudence and becomes a mere adjunct to it or sociology of law has an object of knowledge the reality of which is ambiguous.

The concept of law may be accepted as false, on two levels.[113] First it may be considered false as a concept for the sociologist's own use. From this by itself it follows that 'law' cannot be an object of knowledge at all, that 'law' does not exist. What evidently does exist, however, is a socially prevalent *belief in* 'law'. At this second level the concept of 'law' may be considered false as a concept employed by the people being sociologically studied. The falsity at this second level enables the sociologist to substitute, at the first level, a true concept of that belief as a socially prevalent fallacy.

Under this new concept the sociologist will have, initially, a dual object of knowledge: (a) the socially prevalent fallacious belief in 'law' and (b) those suggestions and demands that are transmuted into 'legal' norms through that belief. From these initial objects of knowledge it should be possible to determine a unified object of knowledge in which the belief is seen as constituting the alien form of the suggestion or demand. The alien form, the legal norm, is the form in which the alienated suggestion or demand appears with apparent immediacy: the sociologist needs to mediate and supersede that form. Since the question is one of the object of knowledge, that supersession must be accomplished in theory before the sociologist can proceed to empirical inquiry.

Such a new concept has been presented in embryo during my argument and now requires a name. I have found it impractical to drop the word 'law'. The new concept may, therefore, be named 'law' — provided that this word is used as the word 'religion' is used in atheistic sociology of religion. That is, the word may be used in a sociological sense while mentioning[114] that the people being sociologically studied use it themselves in an objective-idealistic sense.[115]

If the word 'law' is used in this sense, determinations under the concept that it signifies will be the task of a coherent sociology of law, with which a thoroughly relativised jurisprudence would be identical.[116]

Notes

1. This paper summarises some of the arguments in a doctoral thesis in jurisprudence which at the time of writing (February, revised September, 1979) is shortly to be submitted to University College London. These arguments are presented here in a highly distilled form and the number of references has been greatly reduced.

2. As to any social scientist. The word 'sociology' will be used here rather loosely.

3. Durkheim 1887/1888, p. 47.

4. Llewellynese – he was a German by origin.

5. Llewellyn and Hoebel, 1941, p. 41; actually written by Llewellyn (Hoebel, 1964, p. 740 n23).

6. Cf. Abel, 1973, p. 187; Ziegert, 1979, pp. 234-5, 254-7, 263.

7. Carlen, 1976, pp. 12 *passim*.

8. Cf. Hegel, 1832/1895, vol. I, pp. 160-99; Lukács, 1923/1971, pp. 162-3.

9. From what is said here it may appear that my position is one of extreme subjective idealism, even solipsism. In the thesis it is argued that solipsism is a false problem and every form of idealism is rejected.

10. Cf. M. Douglas, 1973, p. 10. Douglas recognises the philosophical difficulties of such a position. Others have maintained some residue of a reality which has specificity independently of being known (Lee, 1959, p. 2; Kuhn, 1962/1970; Berger and Luckmann, 1966/1971). I think I have made some headway toward making such a position tenable, but the argument is too involved to include here.

11. Schutz and Luckmann, 1973/1974, pp. 3-15.

12. Cf. J D. Douglas, 1971, pp. 15-17.

13. Cf. Marx: 'Supersession of *alienation* may be identified with supersession of *objectivity [Gegenständlichkeit]*' (1844/1962; and see 1844b/1975) . See also the *general* concept of 'fetishism' to be found in his *Theories of Surplus Value* (1862-3/1963-71). Also Simmel, 1900/1978, pp. 59-79 *passim*; Quine, 1951; Schmidt, 1962/1971; Kolakowski, 1966/1969, p. 141; Schacht, 1970/1971; Mészáros, 1970/1972; Poole, 1972, pp. 44-6; Putnam, 1979.

14. Cf. Kafka, 1914/1953, Ch. 9; Althusser, 1965b/1970, pp. 93-6, 1969-70/1971, pp. 160-70.

15. A might, for example, distinguish between 'Catholics and all those who fail or refuse, for one reason or another, to recognize consciously their actual and inescapable incorporation into the supernatural order and their call to actual, full, and living membership in the authentic Church of Christ' (Hanley, 1947, p. viii). Cf. Carroll, 1894/1939; Winch, 1958/1963, pp. 55-7; Berger and Luckmann, 1966/1971, pp. 132-3; Poole, 1972, pp. 46-7.

16. Roughly, in Althusser's sense.

17. Roughly, in Berger's and Luckmann's sense (1966/1971, pp. 132-3).

18. Feuerbach, 1841/1957. If this self is a social self, and the sum of individuals in a society not different in substance from the sum of their social

relations (Marx, 1844a/1975, p. 299, 1845/1976, p. 4), Feuerbach's theory of religion is complementary to Durkheim's (1912/1915, pp. 225, 347). However, for simplicity of argument I will stick here to Feuerbach's theory with respect to 'God', although I will assume both theories when dealing with secular alleged absolute subjectivity.

19. On the meanings of 'natural law' and 'positive law', and their mutual relationship, see in particular Pollock, 1900/1961; Kelsen, 1927-8, 1928/1964, 1961/1968; Kuttner, 1936; Hall, 1949; Verbeke, 1964/1966. For a time there was a notion of 'divine' as well as 'human' positive law (e.g. Grotius, 1631/1953, vol. 1. p. 7).

20. Cf. Pound, 1909, p. 464; Weber, 1922/1954, pp. 35, 64; Stone, 1964/1968, pp. 187-9. For an example, see Radbruch 1914/1950, pp. 212-13. The three claims are stated, in different terms, by Hunt (1976, p. 185).

21. Kelsen, 1925/1966, pp. 76-80, 1962/1963, 1964; Goodhart, 1932/1933, p. 2. For examples of personification of positive law see Salmond, 1902/1966, pp. 323-5. Consider also Kelsen's contention that 'the state', through juristic eyes, is no more than a personification of the unity of the legal order and therefore identical with the legal order (e.g. 1934/1970, Ch. 6).

22. Maine, 1883, pp. 360-1, Gény, 1899/1954, vol. 1, pp. 129-30; Chloros, 1955; Villey, 1967/1969; MacCormick, 1973/1974, esp. pp. 105, 109.

23. Rommen, 1936/1947, pp. 172-3. I will use the word 'deontic' instead of 'normative' since Kelsen, to whom I am referring several times, uses the latter in a special sense.

24. Huizinga, 1919/1955, Chs. 15-17.

25. Cf. Kelsen, 1925/1966, p. 76.

26. Berman, 1977, p. 899. Cf. *CLH* I, p. 432; Rashdall, 1895/1936, vol. 1, p. 124; Llewellyn, 1940, p. 1357.

27. Engels, 1884/1975, p. 355; *CLH* I, *passim*; Anderson, 1974, pp. 24-9, 424-6. See also, however, Wieacker, 1960/1963.

28. *CLH* I. pp. 139-43.

29. Franklin, 1963; Kelley, 1970.

30. Savigny, 1814/1973, pp. 114-15 (translation, 1814/1831, pp. 46-7).

31. Maine, 1861/1906.

32. Maine, 1865/1890, pp. 264-72.

33. Maine, 1875/1890, pp. 238-9.

34. Maine, 1883, pp. 360-1.

35. Marx, 1873/1976, p. 103.

36. Maitland, 1888/1957, pp. 56-7; Baker, 1972/1975, p. 3; Midgley, 1975.

37. Howe, 1957-63, esp. vol. 1, p. 269.

38. Holmes, 1897, p. 476.

39. Ibid.

40. Quoted in Konefsky, 1968, p. 491.

41. Holmes, 1897, p. 477. Cf. 1899, p. 460.

42. Holmes, 1897, p. 474.

43. Holmes, 1881/1963, pp. 5, 168, 1897, p. 459, 1899, p. 444.

44. Holmes, 1897, p. 474.

45. Ibid., p. 457. He did, however, prefer that students should read economics rather than Roman law (ibid., pp. 474-6).

46. Ibid., p. 464.

47. Ibid., pp. 473-4.

48. Pound 1943, pp. 2, 3.

49. Pound, 1947, p. xv. As Friedmann says, it is not sociology of law but 'sociologically oriented teleology of law' (1961-2, p. 3).

50. Pound, 1932, p. 485, 1959, vol. 1, p. 350.

51. Pound, 1932, p. 487, 1943, p. 20; Dewey, 1916/1970, p. 827.

52. Pound, 1910, p. 21.

53. Pound, 1959, vol. 1, pp. 105, 108, 166. Cf. 1905, p. 341, 1952. See also Holmes, 1918, p. 41.

54. Pound, 1909, p. 464.

55. Cowan, 1947, pp. 137-8; Wigdor, 1974, pp. x, 283-7; Hunt, 1978, Ch. 2.

56. See generally Rumble, 1968; Twining, 1973. Scandinavian 'legal realism' will not be considered here, since it is a philosophical rather than a sociological movement. My eventual conclusion parallels this movement's rejection of the concept of a supra-individual 'ought', but does not follow its rejection of practical rationality.

57. Gray, 1909/1972.

58. Llewellyn, 1940, p. 1364.

59. Llewellyn, 1929/1962, pp. 3-5. Cf. 1940, pp. 1357-67; Althusser, 1965a/ 1970, pp. 26-7. Llewellyn characterises the legal as 'ideology', but in no clear sense (1940, p. 1392).

60. Llewellyn, 1930/1977, p. 107.

61. See Hoebel, 1964, p. 738 n13.

62. In which capacity he set aside his jurisprudential views (Berman, 1971/1974, p. 30+n10 (on p. 148)).

63. Arnold, 1935/1962, Chs 2 and 3.

64. Arnold, 1960, p. 1311.

65. See, particularly, the writings of Glendon Schubert.

66. Cf. Holmes, 1897, p. 457.

67. Twining, 1974, pp. 161, 167.

68. Stone, 1946/1968, p. 25.

69. Twining, 1974, p. 158.

70. Campbell, 1974, pp. 24-5. Cf. Twining, 1974, pp. 157-8.

71. Gény, 1899/1954, vol. 1, p. 384.

72. Willock, 1974, pp. 3, 4, 9, 11, 12.

73. Lloyd, 1964/1976, pp. 7, 327.

74. Dworkin, 1972/1977, pp. 66-8.

75. Campbell, 1974, p. 22; Willock, 1974, p. 8.

76. Kafka, 1914/1953, Ch. 9; Kraft, 1928-9; Arnold, 1935/1962, pp. 59-71; Berman, 1971/1974.

77. E.g. Lukács, 1920/1971.

78. E.g. Seagle, 1941, p. 5.

79. Harvey, 1944, p. 42. See also Cohen, 1978.

80. See e.g. the two halves of Hunt, *The Sociological Movement in Law* (1978).

81. Campbell and Wiles, 1976; cf. Willock, 1974, pp. 3, 4. Some of what goes under the name 'sociology of law' is really 'socio-legal': for example, the 'sociology of law' of Ehrlich is mainly inquiry into what social factors a judge may properly take into account when deciding a case (1913/1975, 1922; cf. 1903/1969; Ziegert, 1979).

82. Cf. Hunt, 1978, p. 45.

83. Bankowski and Mungham, 1976.

84. Cf. Austin, 1832/1970, vol. 1. pp. 22-4.

85. Cf. Radbruch, 1914/1950, p. 213; Kelsen, 1934/1970, pp. 344-6, 1945/ 1961, pp. 380, 386-7, 1948/1957, pp. 202-3, 1952, pp. 432, 444-5; Raz, 1974/ 1975, pp. 500-2, 1975, pp. 150-2.

86. Jurisprudential theorists tend, when they leave the plane of the abstract for that of the actual, to fall into the terms of their 'home' legal order, and even to work in the abstract in those terms. Cf. Goodhart, 1932/1933, pp. 1, 2.

87. That is, the 'bindingness' of legal norms is annullative rather than positive.

88. The analysis of evolutionism is based on a study of Spencer and, in some respects, on a study of Hobbes.

89. See, in Marx, especially the discussion of 'the fetishism of capital' in *Theories of Surplus Value* (1862-3/1963-71: index references).

90. Cf. Lukács, 1923/1971, pp. 88-91, 96-103; Weber, 1919-20/1927, pp. 275-7, 279.

91. See generally Marx on 'commodity fetishism' (1963-6/1933, pp. 142, 164, 166 (translation, 1863-6/1976, pp. 1046, 1058); 1867/1976, pp. 163-77), where it is important to note that his emphasis is not on 'reification (*Verdinglichung*)' so much as on 'objectivation (*Versachlichung*)'; Lukács, 1923/1971; Goldmann, 1958/1959; Ranciére, 1973.

92. Cf. Marx, 1862/1975, p. 120; Engels, 1875/1975; Macpherson, 1962/1964.

93. Lovejoy, 1933/1936, Ch. 9; Nisbet, 1972.

94. There is a religiose, involutionist element even in Spencer.

95. E.g. Kelsen's campaign against personification of the state (see n21 above).

96. Duiguit, 1913/1970, pp. xlii, xliii.

97. Engels, 1890/1975, pp. 399, 400; Lukács, 1923/1971, pp. 95-7.

98. Marx, 1867/1976, pp. 125-6.

99. Kaulla, 1936/1940, Ch. 2.

100. In Marxist terms, this legal aspect is part of the 'basis' (cf. Engels, 1877-8/1975, p. 109; Godelier, 1977/1978; Kinsey, 1978), while the legal *determination* (to be discussed in a moment) is part of the 'superstructure'.

101. Cf. Engels, 1887/1975, p. 270; Seagle, 1941, pp. 27, 371. See also Braverman, 1974, Ch. 13.

102. Cf. Pashukanis, 1924/1970, p. 110 (this seems the most reliable translation from the Russian); Kelsen, 1934/1970, pp. 168-74. The analysis of a legal aspect of the object and the subject could be extended into analysis of the social relation in respect of the object (cf. Pashukanis, 1924/1970, p. 107).

103. E.g. Llewellyn, 1940, p. 1364; Kelsen, 1941/1957, 1950, p. xiii.

104. E.g. in Kelsen.

105. Chroust, 1974, pp. 8 ff.

106. In this paper I have had to neglect the existence of some of the modern capitalist ideological tendencies in classical society.

107. Pound, n53 above; Laski, quoted in Lloyd, 1959/1979, p. 405 n41; Villey, 1962/1969, p. 135.

108. Cf. Maquet, 1958-9.

109. Kafka, 1914/1953, Ch. 9. Kafka had a doctorate in law and held a legal post.

110. Kelsen, 1911/1960, esp. pp. 17-23, 1964. See, further, my 'The Basic Norm as Fiction' (forthcoming, *Juridical Review*).

111. Cf. Mandel, 1976, p. 20.

112. Althusser, 1969-70/1971, p. 161.

113. Cf. Bohannan, 1963, pp. 11-13, 51.

114. Cf. Searle, 1969, pp. 73-6.

115. And similarly for words the meaning of which depends on that of 'law' − 'crime', 'property' and so on − and for other words, such as 'state', in so far as their meaning depends on that of 'law'.

116. These conclusions on the nature of law are, in their practical implications, very far from being anarchistic − the suggestions and demands, or at least the demands, can be enforced − nor do they entail any very important changes in actual legal orders, except that the rejection of legal absolutism entails abolition of death penalties.

References

Abel, R.L. (1973) 'Law Books and Books about Law'. *Stanford Law Review*, 26, pp. 175-228

Althusser, L. (1965a/1970) 'From *Capital* to Marx's Philosophy'. In L. Althusser and E. Balibar, *Reading Capital*. London: New Left Books

—— (1965b/1970) 'The Object of *Capital*'. In Althusser and Balibar *Reading Capital*

—— (1969-70/1971) 'Ideology and Ideological State Apparatuses'. In L. Althusser, *Lenin and Philosophy and Other Essays*. London: New Left Books

Anderson, P. (1974) *Lineages of the Absolutist State*. London: New Left Books

Arnold, T.W. (1935/1962) *The Symbols of Government*. New York: Harcourt, Brace and World

—— (1960) 'Professor Hart's Philosophy'. *Harvard Law Review*, 73, pp. 1298-1317

Austin, J. (1832/1970) *Lectures on Jurisprudence*, 3 vols. New York: Franklin

Baker, J.H. (1972/1975) 'The Dark Age of English Legal History 1500-1700'. In D. Jenkins (ed.), *Legal History Studies 1972*. Cardiff: University of Wales Press

Bankowski, Z. and Mungham, G. (1976) *Images of Law*. London: Routledge and Kegan Paul

Berger, P.L. and Luckmann, T. (1966/1971) *The Social Construction of Reality*. Harmondsworth: Penguin

Berman, H.J. (1971/1974) *The Interaction of Law and Religion*. London: SCMP

—— (1977) 'The Origins of Western Legal Science'. *Harvard Law Review*, 90 pp. 894-943

Bohannan, P. (1963) *Social Anthropology*. New York: Holt, Rinehart and Winston

Braverman, H. (1974) *Labor and Monopoly Capital*. New York: Monthly Review Press

Campbell, C.M. (1974) 'Legal Thought and Juristic Values'. *British Journal of Law and Society*, 1 pp. 13-30

—— and Wiles, P. (1976) 'The Study of Law and Society in Britain'. *Law and Society Review*, 10, pp. 547-78

Carlen, P. (1976) *Magistrates' Justice*. London: Robertson

Carroll, L. (1894/1939) 'What the Tortoise said to Achilles'. In L. Carroll, *Complete Works*. London: Nonesuch Press

Chloros, A.G. (1955) 'Some Aspects of the Social and Ethical Element in Analytical Jurisprudence'. *Juridical Review*, 67, pp. 79-102

Chroust, A.-H. (1974) 'The Philosophy of Law of St Thomas Aquinas: his Fundamental Ideas and Some of his Historical Precursors'. *American Journal of Jurisprudence*, 19, pp. 1-38

CLH I (1968) Various authors, *A General Survey of Events, Sources, Persons and Movements in Continental Legal History* (*Continental Legal History* series, vol. 1). South Hackensack, NJ: Rothman. New York: Kelley

Cohen, J. (1978) 'The Political Element in Legal Theory: a Look at Kelsen's Pure Theory'. *Yale Law Journal*, 88, pp. 1-38

Cowan, T.A. (1947) 'Legal Pragmatism and Beyond'. In P. Sayre (ed.), *Interpretations of Modern Legal Philosophies. Essays in Honor of Roscoe Pound*. New York: Oxford University Press

Dewey, J. (1916/1970) 'Progress'. In J. Dewey, *Characters and Events*, vol. 2, pp. 820-30. New York: Octagon

Douglas, J.D. (1971) *American Social Order*. New York: Free Press. London:

Collier-Macmillan
Douglas, M. (1973) Introduction. In M. Douglas (ed.), *Rules and Meanings*.
Harmondsworth: Penguin
Duguit, L. (1913/1970) *Law in the Modern State*. New York: Fertig
Durkheim, E. (1887/188) 'Cours de Science Sociale: Leçon d'Ouverture'. *Revue
Internationale de l'Enseignement*, 15, pp. 23-48
—— (1912/1915) *The Elementary Forms of the Religious Life*. London: Allen
and Unwin
Dworkin, R. (1972/1977) 'The Model of Rules II'. In R. Dworkin, *Taking Rights
Seriously*. London: Duckworth
Ehrlich, E. (1903/1969) 'Judicial Freedom of Decision: its Principles and
Objects'. In (various authors) *Science of Legal Method* (Modern Legal Philos-
ophy series, vol. 9). New York: Kelley. South Hackensack, NJ: Rothman
—— (1913/1975) *Fundamental Principles of the Sociology of Law*. New York:
Arno Press
—— (1922) 'The Sociology of Law'. *Harvard Law Review*, 36, pp. 129-45
Engels, F. (1875/1975) 'Letter to Lavrov, 12-17 November 1875'. In K. Marx and
F. Engels, *Selected Correspondence*. Moscow: Progress
—— (1877-8/1975) *Anti-Dühring*. London: Lawrence and Wishart
—— (1884/1975) 'Letter to Kautsky, 26 June 1884'. In Marx and Engels,
Selected Correspondence. Moscow: Progress
—— (1887/1975) 'Juristic Socialism'. In K. Marx and F. Engels, *On Religion*.
London: Lawrence and Wishart
—— (1890/1975) 'Letter to Schmidt, 27 October 1890'. In Marx and Engels,
Selected Correspondence. Moscow: Progress
Feuerbach, L. (1841/1957) *The Essence of Christianity*. New York: Harper
Franklin, J.H. (1963) *Jean Bodin and the Sixteenth-Century Revolution in the
Methodology of Law and History*. New York: Columbia University Press
Friedmann, W.G. (1961-2) 'Sociology of Law'. *Current Sociology*, 10/11, pp.
1-16
Gény, F. (1899/1954) *Méthode d'interprétation et Sources en Droit Privé Positif*,
2 vols. Paris: Librairie Générale de Droit et de Jurisprudence
Godelier, M. (1977/1978) 'Infrastructures, Societies and History'. *New Left
Review*, 112, pp. 84-96
Goldmann, L. (1958/1959) 'La Réification'. In L. Goldmann, *Recherches
Dialectiques*. Paris: Gallimard
Goodhart, A.L. (1932/1933) 'Some American Interpretations of Law'. In W.I.
Jennings (ed.), *Modern Theories of Law*. London: Oxford University Press
Gray, J.C. (1909/1972) *The Nature and Sources of the Law*. Gloucester, Mass:
Smith
Grotius, H. (1631/1953) *The Jurisprudence of Holland*, 2 vols. London: Oxford
University Press
Hall, J. (1949) 'Concerning the Nature of Positive Law'. *Yale Law Journal*, 58,
pp. 545-66
Hanley, T.R. (1947) Translator's Preface. In H.A. Rommen, *The Natural Law*.
St. Louis: Herder
Harvey, C.P. (1944) 'A Job for Jurisprudence'. *Modern Law Review*, 7,
pp. 42-54
Hegel, G.W.F. (1832/1895) *Lectures on the Philosophy of Religon*. London:
Routledge and Kegan Paul, 1962 reprint
Hoebel, E.A. (1964) 'Karl Llewellyn: Anthropological Jurisprude'. *Rutgers Law
Review*, 18, pp. 735-44
Holmes, O.W. (1881/1963) *The Common Law*. Boston: Little, Brown
—— (1897) 'The Party of the Law', *Harvard Law Review*, 10, pp. 457-78

—— (1899) 'Law in Science and Science in Law'. *Harvard Law Review*, 12, pp. 443-63
—— (1918) 'Natural Law. *Harvard Law Review*, 32, pp. 40-4
Howe, M. DeW. (1957-63) *Justice Oliver Wendell Holmes*, 2 vols. Cambridge, Mass: Belknap Press
Huizinga, J. (1919/1955) *The Waning of the Middle Ages*. Harmondsworth: Penguin
Hunt, A. (1976) 'Law, State and Class Struggle'. *Marxism Today*, 20, pp. 178-87
—— (1978) *The Sociological Movement in Law*. London: Macmillan
Kafka, F. (1914/1953) *The Trial*. Harmondsworth: Penguin
Kaulla, R. (1936/1940) *Theory of the Just Price*. London: Allen and Unwin
Kelley, D.R. (1970) 'The Rise of Legal History in the Renaissance'. *History and Theory*, 9, pp. 174-94
Kelsen, H. (1911/1960) *Hauptprobleme der Staatsrechtslehre entwickelt aus der Lehre vom Rechtssatze*. Aalen: Scientia
—— (1925/1966) *Allgemeine Staatslehre*. Bad Homburg von der Höhe: Gehlen
—— (1927-8) 'Naturrecht und positives Recht'. *Revue Internationale de la Théorie du Droit*, 2, pp. 71-94
—— (1928/1964) 'Die Idee des Naturrechts'. In H. Kelsen, *Aufsätze zur Ideologiekritik*. Neuwied: Luchterhand
—— (1934/1970) *The Pure Theory of Law*. Berkeley: University of California Press
—— (1941/1957) 'The Law as a Specific Social Technique'. In H. Kelsen, *What is Justice?* Berkeley: University of California Press
—— (1945/1961) *General Theory of Law and State*. New York: Russell and Russell
—— (1948/1957) 'Absolutism and Relativism in Philosophy and Politics'. In H. Kelsen, *What is Justice?* Berkeley: University of California Press
—— (1950) *The Law of the United Nations*. London: Stevens
—— (1952) *Principles of International Law*. New York: Rinehart
—— (1961/1968) 'Naturrechtslehre und Rechtspositivismus'. In H. Kelsen, A. Merkl and A. Verdross, *Die Wiener rechtstheoretische Schule*. Vienna: Europa V
—— (1962/1963) 'Die Grundlage der Naturrechtslehre'. In F.-M. Schmölz (ed.), *Das Naturrecht in der politischen Theorie*. Vienna: Springer
—— (1964) 'Die Funktion der Verfassung'. *Forum* [Vienna], 11, pp. 583-6
Kinsey, R. (1978) 'Marxism and the Law: Preliminary Analyses'. *British Journal of Law and Society*, 5 pp. 202-27
Kolakowski, L. (1966/1969) *The Alienation of Reason*. Garden City, NY: Doubleday (Anchor)
Konefsky, S.J. (1968) 'Oliver Wendell Holmes'. In D.L. Shills (ed.), *International Encyclopedia of the Social Sciences*, vol. 6, pp. 490-3. New York: Macmillan and Free Press. London: Collier-Macmillan
Kraft, J. (1928-9) 'Über das methodische Verhältnis der Jurisprudenz zur Theologie'. *Revue Internationale de la Théorie du Droit*, 3, pp. 52-6
Kuhn, T.S. (1962/1970) *The Structure of Scientific Revolutions*. Chicago: University of Chicago Press
Kuttner, S. (1936) 'Sur les Origines du Terme "Droit Positif" '. *Revue Historique de Droit Français et Étranger* (4e sér.), 15, pp. 728-40
Lee, D. (1959) Introduction. In D. Lee, *Freedom and Culture*. Englewood Cliffs, NJ: Prentice-Hall
Llewellyn, K.N. (1929/1962) 'A Realistic Jurisprudence – the Next Step'. In K.N. Llewellyn, *Jurisprudence*. Chicago: University of Chicago Press
—— (1930/1977) *The Bramble Bush*. Dobbs Ferry, NY: Oceana

—— (1940) 'The Normative, the Legal, and the Law-jobs: the Problem of Juristic Method'. *Yale Law Journal*, 49, pp. 1355-400
—— and Hoebel, E.A. (1941) *The Cheyenne Way*. Norman: University of Oklahoma Press
Lloyd, Lord (1959/1979) *Introduction to Jurisprudence*. London: Stevens
—— (Lloyd, D.) (1964/1976) *The Idea of Law*. Harmondsworth: Penguin
Lovejoy, A.O. (1933/1936) *The Great Chain of Being*. Cambridge, Mass: Harvard University Press
Lukács, G. (1920/1971) 'Legality and Illegality'. In G. Lukács, *History and Class Consciousness*. London: Merlin Press
—— (1923/1971) 'Reification and the Consciousness of the Proletariat'. In Lukács, *History and Class Consciousness*
MacCormick, N. (1973/1974) 'Law as Institutional Fact'. *Law Quarterly Review*, 90, pp. 102-29
MacPherson, C.B. (1962/1964) *The Political Theory of Possessive Individualism*. London: Oxford University Press
Maine, H.S. (1861/1906) *Ancient Law*. London: Murray (this edn with notes by Pollock)
—— (1865/1890) Address to University of Calcutta, II'. In H.S. Maine, *Village-communities in the East and West*. London: Murray
—— (1875/1890) 'The Effects of Observation of India on Modern European Thought'. In Maine, *Village-communities*
—— (1883) *Dissertations on Early Law and Custom*. London: Murray
Maitland, F.W. (1888/1957) 'Why the History of English Law is not Written'. In V.T.H. Delany (ed.), *Frederick William Maitland Reader*. New York: Oceana
Mandel, E. (1976) Introduction. In K. Marx, *Capital*, vol. 1. Harmondsworth: Penguin
Maquet, J.J. (1958-9) 'Le Relativisme Culturel'. *Présence Africaine* (n.s.), 22, pp. 65-73; 23, pp. 59-68
Marx, K. (1844/1962) ['Marx über sein Verhältnis zu Hegel und Feuerbach.'] In K. Marx and F. Engels, *Werke*, vol. 3, p. 536. Berlin: Dietz
—— (1844a/1975) *Economic and Philosophic Manuscripts of 1844*. In K. Marx and F. Engels, *Collected Works*, vol. 3, pp. 229-346. London: Lawrence and Wishart
—— (1844b/1975) 'Hegel's Construction of the Phenomenology'. In Marx and Engels, *Collected Works*, vol. 4, p. 665
—— (1845/1976) 'Theses on Feuerbach'. In Marx and Engels *Collected Works*, vol. 5, pp. 3-5
—— (1862/1975) 'Letter to Engels, 18 June 1862'. In Marx and Engels, *Selected Correspondence*. Moscow: Progress
—— (1862-3/1963-71) *Theories of Surplus Value*, 3 vols. London: Lawrence and Wishart
—— (1863-6/1933) *Das Kapital* Erstes Buch. 'Der Produktionsprozess des Kapitals'. Sechstes Kapitel. 'Resultate des unmittelbaren Produktionsprozesses'. *Archiv Marksa i Engel'sa*, 2 (7), pp. 1-267.
—— (1863-6/1976) 'Results of the immediate process of production'. In K. Marx, *Capital*, vol. 1. Harmondsworth: Penguin
—— (1867/1976) *Capital*, vol. 1. Harmondsworth: Penguin
—— (1873/1976) Postface to the second edn of *Capital*, vol. 1.
Mészáros, I. (1970/1972) *Marx's Theory of Alienation*. London: Merlin Press
Midgley, T.S. (1975) 'The Rôle of Legal History'. *British Journal of Law and Society*, 2, pp. 153-65
Nisbet, H.B. (1972) *Goethe and the Scientific Tradition*. London: Institute of

Germanic Studies, London University

Pashukanis, E.B. (1924/1970) *La Théorie Générale du Droit et le Marxisme*. Paris: Études et Documentation Internationales

Pollock, F. (1900/1961) 'The History of the Law of Nature'. In F. Pollock, *Jurisprudence and Legal Essays*. London: Macmillan

Poole, R. (1972) *Towards Deep Subjectivity*. London: Allen Lane

Pound, R. (1905) 'Do We Need a Philosophy of Law?' *Columbia Law Review*, 5, pp. 339-53

—— (1909) 'Liberty of Contract'. *Yale Law Journal*, 18, pp. 454-87

—— (1910) 'Law in Books and Law in Action'. *American Law Review*, 44, pp. 12-36

—— (1932) 'Jurisprudence'. In E.R.A. Seligman (editor-in-chief), *Encyclopaedia of the Social Sciences*, vol. 8, pp. 477-92. New York: Macmillan

—— (1943) 'Sociology of Law and Sociological Jurisprudence'. *University of Toronto Law Journal*, 5, pp. 1-20

—— (1947) Preface. In G. Gurvitch, *Sociology of Law*. London: Routledge and Kegan Paul

—— (1952) 'Natural Natural Law and Natural Positive Law'. *Law Quarterly Review*, 68, pp. 330-6

—— (1959) *Jurisprudence*, 5 vols. St Paul: West

Putnam, H. (1979) 'Il Existe au Moins une Vérité "a priori" '. *Revue de Métaphysique et de Morale*, 84, pp. 195-208

Quine, W.V. (1951) 'Two Dogmas of Empiricism'. *Philosophical Review*, 60, pp. 20-43

Radbruch, G. (1914/1950) 'Legal Philosophy'. In *The Legal Philosophies of Lask, Radbruch, and Dabin* (*Twentieth Century Legal Philosophy* series, vol. 4). Cambridge, Mass.: Harvard University Press

Rancière, J. (1973) *Lire le Capital III*. Paris: Maspero

Rashdall, H. (1895/1936) *The Universities of Europe in the Middle Ages*, 3 vols. Oxford: Clarendon Press

Raz, J. (1974/1975) 'The Institutional Nature of Law'. *Modern Law Review*, 38, pp. 489-503

—— (1975) *Practical Reason and Norms*. London: Hutchinson

Rommen, H.A. (1936/1947) *The Natural Law*. St Louis: Herder

Rumble, W.E. (1968) *American Legal Realism*. Ithaca, NY: Cornell University Press

Salmond, J. (1902/1966) *Jurisprudence*. London: Sweet and Maxwell

Savigny, F.C. von (1814/1831) *Of the Vocation of our Age for Legislation and Jurisprudence*. London: privately printed

—— (1814/1973) 'Vom Beruf unserer Zeit für Gesetzgebung und Rechtswissenschaft'. In H. Hattenhauer (ed.), *Thibaut und Savigny. Ihre programmatischen Schriften*. Munich: Vahlen

Schacht, R. (1970/1971) *Alienation*. London: Allen and Unwin

Schmidt, A. (1962/1971) *The Concept of Nature in Marx*. London: New Left Books

Schutz, A. and Luckmann, T. (1973/1974) *The Structures of the Life-world*. London: Heinemann

Seagle, W. (1941) *The Quest for Law*. New York: Knopf

Searle, J.R. (1969) *Speech Acts*. Cambridge: Cambridge University Press

Simmel, G. (1900/1978) *The Philosophy of Money*. London: Routledge and Kegan Paul

Stone, J. (1946/1968) *The Province and Function of Law*. Buffalo, NY: Hein

—— (1964/1968) *Legal System and Lawyers' Reasonings*. Sydney: Maitland

Twining, W. (1973) *Karl Llewellyn and the Realist Movement*. London: Weidenfeld and Nicolson

—— (1974) 'Some Jobs for Jurisprudence'. *British Journal of Law and Society*, 1, pp. 149-74

Verbeke, G. (1964/1966) 'Aux Origines de la Notion de "Loi Naturelle" '. In *La filosofia della natura nel medioevo. Atti del Terzo Congresso Internazionale di Filosofia Medioevale*. Milan: Società Editrice Vita e Pensiero

Villey, M. (1962/1969) 'François Gény et la Renaissance du Droit Natural'. In M. Villey, *Seize Essais de Philosophie du Droit*. Paris: Dalloz

—— (1967/1969) Ontologie Juridique. In Villey, *Seize Essais de Philosophie du Droit*

Weber, M. (1919-20/1927) *General Economic History*. London: Allen and Unwin

—— (1922/1954) *Max Weber on Law in Economy and Society*. Cambridge, Mass: Harvard University Press

Wieacker, F. (1960/1963) 'Éclipse et Permanence du Droit Romain'. In Centre d'Études Supérieures de la Renaissance, *Pedágogues et Juristes*. Paris: Vrin

Wigdor, D. (1974) *Roscoe Pound: Philosopher of Law*. Westport: Greenwood Press

Willock, I.D. (1974) 'Getting on with Sociologists'. *British Journal of Law and Society*, 1, pp. 3-12

Winch, P. (1958/1963) *The Idea of a Social Science and its Relation to Philosophy*. London: Routledge and Kegan Paul

Ziegert, K.A. (1979) 'The Sociology behind Eugen Ehrlich's Sociology of Law'. *International Journal of the Sociology of Law*, 7, pp. 225-73

6 STATE, REDUNDANCY AND THE LAW

Bob Fryer

> Few workers are so unrealistic as those in Britain, led by the extreme
> left, who oppose on principle all reductions in the number of jobs in
> a particular enterprise. It is obvious that in a dynamic society jobs
> must be redistributed among enterprises and occupations.
>
> Frederick Meyers (1964), *Ownership of Jobs:*
> *a Comparative Study*

Industrial and Occupational Change in Britain

The years since the end of the Second World War have witnessed
remarkable transformations in the industrial and occupational structure
of Britain. In particular, large-scale reductions in employment have
occurred in sectors of the British economy which were still, after the
Second World War, major employers of labour, especially of manual
labour. In 1948, agriculture still employed over three-quarters of a
million workers; by 1958, 200,000 jobs had disappeared, by 1968 a
further 200,000 had gone and by 1975[1] agriculture and horticulture
together employed 371,500. Other dramatic declines in numbers were
brought about in coal mining (over three-quarters of a million in 1948;
only marginally fewer in 1958; 427,500 in 1968; and 297,500 in 1975),
shipbuilding (244,900 in 1948; 214, 900 in 1958; 155,600 in 1968; and,
in the whole of shipbuilding and marine engineering, there was employment for only 185,000 in 1975), manufacture of locomotives, carriages
and wagons (178,000 in 1948; 158,800 in 1958; 59,500 in 1968; and
42,800 in 1975), cotton spinning and weaving (291,700 in 1948;
235,400 in 1958; 175,600[2] in 1968; and 101,800 in 1975) and
railways (572,400 in 1948; 494,600 in 1958; 293,100 in 1968; and
219,200 in 1975).[3] Similar wholesale drops in employment were
brought about in fishing, docks, boot and shoe manufacture and
private domestic service. Over the same period, other industries
enlarged their share of the British labour force — chemicals, plastics,
printing and publishing, education, medical and health services,
electrical and electronic manufacture and, at least up to 1968, the
production of motor vehicles (280,300 in 1948 up to 474,600 in
1968).[4] Accompanying these shifts in industrial structure have been
equally dramatic occupational changes, with the decline of manual
work, the growth of white-collar employment in general and dramatic

136

increases in scientific and technical work and in the feminisation of
routine clerical jobs (Bain, 1974).

The blunt figures mask more than they reveal: much of the transformation has struck hard at traditional working-class employment,
very often of a community-based or highly localised kind and not
infrequently regionally specific. Hand in hand with the destruction of
jobs has gone the elimination of traditional areas of working-class
housing and fragmentation of working-class communities. Huge shifts
of employment and occupation have been mirrored in changes in the
structure and composition of British trade unions. Behind the losses in
jobs lie equally important changes in the organisation of production
and structure of industrial relations including a significant decline in
skilled manual work. In each of these arenas of change and challenge to
working-class organisation, the state has played a significant (if
ultimately limited) part, often through the specific apparatus of the
law. In short, the terms of class struggle in Britain may have altered
little in the last thirty years or so, but its location and the forms of class
organisation have certainly changed and state redundancy policy has
played a part in that transformation. This chapter sets out to trace the
halting development of state facilitation of dismissals, through the
development of a redundancy programme underpinned eventually by
the law. Legal regulation of redundancy has been credited with an
apparently dramatic diminution of opposition to closures and
sackings, but redundancy and state policy alone have proved insufficient
to transform the labour process.

The Processes of Industrial and Occupational Change

Many processes have contributed to the signal transformation of the
industrial and occupational structure of Britain: so-called 'natural
wastage', whereby numbers run down by virtue of non-replacement of
leavers and retired workers; alterations in recruitment policies and in
demand for labour, whereby there are fewer new entrants to traditional
jobs; and, the specific focus of this paper, redundancies and closures,
the collective dismissal of workers. Needless to say, each of the
processes is related to the others, especially when redundancy occurs or
is in prospect. Indeed, 'voluntary leaving' in anticipation of excess
labour supply is a well-known phenomenon, often losing workers
entitlement to financial compensation under the terms of the Employment Protection Consolidation Act 1978 or (where they exist) under
the terms of the relevant collective agreement. 'Voluntary leaving' has
also proved a mixed blessing for capital, for it is likely that the young,
more versatile and more heavily indebted workers will cut their losses

and anticipate redundancy rather than await meagre compensation and
face competition in the external labour market. But, for obvious
reasons, these are the very workers whom an employer will wish to
retain if any are to be retained at all.

Remarkably, in a society obsessed by the regular examination of
economic and industrial indicators — strike statistics, balance-of-
payments figures, wage and earning rates, gold and dollar reserves and
even unemployment percentages — we do not know how many people
lose their jobs by way of redundancy in Britain each year. That rather
awkward formulation, 'lose their jobs by way of redundancy', is
deliberately chosen and includes all those men and women whose
employment in a particular place with a particular employer ceases
because the employer embarks upon a policy of (usually) collective
dismissals. This loose definition contrasts both with the legal definition
of what constitutes individual redundancy, which qualifies the
redundant worker for consideration for financial payment under the
terms of the Employment Protection Consolidation Act (previously the
Redundancy Payments Act 1965) and with the quarterly statistics
of redundancy payments published by the Department of Employment. All we know for certain is the number of persons receiving
redundancy payments — *not* those declared redundant within the
meaning of the Act, nor those leaving within the period of the general
warning often given or the statutory period of consultation laid on
employers intending to initiate redundancies under the terms of
Part IV of the Employment Protection Act 1975. These latter are so-
called 'voluntary leavers' who have no legal entitlement to redundancy
pay and, together with those who are declared 'redundant' according
to the statutory definition but who fail to qualify for payment by
virtue of their age or length of service with the employer represent the
hidden side of the impact of redundancy in contemporary Britain.
Thus, all we know for certain is that, since the first full year of
operation of the Redundancy Payments Act, the numbers who have
received payments are as set out in Table 6.1.

Some workers not declared redundant within the meaning of the
law and some receiving statutory payments receive supplementary
severance pay from employers' own schemes often resulting from
collective agreements with trade unions. Elsewhere, I have argued that
the total *paid* redundants are exceeded by unpaid redundants by at
least two to three times, and that number excludes any 'voluntary
leavers' (Fryer, 1973a). In short, we can only hazard a guess at the numbers
who lose their jobs by way of redundancy. More importantly, we have
little idea of the numbers of workers, workplaces or communities for
which the occurrence of redundancy results in a realignment of class
forces, bearing in mind that redundancy, especially partial closures

Table 6.1: Numbers Receiving Redundancy Payments

Year	Number	Average payment
1966	137,208	£193.0
1967	241,581	£207.6
1968	264,506	£233.8
1969	250,764	£246.8
1970	275,563	£263.2
1971	370,221	£292.3
1972	297,112	£328.2
1973	176,919	£376.3
1974	182,161	£403.8
1975	340,215	£524.0
1976	313,728	£602.9
1977	267,234	£619.0

affecting only a proportion of workers, strikes at the very roots of collective working-class organisation by interposing the individual calculus of payments and/or chances of dismissal between the worker and collective resistance to redundancy. The majority of redundancy studies have focused upon the consequences of redundancies for individuals, families, participation rates, local communities etc. Seldom have there been accounts of either the course of the redundancies or the consequences for those workers left behind once the dismissals have been effected, although it is clear that redundancy short of total closure inevitably entails a reconstruction of relations at the point of production.

Despite these significant difficulties in the way of achieving a full understanding of the contribution of redundancy to the reconstruction of production and industrial relations over the past thirty years, a glance at the changes in employment suggests a number of important lines of inquiry. Most striking is the quickening pace of decline after 1958: the 1960s were years in which job losses fed upon job losses. Over the decade 1961-71 the percentage *annual* loss in employment for particular industries was as follows: mining and quarrying, 6.0 per cent; agriculture, forestry and fishing, 2.5 per cent; shipbuilding and marine engineering, 3.2 per cent; textiles, 2.9 per cent; clothing and footwear, 1.5 per cent. For the last five years of the decade, from 1966-71, the pace of decline quickened (except for shipbuilding) and the annual percentage losses were: mining and quarrying, 7.2 per cent; agriculture, forestry and fishing, 3.6 per cent; shipbuilding and marine engineering, 1.2 per cent; textiles, 4.3 per cent; clothing and footwear, 2.3 per cent (statistics from Unit for Manpower Studies, 1975). Over this same decade, 1961-71, the labour force grew by more than one and a quarter millions from 23.8 millions to 25.1 millions, with much of this growth coming from the increased numbers of married women in paid employment, many in part-time jobs (Unit for Manpower Studies, 1975;

Ministry of Labour, 1967).

What all of these figures suggest is that inquiry should focus upon developments in the 1950s and differences between the 1950s and 1960s and between the early and late 1960s which facilitated the increase in the restructuring of employment in Britain. In particular, it is necessary to explore how far redundancy featured in this restructuring and to discover the respective contributions of labour, capital and especially of the state and law to the development of redundancy policy.

From Unemployment to Redundancy

Before the Second World War there existed a profusion of studies and advocated policies in respect of the problem of unemployment. From a range of analytic and political perspectives, it was suggested that unemployment was a question of the unsatisfactory, ill-organised or irrational operation of the labour market. As Beveridge's first study put it, unemployment was a problem of 'business organisation' in which the resolution lay in the twin policies of 'smoothing industrial transitions' and 'diminishing the extent of the reserves required for fluctuation or their intervals of idleness'. For Beveridge in this early study 'unemployment was a question not of the scale of industry but of its organisation, not of the volume of demand for labour but of its change and fluctuations' (*Unemployment*, p. 193). The organisation of the labour market was then denounced as cumbersome, antiquated and wasteful with harmful effects upon the mentality of labour, especially marked in the case of casual labour.

> Thrift, sobriety, adaptability and initiative are good things for many reasons. They are all apt to be too good for the casual labourer. The individual here and there may rise superior to overwhelming odds. The man is inevitably demoralised by a system of employment which panders to every bad instinct and makes every effort at good hard and useless; which by turning livelihood into a gamble goes far to take from idleness, slovenliness and irresponsibility their punishment and from assiduity its reward. The casual labourer is the rock upon which all hopes of thrift and self-help or trade union organisation, no less than all schemes of public assistance, are shattered. (Beveridge, *Unemployment*)

In the aftermath of the Second World War, a combination of the smashing of industrial competitors, Marshall aid, post-war reconstruction, government policy, Keynesian economic policy and the Korean boom appeared to have eliminated unemployment. Some commentators effusively spoke of the 'affluent' and 'post-capitalist' society, especially when the Tory Governments of the 1950s failed to dismantle the apparatus of the welfare state. Not only was unemployment a problem of the past, so was its corollary, the class war. Sociologists spoke of 'embourgeoisement',[6] preferred 'status' to 'class', discovered the 'privatised' worker and advanced the revisionist theme of 'convergence'. Unfortunately, neither the commentators nor the state functionaries could be depended upon.

First of all, they had both failed to read and take lessons from Beveridge's later classic, *Full Employment in a Free Society* (1944) which not only argued the clear case for full employment as a counter to class war but, more importantly, set out the consequences under conditions of capitalist democracy of a full employment policy. Second, neither commentators nor the state functionaries had noticed, or were willing to take the implications of, the developing crisis that was gripping whole sections of the British economy. From the late fifties through to the mid-1960s cotton, railways, coal, docks, motor vehicles, steel, shipbuilding and aerospace experienced crises which were resolved partly by resort to redundancy. The redundancies attracted the attention of a small band of academics who variously examined the labour market, community, family and individual consequences of the redundancies. They in turn failed to appreciate not simply that redundancy was a specific form of collective dismissal, to be understood in the context of the respective positions of contemporary capital and labour, but also that a proper understanding of the class context of redundancy posed especial tasks for the capitalist state (see Mukherjee, 1973, and Wood, 1978). The learning of this last lesson has been slow, fragmentary and incomplete under successive political administrations.

Redundancy as a Form of Collective Dismissal

There was nothing new about 'workers' being 'dismissed' by 'employers'. In any society where a group or individual has the power, both material and cultural, to fracture the relationship of others to the principal means of subsistence, 'redundancy' must remain a potential channel for the realisation of the interests of the powerful. Under capitalism it is capital's ability unilaterally to terminate its relation with specific labour, thus preventing workers from realising subsistence through that relation by the sale of their labour power, that characterises the class context of dismissal. Irrespective of whether redundancy leads to unemployment, whether 'frictional', 'structural', short or long term, it is the manifestation of class conflict in the instance of redundancy that merits attention. In different industries at different points in time collective dismissals have more or less salience in the portfolio of policies open to capital in its quest for accumulation. Similarly, the *form* of those dismissals also varies according to circumstances. The factors which determine capital's evaluation of mass dismissal as both a means of and necessity for advancing its interests, include crucially the state of working-class organisation, in general and at the point of production in question.

In Britain of the 1950s, when the term 'redundancy' began to be widely used to describe dismissals,[7] it was the working-class outcry about temporary struggle against specific mass dismissals, against a background growth of relatively autonomous shop-floor power in the shape of restrictive labour practices and shop-steward organisation, that prompted the state's search for redundancy policies which could secure working-class acquiescence through a combination of procedural reform and financial inducement.

It had been precisely under conditions of buoyant demand for labour, low levels of unemployment and rising standards of living in the 1950s that opposition to redundancies had grown. Admittedly, in some industries such as motors, worker hostility to redundancy was more poignant in times of sudden slumps and 'overnight' announcements of mass dismissals such as in BMC and Standard Motors in 1956. As Turner and Bescoby in the early 1960s remarked:

> the post-war development of strikes against redundancy . . . suggests that workers' conceptions of their basic standards have been enlarged since pre-war days, and now include job security: nearly a quarter of all the strikes, and rather more than a quarter of all the time lost from disputes in the car firms since the war are attributable to dismissals or to issues arising from a lack of employment. (1962)

In this climate of opposition to redundancy, the AEU policy, advocating a 'right to work', was often singled out for criticism by those advocating 'rational' approaches to reductions of labour forces (i.e. redundancy). The AEU policy, it was said, 'was militantly advanced particularly by Communist and extreme leftist groups' (Meyers, 1964). The AEU National Committee adopted the following resolution in 1957:

> This National Committee declares that compensation is no solution to the problem of 'Right to Work' and 'Full Employment'. Therefore we instruct the Executive Council to conduct a national campaign against redundancy and unemployment and for the 'Right to Work'.

Furthermore this National Committee instructs our Executive Council to issue or cause to be issued, through the District Committee, suitable propaganda material on the question of the 'Right to Work'.

That where redundancy is threatened we instruct our Executive Council to warn the employers that this Union will move into action to safeguard the livelihood of our members and will demand the 'Right to Work' and that the necessary action will be taken to enforce our demands.

The resolution was reaffirmed the following year and it was proposed to establish agreements forbidding redundancies where there was no suitable alternative work and to institute work-sharing arrangements backed up by a guaranteed weekly wage. In 1959 the policy was further extended to include the advocacy of overtime bans and shorter working weeks where redundancy threatened. The paradox of this situation was many sided. First, as Meyers noted, 'it was in a period of full employment that plant-level reactions to reductions in force made it apparent that many British workers were not satisfied with alternative job opportunities; they sought continued tenure in the jobs they need' (1964). Second, it remained true, as Goodrich had observed almost forty years earlier, that 'even the most elaborate of the expedients . . . are directed toward the end, not of decreasing irregularity of employment but merely of distributing more equally the incidence of its hardships' amongst workers (1920 and 1975, p. 82). Third, this stance was adopted when British management still clung to the ideology of managerial prerogative in respect of dismissals while, in practice, so uncertain were British managers about the potential response to sackings, there was great reluctance to engage in collective bargaining about redundancy in advance of any particular need to dismiss workers or sometimes even at all. Fourth, some senior trade union officials opposed, in practice, the 'no redundancy' policies of the shop steward and rank and file. As Clegg rather tendentiously remarked, the AEU was 'hampered by' its resolution of no redundancy but 'most trade union leaders, however, being reasonable men, acknowledge that redundancies must occur' (1965).

Against this background of worker opposition to redundancy, there was developing an increasing alarm about labour hoarding, restrictive practices, immobility of labour, underemployment, inflexibility and the growing autonomy of the shop floor. This line of argument developed into a well-orchestrated crescendo in the early 1960s and influenced both the rhetoric and direction of Labour government policy. But this was more sophisticated than a modernised version of the standard blaming of workers for the problems of capital. Criticism was directed also at employers for failures of management and at governments for incoherent economic management. Moreover, there gradually emerged a realisation that workers could not be simply forced into economic and industrial change but had to give their active 'consent', although often the strategy chosen was geared more to undermining and fragmenting worker solidarity. Even so, from the post-war Conservative opposition's *Industrial Charter* (the brainchild of Butler aided by McLeod and Powell) through to *Positive Employment Policies* in January 1958 produced by the Ministry of Labour (McLeod was, by then, Minister of Labour), the argument emerged in public policy that workers should be won to the aims and plans of management, by information, explanation and leadership. The path to industrial efficiency and high productivity depended upon the 'active co-operation of employees at all levels'. *Positive Employment Policies* would include job satisfaction, opportunity for advancement, security and redundancy. This latter would involve consultation, reduction in overtime and recruitment and (limited) short-time working, and agreement about the order of redundancy, length of notice and compensation to long-service employees.

In subsequent years, the paternalism of *Positive Employment Policies* gave way to advocacy of pluralistic bargaining relations, particularly productivity bargaining. As Allan Flanders, the leading theoretician of productivity bargaining, insisted, the prize was no less valuable: it was only by learning to share control that management would regain it. By this time, the mid-1960s, the rationalisation of manpower resources had become a focus of public policy, alongside the reconstruction of wages systems, the elaboration of procedural arrangements and the incorporation of shop-floor representation. In all of this, redundancy had its part to play. Increasingly, as the need for large-scale dismissals became identified as a necessary and normal phase in the reorganisation of a wide cross-section of British industry, the call was intensified for a coherent strategy for redundancy. As Beveridge had properly understood, only the state was in a position to give a lead in the establishment of such a strategy but, in the face of hostility and indifference by the official representatives of labour and capital, the lead it gave was late, hesitating and incomplete.

Beveridge, Capital and the State

Beveridge had grasped what capital was incapable of grasping (because of internal divisions and the uneven experience of crisis) and what the state seemed to be unwilling to accept, that a full employment policy *tout court* was likely to be not only merely pious but also unworkable.

Beveridge's aim, in arguing for his own, liberal version of full employment (the creation of a sellers' market for labour), was designed to
preserve what he identified as 'all the essential springs of material
progress in the community, to leave to special efforts its rewards, to
leave scope for change, invention, competition and initiative'
(Beveridge, 1944, p. 20).

State action to implement the policy was required in three areas:

1. maintaining at all times adequate total outlay, by which he meant
   the deployment of sufficient money to meet demand for the products
   of contemporary industry, including all goods and services for public
   and private consumption;
2. controlling the location of industry;
3. securing the organised mobility of labour.

Beveridge understood well the implication of the policy he was advocating. 'Full employment cannot be won and held without a great
extension of the responsibilities and powers of the State.' In particular,
it was emphasised that responsibility for total outlay could rest only
with the state: 'no one else has the requisite powers; the condition will
not get satisfied automatically' (1944, p. 29). Beveridge's comprehensive proposals in this first area included a new type of budget, the
direction of outlay to social priorities, the expansion of outlay through
taxation, the acceptance of planning as the basis for achieving the
common objective (as he saw it) of full employment and the creation of
new ministries. Beveridge also saw the role of the state as being central
to industrial location:

> For an effective attack upon mass unemployment, as much as for
> an effective attack upon the evils of urban congestion, control over
> the location on industry is indispensable. This control must be both
> negative, prohibiting undesirable location, and positive, encouraging
> desirable location. (1944, p. 170)

In principle, Beveridge saw no real contradiction 'between the interests
of producers and consumers in respect of industrial location'.

The third area for action, to ensure the organised mobility of labour,
Beveridge saw as a joint task to be undertaken by the state, managers
and the workers themselves. The other side of the coin of 'unlimited
demand for labour' in a policy of full employment was 'the abolition
of nearly all qualitative restrictions on the use of manpower' (1944,
p. 171). This implied controlling the flow of 'adaptable juveniles',
abolishing casual employment, ending the 'aimless, unguided search
for work which is involved in the hawking of labour from door to

door' (1944, p. 172), by the extended use of labour exchanges and the removal of two kinds of obstacle to the fluidity of labour – the unwillingness of individuals to change jobs and the restriction on entry to particular trades. Where individuals were concerned 'a just consequence of a full employment policy would lie in the stiffening of conditions of unemployment benefit' for the long-term unemployed. Trade unions should also 'reconsider' their restrictions, rules and customs with respect to methods of work, types of labour, demarcation of trades and entry into employment. Without such a reconsideration, a policy of 'outlay' for full employment would fail: just as the state was accepting new responsibilities, so too should the unions (1944, p. 174-5). What was required was not perpetual motion, but flexibility of labour (p. 175).

As already noted, Beveridge recognised that the proposals he was advocating would require changes in the apparatus of the state, including a new Ministry of National Development to control the location of industry and an expanded Ministry of Labour to undertake 'man-power planning' (sic) and to secure through co-operation of employers and workers the organised mobility of labour. The Ministry of Finance would be concerned with all forms of 'outlay', both public and private, and would have access to a new institution to be known as a National Investment Board to execute the policy with powers of 'obtaining intelligence, of giving assistance and of regulating investment' (1944, p. 177). To oversee the reform of the state, the supreme direction of the country 'must be in the hands of men (sic) with leisure from the daily routine of vast departments, men able to decide quickly, but with time to read, think and discuss before they decide' (1944, p. 180). What Beveridge envisaged was a Supreme Cabinet of three.

Given the adoption of a policy of full employment, in addition to the three main areas for action already identified, Beveridge went on to sketch out other fundamental implications of the policy. Full employment would 'give a new turn to all social relations' (1944, p. 194) and Beveridge picks out for especial comment 'the problem of industrial discipline and efficiency; of the determination of wages; of the determination of prices; and of the treatment of monopolies and trade associations' (1944, pp. 194-207). These are the so-called 'internal implications of full employment'. On the first score, efficiency and discipline, Beveridge unequivocally insisted that full employment should 'not mean that everyone has security in his present job even if he behaves well in it; still less does it mean that he has security if he behaves badly' (1944, p. 197). The best way of ensuring industrial discipline was first to remove the fear of unemployment which had been a fertile source of restriction of output and opposition to change, and second to use fellow workers to keep idlers and shirkers up to the mark. 'Workmen have no love for idlers' and, if management can promote 'participation' and workpeople be made to feel 'partners in the enterprise', then the democratic solution to the problem of efficiency and discipline will reside in enlightened management and the imposition of high standards by workers themselves rather than in starvation and fear.

A policy of full employment, argued Beveridge, must also beware the dangers of sectional wage bargaining 'pursued without regard for its effects upon prices'. The problem was that there was 'no inherent mechanism in our present system which can with certainty prevent competitive sectional bargaining for wages from setting up a vicious spiral of rising prices under full employment' (1944, p. 199). Beveridge made two proposals here. First, the TUC should devise a 'unified wage policy' designed to ensure that the claims of individual unions are 'judged with reference to the economic situation as a whole' and second, there should be some form of compulsory arbitration so that wages might be 'determined by reason, in the light of all the facts and with some regard to general equities and not simply by the bargaining power of particular groups of men' (1944, p. 200). For employers, the correlative to acceptance of these proposals by trade unions would be opening up the books showing 'all facts as to profits, costs and margins' to arbitrators and expert staff for criticism (1944, p. 200). The state, for its part, would have to adopt a stable price policy, for, 'the successful working of a full employment policy . . . will depend ultimately on the degree of responsibility with which bargaining is conducted'. Integral to the policy would be a stable price policy which ensured that wages would rise 'both in money terms and in real terms as productivity per head increases' (1944, p. 200). Finally, with respect to monopolies and trade associations, the state should be prepared to explore three stages of control: supervision, regulation and public ownership.

Taken together, the 'internal considerations' set out by Beveridge raised questions of the future of private enterprise. In particular, the central question appeared to be whether working-class co-operation could be secured 'under conditions of enterprise conducted for private profit' (p. 206). Beveridge preferred to remain agnostic and to leave these wider issues, 'economic, political and moral', until they were reached. His own proposals, he argued, were designed to take Britain round the next corner whilst preserving her 'essential freedoms' and were not logically inconsistent with the persistence of capitalism.

Ultimately, it was Beveridge's failure to analyse the contradictions of the state policies he advocated, when taken in conjunction with what he saw as the essential British liberties of social democracy and the persistence of private capital, which constituted the fundamental flaw in his analysis and prescriptions. This unwillingness of Beveridge to locate the question of employment within an acceptance of a developed class analysis is all the more surprising in view of his key defence of his policy which recognised that the central danger of unemployment was not loss of material wealth but class hatred:

> The greatest evil of unemployment is not the loss of additional material wealth which we might have with full employment. There are two greater evils: first, that unemployment makes men seem useless, not wanted, without a country; second, that unemployment makes men live in fear and that from fear springs hate.
>
> So long as chronic mass unemployment seems possible, each man appears as the enemy of his fellows in a scramble for jobs. So long as there is a scramble for jobs it is idle to deplore the inevitable growth of jealous restriction of demarcations, of organised or voluntary limitation of output, of resistance to technical advance.
>
> [Hence the text on the title page of the report for which Beveridge is indebted to his wife: 'misery generates hate'.]

It is possible that Beveridge's reluctance to embrace a class analysis of the problems of full employment contributed to the failure of capital and the state to accept the practical implications of his arguments. A more likely reason for that failure is that Beveridge, the state and representatives of capital alike did not have to hand an analysis which enabled them to foresee the crisis that was to envelop large sections of British capital and British capital as a whole at the end of the 1950s and throughout the two following decades. Even if they had enjoyed access to such an analysis, the internal politics of capital and state and their respective relations with the organised working class would have placed obstacles in the path of a comprehensive approach to the corollaries of full employment in a capitalist society set out by Beveridge.

In the event, not only was there a failure to develop the required total policy for dealing with the new social relations engendered by and engendering full employment, there was even an absence of any-thing resembling the proper establishment of a key fragment of such a total policy, namely a policy or series of policies in relation to redund-ancy. Admittedly, more progress was made in respect of redundancy policy than in other arenas of class confrontation, namely incomes policy, price stabilisation, industrial location, control over mono-polies, industrial training and retraining, direction of investment, the elimination of job control and restrictive work practices, technical and scientific innovation, arbitration and mediation of industrial disputes and accommodation of shop-floor power in the shape of shop stewards.

Without a coherent policy embracing and relating all of these features
of industrial restructuring, it was hardly to be expected that the
problems of full employment could be tackled by redundancy policy
alone, although it must be said that from the late 1950s, where it
existed at all, the success of redundancy policy in defusing working-
class resistance to mass dismissals was remarkable.

The Construction of Redundancy Policy

Throughout the 1950s neither collective bargaining between capital
and labour nor unilateral action by employers in privately owned
industry had established provisions for redundancy on a large scale. The
Tinplate Labour Fund had been established in 1946 to deal with the
run-down of the old hand mills in South Wales. But this was very much
the exception. The Ministry of Labour's survey, *Security and Change*,
published in mid-1961, gave details of some 236 policies covering only
1,105,000 workers. As the tables below show, in more than half of the
policies (143) there was no provision even for severance payments and
just under half (106) gave neither extra notice nor severance payments
to those declared redundant. Many redundancy policies amounted only
to a statement of general principles to be followed in case of
redundancy, including restrictions on recruitment, consultation with
trade unions, co-operation with employment exchanges and a preference order for the discharge of workers, beginning with those with
shortest service (other things being equal).

By far the most comprehensive redundancy policies either were to
be found in the state sector, in nationalised industries, or were under-
written by the state. In railways there was an industry-wide agreement
in February 1958 while the Coal Board's scheme included lump-sum
compensation, early pensions, weekly unemployment supplements,
transfer arrangements, removal allowances, the provision of housing
and 'settling in' grants. There were also schemes in the airlines, gas and
electricity supply. However, probably the most complete policy for
redundancy and restructuring was to be found in the cotton industry
in a scheme of rationalisation underpinned by the Cotton Industry Act
1959.[8] The Act made provision for the elimination of excess capacity
in the industry (estimated at 60 per cent in spinning, 29 per cent in
weaving and 25-40 per cent in finishing) by providing for compensation
to capital for smashing up outdated plant and machinery and to capital
and labour for displacement from the industry. It also provided for
financial assistance for re-equipping the industry. As the Bill was
passing its various stages through Parliament, speaker after speaker
showed an awareness not only of the specific circumstances of the

Table 6.2: Warning, Formal Notice and Severance Payment Provisions 1960

	No. of companies irrespective of policy re length of notice or warning	Companies giving 1 week's notice or less		Companies giving notice in excess of 1 week, but without reference to length of service		Companies giving notice in excess of 1 week, graduated according to length of service	
		No extra warning	Extra warning	No extra warning	Extra warning	No extra warning	Extra warning
Totals, irrespective of policy re severance payments	236 (1,105,000)a	71 (285,000)	98 (387,500)	30 (79,000)	12 (45,000)	17 (259,500)	8 (49,000)
No severance payments given	143 (437,000)	46 (52,500)	60 (177,500)	11 (14,000)	6 (12,000)	13 (132,500)	7 (48,500)
Severance payments given, but without reference to length of service	10 (16,500)	4 (5,000)	4 (5,000)	2 (6,500)	–	–	–
Severance payments given graduated according to length of service	83 (651,500)	21 (227,500)	34 (205,000)	17 (58,500)	6 (33,000)	4 (127,000)	1 (500)

Note: a. The numbers in brackets show the total number of employees (works and staff) in the companies concerned.
Source: Ministry of Labour, *Security and Change* (1961).

Table 6.3: Terms of Notice and Severance Payments Analysed by Size of Company (Numbers of Employees), 1960

	Size of Company (total numbers of employees)						
	Under 500	500-999	1,000-1,999	2,000-4,999	5,000-9,999	10,000 and over	Totals
No extra notice,[a] no severance payments	30	26	23	18	5	4	106
Extra notice[a] (i.e. in excess of 1 week); no severance payments	6	8	12	4	4	3	37
No extra notice[a] but severance payments given	8	8	14	15	6	12	63
Extra notice[a] (i.e. in excess of 1 week) and severance payments given	1	3	7	11	6	2	30
Totals	45	45	56	48	21	21	236

Note: a. Other than preliminary warning to individuals.
Source: Ministry of Labour, *Security and Change* (1961).

cotton industry but also of the emergent historical necessity for action on redundancy across a broad front. As Mr Douglas Houghton put it:

> I repeat most emphatically that we are approaching the stage when the question of redundancy in industry will have to be looked at entirely afresh and apart from the normal inadequate compensation for loss of employment which we give under the National Insurance Scheme. We must assume our national responsibilities where they are appropriate in order that our industries may re-shape themselves, that we may embrace new techniques, change the pattern of our industry and go forward fearlessly in meeting the challenge of the future. We can then ensure that those whose livelihood is affected by these changes are adequately dealt with out of the rising national wealth which should be the consequence of these big changes in our industrial activity. (H.C. Debs, 17.6.1959, col. 512)

Despite the provisions of the Cotton Industry Act, which placed cotton redundancies within the wider question of restructuring of the industry, the legislation had limitations within its own terms and especially by comparison with the total policy for employment deployed by Beveridge. Moreover, a further six years elapsed before the Redundancy Payments Act reached the statute book (although it was probably delayed by the 1964 General Election) and, when it was eventually brought forward by the Labour Government in a colourful rhetoric denouncing restrictive practices and labour hoarding, it remained a highly individualistic statute making provision only for proper dismissal, for the calculation of financial compensation for each worker separately according to length of service, age and level of wages, and for a system of individual appeals to tribunals.

The Redundancy Payments Act

The Redundancy Payments Act 1965, introduced by a Labour Government, initially met with no great enthusiasm from either capital or labour, although capital came to see it as having positive advantages in discharging workers and it was later cited to prove the Labour Government's determination to advance the interest of workers by enlarging the welfare state.[9] The Act made provision for severance payments, individually calculated according to age, length of continuous service and level of wages, to workers who were dismissed because their employer had ceased to carry on business or because a cessation or diminution of work of a particular kind had occurred. Only workers with two or more years' service and under retirement age were eligible for compensation. There was some recognition of the likely greater difficulties for older workers and those above the age of forty received one and a half weeks' pay for each year of service after the age of forty up to a maximum of twenty years. Even so, average payments were low, far lower than publicity to occasional 'golden hand shakes' might suggest. The payments were financed partly out of a levy on all employers and partly by the particular employer concerned. Apart from some changes in the rules governing Redundancy Fund and employer components of compensation, no fundamental statutory changes were introduced in the Act until the Industrial Relations Act 1971 introduced the notion of 'unfair selection for redundancy' as part of its provisions in respect of appeals to industrial tribunals alleging unfair dismissal. Further changes were made when the Employment Protection Act 1975 obliged employers to give notice of collective dismissals and to consult with workers and their organisations about any intended redundancies. Although not a statutory duty before 1975, the advocacy of consultation went back a long time and was especially clear in both particular industrial policies (such as steel) and the booklet *Dealing with Redundancies* published by the Department of Employment and Productivity in June 1968 when Barbara Castle was First Secretary and Secretary of State for Employment and Productivity.

Neither the original Act, nor the additional rights under the Industrial Relations Act and additional requirements of employers under the Employment Protection Act, were designed to question the legitimacy of redundancy or to strengthen workers' opposition to redundancy. Common to all three statutes was the establishment of proper procedures calculated to remove redundancy from the realm of collective conflict and to replace class struggle with something approximating the American notion of 'due process'. The statutes make plain that there was nothing wrong with redundancy as a policy, but that in cases of redundancy individuals should be properly selected (according to formulae), properly notified and properly consulted. Aggrieved individuals would have the right to go to industrial tribunals about alleged improper selection or alleged inadequate compensation; aggrieved trade unions might establish that they were inadequately notified or consulted and win a 'protective award' for their members, effectively lengthening their period of notice. Nothing in the legislation to date requires employers to receive consent from either their workforce or local public authorities before implementing a redundancy,[10] although *de facto* 'consent' is often achieved by the increasingly popular tactic of 'voluntary' redundancy, a major fragmentation of shop-floor opposition to collective dismissal.

It is difficult to determine whether or not the Redundancy Payments Act has lessened the incidence of conflict generated by redundancies. After an initial reduction of strikes attributable to redundancy, the number of disputes about redundancy climbed again in the late 1960s and early 1970s and were associated with factory occupations, 'sit-ins', 'work-ins' and experiments in workers' co-operatives.[11] However, all disputes rose in this period, as did the incidence of redundancy.

Table 6.4: Working Days Lost through Stoppages of Work caused by Redundancy Disputes, 1960-1970[a]

Year	Total days lost from all causes (000s)[b]	Days lost from redundancy disputes (000s)[c]	Redundancy loss as per cent of total loss	Index of loss from redundancy disputes (1965=100)	Index of redundancy loss as per cent of total loss (1965=100)
1960	3,049	105.4	3.5	174	167
1961	3,038	147.8	4.9	244	233
1962	5,778	514.5	8.9	848	424
1963	1,997	41.2	2.1	68	100
1964	2,030	101.2	5.0	167	238
1965	2,932	60.7	2.1	100	100
1966	2,395	107.2	4.5	177	214
1967	2,783	31.7	1.1	52	52
1968	4,719	56.4	1.2	93	57
1969	6,925	102.6	1.5	169	71
1970	10,908	254.2	2.3	419	110

Notes: a. All figures relate to Great Britain.
b. Department of Employment Gazette, May each year.
c. Obtained from the Department of Employment: this is a sub-category of the set of causes given in the DE statistics, published as 'Disputes concerning the Employment or Discharge of Workers (Including Redundancy Questions)

Source: S. Mukherjee, *Through No Fault of Their Own* (1973).

What is more difficult to calculate is the lessening of friction because of the provisions of the 1965 Act: however, an early survey showed that three times as many employers felt the Act had made it easier to discharge workers than felt it had made no difference (32 per cent and 11 per cent respectively, 52 per cent thought it made no difference) and 79 per cent of full-time officials were of the view that the Act had 'helped management to get workers to accept changes affecting manpower needs' (Parker *et al.*, 1971).

Evidence also seems to suggest that there has been an increase in redundancy agreements since the 1965 Act, at least in those establishments that have experienced redundancy. Parker reports about half of the employers and the same proportion of union officers saying that

Table 6.5: Working Days Lost through Redundancy Disputes in Eight Industry Groups, 1960-1970 (total days, and index 1965=100)

Year	Mining and quarrying[a]		Metals and engineering		Shipbuilding and marine engineering		Vehicles		Textiles and clothing[b]		Construction		Transport and communication		All other industries and services	
	Index	Number	Index	Number	Index	Number	Index	Number	Index	Number	Index	Number	Index	Number	Index	Number
1960	3951	12,249	82	18,679	13	316	274	65,964	2	124	37	2,451	454	5,466	5	174
1961	2368	7,342	118	26,737	1048	24,637	302	72,768	3	140	108	7,167	287	3,459	162	5,563
1962	4282	13,273	476	107,753	2089	49,103	334	80,285	69	3,573	290	19,203	19519	235,202	176	6,056
1963	0	–	64	14,547	308	7,240	34	8,147	6	300	67	4,444	419	5,048	41	1,421
1964	41	126	94	21,246	52	1,229	270	64,870	1	25	139	9,196	265	3,194	34	1,173
1965	100	310	100	22,663	100	2,351	100	24,060	0	–	100	6,632	100	1,205	100	3,434
1966	936	2,901	125	28,244	3	64	105	25,359	100	5,215	67	4,426	2524	30,410	307	10,545
1967	0	–	82	18,464	72	1,680	14	3,429	0	–	85	5,658	31	374	62	2,124
1968	0	–	98	22,090	300	7,055	81	19,440	40	2,100	62	4,093	0	–	48	1,654
1969	0	–	113	25,622	303	7,126	159	38,190	20	1,065	167	11,060	291	3,511	466	15,993
1970	1778	5,513	522	118,384	270	6,352	297	71,548	19	809	256	16,949	78	934	983	33,743

Notes: a. There were no redundancy disputes in mining and quarrying in 1963, or during 1967-69.
b. As there were no redundancy disputes in this industry group in 1965, the index is based on 1966=100.
Data made available by the Department of Employment.

Source: Mukherjee (1973).

Table 6.6: Number of Stoppages of Work Caused by Redundancy Disputes, 1966-69[a]

Year	Total stoppages from all causes	Stoppages from redundancy disputes	Redundancy stoppages as per cent of all stoppages	Index of stoppages caused by redundancy disputes (1965=100)	Index of redundancy stoppages as per cent of total stoppages from all causes (1965=100)
1960	2,832	47	1.7	84	71
1961	2,686	70	2.6	125	108
1962	2,449	114	4.7	204	196
1963	2,068	70	3.4	125	142
1964	2,524	51	2.0	91	83
1965	2,354	56	2.4	100	100
1966	1,937	53	2.7	95	113
1967	2,116	53	2.5	95	104
1968	2,378	47	2.0	84	83
1969	3,116	68	2.2	121	92

Note: a. More recent data for stoppages solely from redundancy disputes are not available.
Source: Mukherjee (1973).

Table 6.7: Number of Workers Involved in Redundancy Disputes, 1966-69[a]

Year	Total number of workers involved in stoppages from all causes	Workers involved in stoppages from redundancy disputes	Workers involved in redundancy stoppages as per cent of total workers in stoppages from all causes	Index of number of workers involved in stoppages from redundancy disputes (1965=100)	Index of workers in redundancy disputes as per cent of workers involved in stoppages from all causes (1965=100)
1960	701,500	22,791	3.2	62	58
1961	672,900	72,819	10.8	195	196
1962	4,296,600	343,499	8.0	920	146
1963	455,200	26,154	5.7	70	104
1964	701,500	16,569	2.4	44	44
1965	673,500	37,322	5.5	100	100
1966	415,400	24,679	5.9	66	107
1967	551,800	21,440	3.9	57	71
1968	2,074,000	45,844	2.2	123	40
1969	1,426,600	47,930	3.4	128	62

Note: a. More recent data for number of workers involved in stoppages solely from redundancy disputes are not available.
Source: Mukherjee (1973).

there were such agreements. In 1973, Industrial Relations Review and Report reported 61 per cent of respondents as having a written agreement and a BIM survey of 350 companies in mid-1974 found that 60 per cent had redundancy polices of which a quarter had introduced their policies before 1965 and 65 per cent had agreed their policies with manual unions and over 40 per cent with clerical unions (see also Gennard, 1979, pp. 38-42). In some industries, such as steel and docks, elaborate agreements have been negotiated in respect of planned closures and dismissals (Jones, 1974, for example).

Limitations of Redundancy Policy

For all its undoubted value to individual capitals, in helping to get rid of workers quietly (and, usually, very cheaply), and to the state, in offering some palliative to a significant aspect of organised class conflict, it is far from certain that redundancy policy has contributed greatly to the wider objective of reconstructing the basis of private accumulation in Britain through the radical restructuring of labour organisation. Undoubtedly, a great deal of such reconstruction has been achieved. But it would be wrong to overestimate it, to minimise workers' successful resistance to it and to overlook the unintended consequences of 'shaking out'[12] workers not to productive, profit-making employment but to public and other service jobs.

Many dismissed workers are, in any case, old, infirm and either unable or unwilling to take on jobs in industrial production once they have been made redundant. Others simply enlarge the ranks of the unemployed. Some, at least in the early days, even returned to the jobs from which they had been declared redundant.

Admittedly, state redundancy policy cannot be viewed alone, and there is a surface plausibility to the coherence of a state strategy that began with redundancy arrangements in the late 1950s (railway workshops, cotton, coal) and runs through the NEDC, Contracts of Employment Act, Industrial Training Act, Redundancy Payments Act, National Plan, Industrial Reorgansiation Corporation, National Board for Prices and Incomes, Prices and Incomes Act, Donovan Commission, Commission on Industrial Relations, *In Place of Strife* and (missing out the Tory years) the various stages of the social contract. But such superficial coherence masks wide variations, failures, misdirections, miscalculations, shifts in policy and inadequacies of strategy. Chiefly, it leaves out the nature of class struggle with its range and variation of workers' opposition to and acceptance of redundancy and other measures designed to reinvigorate British capital. This does not mean that redundancy has not been significant and, in some major areas of employment, devastating. Nor does it mean that the stuttering policy of procedural embellishment (and diversion) in respect of redundancy does not constitute a specific form of mass dismissal. However, redundancy policy alone and state redundancy policy in particular, for all its staggering impact, cannot amount to an integrated strategy for the restructuring of capital-labour relations. Redundancy policy needs to be closely articulated with a whole range of other policies: state redundancy policy requires detailed elaboration and supplementation by plant and company-level *substantive* as well as *procedural* arrangements for redundancy. Each of those developments depends upon class organisation and class politics and the successes and failures themselves need to be located in a sensitive account of class struggle.

That it took an initiative of the state — in both the state sector of employment and through statutory provision — to initiate a minimal but economy-wide redundancy policy is clearly significant. But the policy itself and its legal form were inherently limited and dependent upon further action from capital and acquiescence from labour. Moreover, as the new wave of redundancies of the late 1970s and early 1980s has swept across whole sections of the British economy, the limitations of state policy and its legal construction have become obvious. Put shortly, the law may be useful in helping employers to sack workers (or to persuade workers to accept sackings), but capital's chief objective is not to sack workers but to realise surplus value. In that endeavour, legal regulation, whether of employment or even of incomes, is inadequate unless accompanied by a concerted attack upon working practices at the point of production. As Leyland's Michael Edwardes has realised, there are many battles that the capitalist state alone cannot wage and announcements of the replacement of class struggle by state corporatism in this as in other spheres have proved premature.

Notes

1. Latest available detailed figures.
2. Underestimates decline because of change in industrial classification after 1958.
3. From *British Labour Statistics Historical Abstracts* and *British Labour Statistics, 1976.*
4. By 1975 this had fallen to 448,300.
5. And we have known that number only since the passing of the Act in 1965.
6. Later in the mid-1960s, the thesis was, of course, subjected to a sustained conceptual and empirical critique by Goldthorpe and others.
7. Before then, as in the restructuring of the cotton industry under the Cotton Spindles Act 1936, redundancy often referred to excess capacity in plant and machinery or to superfluity of labour rather than to its dismissal. For an extended consideration of the origins of the term 'redundancy' see Fryer,

'Redundancy and the Restructuring of Work', forthcoming.

8. For accounts of redundancy policy in the 1960s on railways, cotton, steel and telecommunications see Smith (1966).

9. For a detailed analysis of the ideology of the Act and critique of optimistic mythology associated with it, see Fryer 1973a and 1973b.

10. Here practice differs from West Germany and France. It is possible to speculate on the reasons for variation. Consent from German works councils or from French public authorities may be less imponderable than from British shop stewards or (Labour) local authorities.

11. Trade union officers reported continued use of sanctions in over one third of workplaces affected by redundancy (Parker *et al.*, 1971, p. 135). See also Gennard (1979), Table 10, p. 62 which demonstrates the increased proportion of stoppages attributable to redundancy in 1971 and 1972.

12. The phrase, not surprisingly, comes from a speech by Harold Wilson in introducing the 'July measures' of July 1966.

References

Bain, G.S. (1974) 'The Labour Force'. In Halsey (ed.), *Trends in British Society*
Beveridge, W.H. (1909 and 1930) *Unemployment: a Problem of Industry*
—— (1944) *Full Employment in a Free Society*
BIM (1974) *Redundancy Policies*
British Labour Statistics (various years, 1968 onwards)
Clegg, H.A. (1965) 'Mobility of Labour'. *NPB Review*
Department of Employment (1968) *Dealing with Redundancies*
—— (various years) *Gazette*
Fryer, R.H. (1973a) 'The Myths of the Redundancy Payments Act' *Industrial Law Journal*
—— (1973b) 'Redundancy, Values and Public Policy'. *Industrial Relations Journal*
—— (1975) *Redundancy and Control*
Gennard, J. (1979) *Job Security and Industrial Relations*
Goodman, G. (1962) *Redundancy in the Affluent Society*
Goodrich, C. (1920 and 1975) *The Frontier of Control*
IRRR (May 1973) 'Redundancy Procedures'
Jones, K. (1974) *The Human Face of Change*
Meyers, F. (1964) *Ownership of Jobs*
Ministry of Labour (1958) *Positive Employment Policies*
—— (1961) *Security and Change*
—— (1967) *Occupational Changes 1951-61*. Manpower Studies No. 6
Mukherjee, S. (1973) *Through No Fault of Their Own*
Parker, S.R. *et al.* (1971) *Effects of the Redundancy Payments Act*
Smith, A.D. (1966) *Redundancy Practices in Four Industries*
Turner, H.A. and Bescoby, J. (1962) 'Strikes, Redundancy and the Demand Cycle'.
Unit for Manpower Studies (1975) *Changing Structure of the Workforce*
Wood, S. (1978) 'Approaches to the Study of Redundancy'. *Industrial Relations Journal*

7 THE LAW AND THE USE OF TROOPS IN INDUSTRIAL DISPUTES

Christopher Whelan

The Myth

The idea that troops could be used on a regular basis in industrial disputes is publicly rejected by virtually everyone connected with such matters. The statements one finds on the subject support notions of limitations on military intervention, and rationalise the intervention that does occur on grounds of emergency or last resort. This was not always the case; in the last century, troops were regularly used as police to suppress disorder and to protect blacklegs, those who do the work of strikers. Troops were also used as blacklegs themselves; by 1917, however, this role had been repudiated.[1] Their intervention occasionally led to shots being fired and to some deaths. Several miners were shot in 1893 and 1894 strikes and, in 1911, two men were shot in Llanelli, and two in Liverpool.

In fact, the role of troops as blacklegs continued after 1917, but in a modified form. The dawning of what may be termed the modern position is best expressed by Winston Churchill in 1919:

> To use soldiers or sailors kept up at the general expense of the taxpayer, to take sides with the employer in an ordinary trade dispute ... would be a monstrous invasion of the liberty of the subject, and would be a very unfair, if not an illegal, order to give to the soldier. But the case is different where vital services affecting the health, life or safety of large cities or great concentrations of people are concerned.[2]

This kind of rhetoric is identical to that used by politicians today when troops are to be used in industrial disputes. Occasionally, one finds an extreme view. According to the former Metropolitan Police Commissioner, Sir Robert Mark, in a speech in 1973,

> It will not, therefore, surprise you when I tell you that the prospect of invoking military force to deal with industrial disputes or political demonstrations has never been contemplated during my thirty-nine years' service and there are, so far as I know, no plans at all for such a contingency.[3]

160

He was not just refering to the use of force, for he added that there has emerged 'a firm and deepening conviction, shared by soldiers, police and public alike that the army has no part to play in Great Britain in matters of political and industrial dispute not involving the overthrow of lawful government by force'.[4]

This latter view is mirrored in legal rhetoric. In one of the leading books on constitutional law, Wade and Phillips, the dilemma can be discovered by looking in different chapters. In their chapter on the armed forces, they begin: 'In the interests of constitutional government and the rule of law, the exercise of the physical might of the modern state must be subject to democratic control.'[5] But in their chapter on Emergency Powers, they declare: 'In times of grave emergency, normal constitutional principles may have to give way to the overriding need to deal with the emergency.'[6] There is thus a presumption throughout the rhetoric of legality, including that of constitutional lawyers, that within a democratic and parliamentary system it would be almost unthinkable that it could be easy to use troops, or that use could be made with virtually no legal accountability. It is this belief, fostered by 'official' sources, that will be compared with the reality; not just the actuality of military intervention, but more in terms of the law under which the use of troops in industrial disputes is regulated.

The Reality

Military Intervention in Industrial Disputes

Since the First World War, troops have been used to offset the impact of disputes which, almost invariably have been a challenge or obstacle to government political and industrial policy. During the 1920s mining industry crises, the mines were under government control. In the 1921 dispute, there was a threat of co-ordinated strike action between the railway, transport workers and mining unions (the Triple Alliance). An emergency was proclaimed, army leave was halted and 60,000 Reserves were called up;[7] 3,500 soldiers were used to protect property, and another 12,000 were stationed in various coalfields during the dispute.[8] Their presence, it was claimed, 'undoubtedly produced a steadying effect'.[9] The cost of the Reserve and Defence Force, and the additional cost to the regular army, totalled just over £8.5 million.[10]

The military played an important role in the extensive government preparations before the General Strike and miners' dispute of 1926. The military, naval and police power of the state was mobilised. The country was divided into eleven areas with a staff of military officers in charge of transport and supplies and plans included the assembling of troops and the navy.[11] The government refused to disclose the movement and the use of troops in the general strike, so it is difficult to determine the extent of their role. As the Secretary for War, Sir Laming Worthington-Evans, observed,

> I do not see that any public interest would be served by disclosing the detail of troop movements during the emergency. I feel sure, however, that this House is grateful to the Army for the efficient and good-tempered manner in which they have performed.[12]

Five hundred and seventy-two naval men were employed in operating power stations, and troops did train their guns on strikers at the London docks while food was being unloaded from ships. Thus, while they were used 'to protect the food supplies, to see that the life of the nation was carried on',[13] troops and armoured cars escorted food convoys with orders to get through at all costs.[14]

Since 1945, military intervention has occurred on about 23 occasions (excluding Northern Ireland). Since 1970, the military have intervened in at least seven disputes[15] and have been standing by, ready to intervene, in another four.[16] Their use, however, has been restricted to a few industries. The docks industry has been the subject of considerable intervention. This is not surprising; as Clement Attlee observed in the 1948 dispute, the government 'had no alternative in the public interest but to utilise Service personnel to safeguard the people's food supplies, particularly those of a perishable nature'.[17] In 1949, troops were twice used to unload ships 'to safeguard the food supplies of the country'.[18] Regulations made after the proclamation of emergency in 1949 provided for an increase in the number of troops. The number was built up as the dispute continued: from 400 in the beginning to 12,792 at the end, working on 130 ships.[19] Troops handled a total tonnage of 140,000 during the four-week strike, including nearly 30,000 tons for export.[20] The number of dockers who had been on strike reached 15,644. Under the emergency regulations, a Port Emergency Committee was set up, and under its authority the work of troops in the docks was regulated. This committee was responsible to the Ministry of Transport and not the Ministry of Labour, thus partially removing possible criticism that the troops were strike breaking. Thus, the committee was not concerned with the conciliation and settlement of the dispute, merely with securing supplies. However, it has been stated that, during Attlee's government, the army was used as 'blacklegs . . . on no less than nine separate occasions'.[21] More recently in the 1970 dispute, 36,500 troops were standing by when a state of emergency was proclaimed, but the union agreed to unload perishables, thus removing the need for army intervention. In the 1972 state of emergency, the RAF was used to fly supplies to offshore islands and the army was used to clear rotting fish.

In the 1960 and 1966 merchant seamen's disputes the navy was used to supply food to the outer islands. However in the 1966 dispute, Harold Wilson told the House of Commons that the navy might be needed because of the greater problem of imports and exports: 'We shall have to take whatever action is needed.'[22]

In recent years the role of troops seems to have increased. The government's (and indeed opposition's) resolve over the handling of civil emergencies has 'stiffened noticeably in the past few months, with ministers overcoming their fastidiousness about strike breaking. Success in handling the firemen's dispute has strengthened their determination.'[23] Before that strike began, the government announced that the armed services would be used as emergency fire fighters, and that preparations were already in hand. Home Secretary Merlyn Rees told the House of Commons that he authorised the chief executive, the chief of police, the chief fire officer and local army commander to talk together about the problems in advance of making firm decisions.[24]

Other military intervention in recent years includes the use of the RAF to supply a strategic radar station during a strike by civil air traffic control assistants in 1977, on the grounds of national security,[25] and use of troops to drive ambulances in the 1979 public employees' dispute. More significantly, troops have been ready to intervene in several other disputes, including petrol tanker drivers' disputes in 1978 and 1979, the dispute involving locker-room workers at Windscale in 1977[26] and the road hauliers' dispute in 1979. The involvement of service personnel in disputes of this nature can be interpreted as an example of intervention as a deliberate instrument of government policy. Furthermore, there are several examples where troops were used in preference to alternative courses of action. In the 1948 and 1949 docks disputes, the government could have instituted prosecutions under an order which prohibited strikes,[27] instead of which they used troops to do dockers' work; in the 1970 electricity supply dispute, power workers could have been prosecuted under an 1875 statute.[28]

The Law[29]

Two statutes deal directly with the use of troops in industrial disputes, the Emergency Powers Acts 1920 and 1964. In addition, there is residual authority to use the military in aid of the civil power under the royal prerogative.

Emergency Powers Act 1964

This Act made permanent a defence regulation first introduced as a wartime measure in 1939, and due to expire in 1964.[30] It allows the

Defence Council, without a proclamation of emergency, and therefore
without consulting Parliament, to authorise the use of service personnel
on 'urgent work of national importance'.[31] The Act was presented as a
'safeguard, and a necessary safeguard . . . a wise exercise in foresight.
It is an insurance policy against contingencies . . . '[32] The wartime regulation had been renewed annually without controversy, and the official
opposition spokesman could not 'offer any objection in principle'[33]
to making it permanent. The wartime regulation had been made to
remove doubts about what constituted a lawful order to soldiers, where
tasks were being performed that could not properly be described as
military. That is, the primary aim of this law was and is to legitimise
military intervention. Between 1947 and 1964, when the regulation was
replaced, troops were used under this regulation on 13 occasions in
industrial disputes, the last occasion being 1960 — two naval vessels
transported food and supplies to the Western Isles during an unofficial
strike by seamen.[34]

The Defence Council, which took over the functions of the
Admiralty, the Army Council and the Air Council in 1964,[35] is a body
established under the royal prerogative with both statutory and prerogative functions. In practice, it issues fresh orders on each occasion
that troops are to be used, specifying the nature of the temporary
employment. Orders may be signed by any two members of the
council. Membership consists of the Secretary of State for Defence
(who chairs the council and is responsible to Parliament for its business), the Minister of State for Defence, the Minister of State for
Defence Procurement, the Parliamentary Under Secretaries of State for
Defence, the Chiefs of the Defence, Naval, General and Air staffs, the
Chief of Personnel and Logistics at the Ministry of Defence (MOD),
the Chief Scientific Officer of the MOD, the Chief Executive (Procurement Executive) of the MOD, the Permanent Under Secretary of State
of the MOD and the First Sea Lord.[36] The council authorised the
employment of service personnel in disputes involving Tower Hamlets
dustmen, 1970, Glasgow firemen, 1973, Glasgow dustmen, 1975, civil
air traffic control assistants, 1977, the national firemen's strike, 1977-8,
and ambulance drivers, 1979. Its function clearly involves a wide
discretion: it is empowered to determine 'urgent work of national
importance'. There is no requirement to consult Parliament, despite the
implications of military intervention.

Emergency Powers Act 1920

Troops can be used under regulations following a proclamation of
emergency where it appears to the government that

there have occurred or are about to occur, events of such a nature as to be calculated, by interfering with the supply and distribution of food, water, fuel or light, or with the means of locomotion, to deprive the community, or any substantial portion of it, of the essentials of life.[37]

The proclamation lasts for one month at a time, and can be extended. Under this proclamation, regulations can be made by Order in Council for securing the essentials of life to the community. This includes powers and duties necessary for the preservation of peace, for securing and regulating the supply of food, water, light and other necessities, for maintaining the means of transit and locomotion, and for any other purposes essential to the public safety and the life of the community.[38] The imposition of compulsory military service or industrial conscription, as well as making it an offence to strike or picket (peacefully), is prohibited.

Both the proclamation and any regulations made are subject to review by Parliament (which, if it is not sitting at the time, must be recalled), and the regulations remain in force for only seven days unless a resolution is passed by both Houses of Parliament providing for their continuance. The regulations have statutory status, but both Houses can, by joint resolution, alter or revoke them.

The 1920 Act was hurried through Parliament as a response to a miners' strike (the mines were under government control) and the threat of co-ordinated strike action by the Triple Alliance: the miners', railwaymen's and transport workers' unions. Royal assent was obtained just one week after the Bill was introduced. The government denied that the strike precipitated the Act, but in 1919 it was revealed that doubts existed as to whether troops could still be relied upon in disputes. A secret circular, drafted in 1919, asked commanding officers whether their troops would assist in strike breaking, where they stood on trade unionism, and what potential there was of agitation.[39]

There have been twelve proclamations of emergency under this Act, five since 1970. Accompanying these have been an array of regulations that have given enormous powers to the government, and 'an all-embracing grip by the State on every citizen'.[40] Regulations have included the power to fix prices, take over vehicles, factories, mines or even land (e.g. in 1926, Hyde Park), impose three-day weeks on industry and other energy conservation, control transport or use troops to work in the mines or in transport, or *in any trade*. This has been said to give the executive an 'absolute right of dictatorship',[41] while the general response to this has been the argument that these regulations are only temporary in effect. In fact, the miners' emergency dispute in 1926 (including the General Strike) lasted seven and a half months, while in 1973-4 it lasted four months.

Reaction to these wide regulations has often been unfavourable. In 1926, for example, one MP told the government: 'You have declared war upon us by these Regulations.'[42] This may appear to be more true when troops are involved.

Military intervention has occurred in seven out of the twelve proclamations of emergency (though, in some instances, intervention preceded the proclamation): 1948, 1949 and 1972 docks, 1921 and 1926 miners, 1965 railways and 1966 merchant seamen; while in the 1970 docks dispute, 36,500 troops were standing by. In contrast to the Emergency Powers Act 1964, the 1920 Act provides for parliamentary scrutiny which could act as a restraint on the executive.[43] However, it is clear from the experience of this Act that the government do have a wide discretion in the Act. For example, the 1920 Act does not permit a proclamation merely to safeguard the national economy; yet, in 1966, a state of emergency was proclaimed in the merchant seamen's dispute. Two reasons for this were given by the Prime Minister: firstly, 'To accept this demand would breach the dykes of our prices and incomes policy',[44] and secondly,

> The reason for the Proclamation was that the main volume of imports into this country – not only food, but also raw materials – is becoming progressively and more damagingly disrupted. This is bound to affect employment fairly quickly, and is also affecting our export trade.[45]

In other words, the basic reason for the proclamation was danger to the national economy, not within the definition of emergency contained in the 1920 Act. Quintin Hogg (later Lord Hailsham) took up this point for the opposition, stating that 'As the Act stands, it would not be a legitimate motivation to take those circumstances into account in declaring an emergency', that is, the 'import and export trade'.[46] He did not argue that such factors could not create an emergency, but that, on technical grounds, the 1920 Act did not cover them. He accordingly proposed that the time may have come 'to examine the phraseology of the Act in the light of contemporary economics'.[47]

Declarations that 'our aim has been to put the power in the hands of recognised constitutional authority of the country',[48] and that 'it is our desire to take every step to make the control of Parliament as complete as possible',[49] are therefore questionable, particularly when it is also realised that since the emergency dispute in 1966 there has been very little parliamentary discussion of the regulations. Instead, codes of regulations have been made following 'the well-established precedents for Regulations of this sort',[50] and discussion has been limited to any additions to the 'corpus'.[51]

Under the 1920 Act then, there is the power to use troops on a wide basis, not merely 'to maintain essential supplies and services' as the Queen's Regulations claim (J11.005a), but when the government deem it a matter of 'public' or 'national' interest. Moreover, troops are backed by 'such force, and no more, as may be necessary to enable them to carry out the duties entrusted to them'.[52] Under the two Emergency Powers Acts, therefore, 'very extensive authority could be exercised by the police and the armed forces'.[53]

Royal Prerogative

In addition to the Emergency Powers Acts, however, both of which relate directly to industrial disputes, there are certain residual powers. According to the Queen's Regulations, which are issued under the royal prerogative, the Defence Council has control (command and administration) over the armed forces.[54] Despite statutes such as the Emergency Powers Acts, which may regulate control of the armed forces in certain matters, their over-all control, disposition and organisation is within the prerogative and, although the ambit of a royal prerogative can be determined by a court of law, the prerogative itself cannot be questioned in a court.[55] As Lord Reid observed in the House of Lords,

> It is in my opinion clear that the disposition and armament of the armed forces, are and for centuries have been, within the exclusive discretion of the Crown and that no one can ever seek a legal remedy on the ground that such discretion has been wrongly exercised.[56]

The scope of the royal prerogative is enormous. Not only is there no legal control, but, according to another House of Lords judge, Lord Parmoor, it 'connotes a discretionary authority or privilege exercisable by the Crown, or the executive, which is not derived from Parliament, and is not subject to statutory control'.[57] In fact, the prerogative is exercised by ministers who are accountable to Parliament. But the extent of the control over the minister remains questionable; the former Home Secretary Roy Jenkins told the House of Commons that Parliament's power to dismiss him or reduce his salary was 'complete Parliamentary control' over his decision to request the use of troops.

Exactly how far the royal prerogative does regulate the armed forces has been called an 'interesting but obscure question'.[58] According to legal authority, the royal prerogative 'is really a relic of a past age, not lost by disuse, but only available for a case not covered by statute'.[59] Statute covers industrial disputes: thus, a leading constitutional lawyer argued that the common law rules on the prerogative in emergencies falling short of war are 'remarkably abstruse',[60] but that 'it cannot mean that troops can lawfully be ordered to do whatever the Crown thinks fit whenever it thinks fit to maintain internal security, irrespective of what necessity requires'.[61]

Once again, however, the legal rhetoric bears little relation, in this case, to the legal reality. Two major differences between this authority and the statutory powers to use troops are, firstly, that no definition of 'emergency' is given and, secondly, that some of the guidelines for the use of troops and their conduct after intervention are kept secret.

Military Aid to the Civil Power

The rules governing what is known as military aid to the civil power are described in the Queen's Regulations,[62] and the Queen commands that they 'be strictly observed on all occasions'.[63] Military aid can be requested 'to maintain peace and public order'; it is also possible 'in very exceptional circumstances for grave and sudden emergencies to arise which in the opinion of the commander demand his immediate intervention to protect life and property. In such emergencies he is to act on his own responsibility.'[64] In the ordinary case, 'Assistance will normally be requested by the chief officer of police and should be confirmed in writing.'[65] The officer to whom the application is made is at once to inform the Ministry of Defence and his immediately superior authority.[66] If a request is received from any other source, the service commander on the spot is to refer the request to the chief officer of police and report it to his superiors. This also applies where the commander acts on his own responsibility to protect life and property in the event of 'very exceptional circumstances' of 'grave and sudden emergencies'.

These regulations have to be read in conjunction with a number of 'related publications'.[67] They are Defence Council Instructions, Land Operations Volume III, Internal Security Doctrine and Instructions (all of which are restricted items and therefore unavailable to the general public), and the Manual of Military Law, Part II, Section V, which is available. This section is headed, 'Employment of Troops in Aid of Civil Power'. The Manual has no formal legal status; its 'main object . . . is to provide officers in general with a readily available means of acquiring such legal knowledge as they may need for the performance of their duties'.[68] The object of Section V 'is to give an explanation of the law relating to the duty of the soldier in case of riot and other disturbances of the peace'.[69]

In fact, the Manual is full of inconsistency and uncertainty. The latest version of Section V of the Manual is dated 1968, whereas the new Queen's Regulations were made in 1975. The central role of the chief officer of police thus contrasts with the regulations before 1975. Following the recommendations of the Committee on the Disturbances at Featherstone,[70] the 1895 Queen's Regulations provided for requests for assistance to be made by the chief constable of a county, the borough mayor or, in cases of emergency, a magistrate acting alone.[71] Thus, the Manual states that a commander 'in all cases where it is practicable, should place himself under the direction of a magistrate'.[72] The Manual discusses at some length the relationship between the magistrate and the commander. These provisions are now practically superfluous and contain inconsistencies. In particular, while the commander should place himself under the direction of a magistrate, a 'commander on the spot, while attaching great weight to the opinion of the magistrate, must himself decide whether military intervention is necessary to deal with the circumstances in which he has been requisitioned'.[73]

Duty to Respond

The Manual is also inconsistent with regard to the duty of the military to respond to a request for assistance, and their duty to take action on their own. According to paragraph 1, there is

> nothing to compel a military commander to seek permission before answering a request for military support in accordance with the terms of Queen's Regulations . . . and indeed he would be wrong to do so if the delay involved would be likely to bring about a worsening of the situation or prejudice the success of his intervention.

This is immediately qualified by paragraph 3, which tells the soldier that 'The law is clear that a soldier must come to the assistance of the civil authority where it is necessary for him to do so but not otherwise.' Paragraph 4 then states: 'A military commander who receives a requisition for troops from a distance is bound to comply if he is not in full possession of the facts.'

Part of the difficulty is the result of a division of responsibility between the soldier and the commander. The Manual correctly observes that 'The common law, which governs soldiers and other citizens alike' imposes an obligation 'to come to the aid of the civil power when the civil power requires his assistance to enforce law and order'.[74] Paragraph 3 states that 'When called to the aid of the civil power soldiers in no way differ in the eyes of the law from other citizens.' But the same paragraph later adds that

> Though there is no legal difference between soldiers and other citizens in respect of the duty to respond to the call of the civil authority, there is, in cases of disturbance where the civil authority

THE POLYTECHNIC OF WALES
LIBRARY
TREFOREST

has not asked for help, a duty to take action laid upon military commanders by Queen's Regulations which is not laid upon other citizens except magistrates and peace officers (QR 1182). Even though the civil authority should give directions to the contrary the commander of the troops, if it is really necessary, is bound to take such action as the circumstances demand.

Thus, according to the Manual, there are circumstances where a military commander is bound to take action (for example, in grave and sudden emergencies), not only in the absence of a request by the civil authority, but also despite their directions to the contrary. This 'startling'[75] interpretation of the old regulations applies to the new regulations, for the decision to act is 'in the opinion of the commander', although he has to report the matter and the action he has taken to the service authorities and the chief officer of police, as soon as possible.[76] There is thus a gap between the law, which applies to citizens and soldiers alike, and the prerogative powers, which, although not law, impose duties which may outweigh the common law and the civil authority.

The Law in Practice

The implications of these powers are immense. The regulations do not define 'grave and sudden emergencies', and the Manual does not explain what is 'really necessary'. Not only is there no legal control of these powers, but also the commander may well exercise these duties according to rules contained in documents that are not available to the public.

It could be argued that such criticisms are academic, for these general powers are not a threat in practice to legitimate industrial action. They are not limited to theory, however, nor to situations other than industrial action, even though they have not been used in such a way in recent years. The potential for such use remains, and there is a precedent. In 1911, troops were used to protect blackleg workers on the railways. The military authorities were granted 'full discretionary powers to move troops along the lines of railways to such points as may enable them to safeguard as far as possible the ordinary working of all necessary traffic'.[77] Local authorities were thus not involved in the requisitioning of troops, and in answer to charges of taking 'illegal or extra constitutional action', Winston Churchill replied 'The military authorities always enjoy power to move troops in their own country . . . whenever it is found to be convenient or necessary.'[78] He described the regulation that restricts use of troops in disorderly cases until requisitioned by local authorities as only 'for the convenience of the War Office and generally of the Government, and has in these circum-

stances necessarily been abrogated in order to enable the military
authorities to discharge the duties with which at this juncture they were
officially charged.'[79]

The constraints presumed to exist in the common law and outlined
in the Manual can also fall short of actuality where there is a request
for military aid. According to Lord Diplock,

> There is little authority in English law concerning the rights and
> duties of a member of the armed forces of the Crown when acting in
> aid of the civil power . . . Where used for such temporary purposes,
> it may not be inaccurate to describe the legal rights and duties of a
> soldier as being no more than those of an ordinary citizen in uniform.
> But such a description is in my view misleading in the circumstances
> in which the army is currently employed in aid of the civil power in
> Northern Ireland.[80]

He stated that, in that situation, a soldier 'is under a duty, enforceable
under military law, to search for criminals if so ordered by his superior
officer and to risk his own life should this be necessary in preventing
terrorist acts'.[81] How this could relate to a sustained industrial protest,
or action such as the Ulster Workers Council strike, is unclear, for the
rules of common law are in their nature *post hoc* rationalisations of
events.

Neither the Queen's Regulations nor the Manual of Military Law
refer to this 'duty', however, and the legal status of the soldier in
Northern Ireland was cloudy until a commission considering legal procedures to deal with terrorist activities reported.[82] This led to the
Northern Ireland (Emergency Provisions) Act 1973, under which
members of HM forces on duty have a number of wide powers relating
to arrest,[83] detention, search and seizure, stopping and questioning,
taking possession of land, detaining, destroying or moving any
property, interfering with any public right, or dispersing assemblies of
more than three people.

Civil/Military Co-ordination

Co-ordination between the military and the police is a basic requisite
in practice for military aid to the civil power. The central role given
to the chief officer of police in the new Queen's Regulations confirms
this. According to the Manual (paragraph 4),

> The civil authority should only requisition troops when satisfied
> that it is or will be impossible to deal with the situation that has
> developed, or is immediately apprehended, by means of all the
> resources of the civil power, that is to say, the local police, supple-

mented by any additional police that can be procured from elsewhere
or by any police reserves or special constabulary that may be
available.

Thus, when the chief officer of police is satisfied that he cannot cope,
he will requisition troops. The procedure in practice has been described
by Sir Robert Mark, as follows:

> permission of the Home Secretary is sought by the chief officer of
> police to invoke military aid and the Minister of Defence, in consul-
> tation with the Home Secretary, who will have considered the views
> of the chief officer of police, will decide whether to authorise the
> ultimate sanction of force by such troops as he may make available.
> Such assistance was formerly sought by police from the magistracy
> rather than the Home Office, but whatever the legal position,
> present practice reflects the emergence of a professional, well-
> organised police service which has inevitably assumed the primary
> responsibility for law and order.[84]

This has now become the 'stock phrase' and 'cumbersome formula'[85]
used by Scotland Yard to describe the procedure. In practice, the Home
Office requests assistance and the Home Secretary consults with the
Minister of Defence. Thus, although the maintenance of order on the
spot has been entrusted almost exclusively to the police,[86] when they
fail to cope with disorder, consultations occur at a national level. Sir
Robert further argued that, after military aid has been approved, 'It is
clearly desirable that both police and the army should then conform to
exactly the same terms of engagement. There is no question of one
service coming under the other.' He concluded that 'In such circumstances, police, army, Home Office and Ministry of Defence must act
in complete accord.'[87]

The 'practice' as outlined by Sir Robert has no basis in the Queen's
Regulations or the Manual of Military Law, the documents available for
scrutiny. It is a far cry from the days of magisterial control. And as
Sir Robert added, triumvirates of the civil, military and police powers
may be set up at several levels to ensure adequate consultation.[88] At
this point, the military have entered most directly into the civil sphere
of our society.[89]

Following the miners' emergency dispute in 1972, Edward Heath
established a new committee, the terms of reference of which have come
to include virtually every possble threat to public safety, from strikes
to terrorism. This has enhanced co-operation between the police and the
military, who have held joint exercises.[90]

In addition, a Civil Contingencies Unit of the Cabinet Office has been established. This unit, the existence of which is not publicly acknowledged, appoints *ad hoc* interdepartmental teams of about four civil servants to handle individual emergencies.[91] It considers requests for troops to be used. It remains a low-key organisation, and its recent involvement included alleviating the consequences of the firemen's strike, and a consideration of the dispute at Windscale. Before that, a team was appointed to handle the consequences of unrest at British Oxygen. It is an executive rather than policy-making body; its status is raised when, in industrial disputes, the Prime Minister takes the Chair. The unit (and the Cabinet Committee) then become an 'action group'[92] with senior Cabinet Ministers in attendance.

Conclusion[93]

According to the Manual of Military Law,

> The merits or demerits of such disputes or unrest are of no concern whatsoever to soldiers, who are solely concerned with the duty and obligation common to all citizens of assisting the civil authority in the maintenance of law and order, and in these situations their principal duty will be the protection of persons and property.[94]

However, the merits of disputes are of primary concern to the government, who can decide when to use troops, and to those involved in the dispute whose strength in collective bargaining is reduced by military intervention.

The use of troops tends to centre on those disputes in the public sector where the real employer is the government itself, a government which is frequently unprepared to meet wage claims. One consequence of the use of troops by government may therefore be to enforce its policy on incomes.

The law that regulates the use of troops in industrial disputes is placed in a context of contingency planning for emergencies; the rhetoric clearly supports this. In fact, the nature of this law, through its somewhat tangled web, allows almost total discretion to the government. It manages this through the rhetoric which emphasises the law's objectivity and its service to the public interest at large. If the use of troops in industrial disputes becomes even more frequent (and their role in the civil sphere of society appears to be increasing), there may be more pressure for a clarification of the controls. In the meantime, the law serves to hide the reality that the law enables any government to use troops in any dispute without effective legal or parliamentary controls.

Notes

1. K.G.J.C. Knowles, *Strikes – A Study in Industrial Conflict* (Blackwells, 1952); other instances of military intervention are described in S. and B. Webb, *The History of Trade Unionism* (Longmans, 1920). Troops were used about twelve times between 1907 and March 1914: H.C. Deb., vol. 60, col. 356.

2. Parliamentary Debates (House of Commons), vol. 116, col. 1511 (cited as H.C. Deb.).

3. Sir Robert Mark, *Policing a Perplexed Society* (George Allen and Unwin, 1977), p. 28.

4. Ibid.

5. E.C.S. Wade and G.G. Phillips, *Constitutional and Administrative Law*, 9th edn (Longmans, 1977), Ch. 23, p. 379.

6. Ibid., Ch. 29, p. 506.

7. H.C. Deb., vol. 114, col. 670; there had already been five 'calls-up' by proclamation since the Naval Reserve Act 1900.

8. Ibid., col. 1074.

9. Sir Laming Worthington-Evans, Secretary of State for War, ibid.

10. Ibid., col. 219.

11. In the 1926 miners' dispute (only), the Army Council was empowered under emergency regulations as a 'competent authority', to requisition land and chattels where they considered possession 'necessary or expedient'.

12. H.C. Deb., vol. 195, col. 124.

13. Sir Laming Worthington-Evans, H.C. Deb., vol. 216, col. 92.

14. See C. Farman, *The General Strike* (London, 1972), pp. 190-2.

15. Docks (1972), firemen (1973, 1977-8), dustmen (1970, 1975), civil air traffic control assistants (1977) and public employees (ambulance drivers) (1979).

16. Docks (1970), nuclear power workers (1977), petrol tanker drivers (1978) and road hauliers (1979).

17. H.C. Deb., vol. 452, col. 1362.

18. H.C. Deb., vol. 466, col. 2163.

19. Cmnd 7851 (1949), Appendix XV.

20. Ibid., Appendix XIII.

21. J. Harvey and K. Hood, *The British State* (London, 1958), pp. 111-12; service personnel were actually used on eleven occasions during Attlee's administration: H.C. Deb., vol. 478, col. 2043.

22. H.C. Deb., vol. 729, col. 42.

23. Peter Hennessy, *The Times*, 10 Feb. 1978, p. 1.

24. Reported in *The Times*, 9 Nov. 1977

25. *Financial Times*, 14 Oct. 1977.

26. See R. Lewis, 'Nuclear Power and Employment Rights', *The Industrial Law Journal* (March 1978).

27. The Conditions of Employment and National Arbitration Order 1940, Statutory Rules and Order No. 1305.

28. Conspiracy and Protection of Property Act 1875.

29. For general law on the armed forces, see *Halsbury's Statutes of England*, 3rd. edn, vol. 29 (Royal Forces) and vol. 38 (War and Emergency).

30. Defence (Armed Forces) Regulations, 1939, Reg. 6: SR and O 1939 No. 1304, in the form set out in Part C of Schedule 2 of the Emergency Laws (Repeal) Act 1959.

31. Emergency Powers Act 1964, s. 2.

32. Henry Brooke, Home Secretary, H.C. Deb., vol. 689, col. 1414.

33. F. Soskice, ibid., col. 1417; other MPs such as S. Silverman and Lord Wedderburn have criticised this, however: in B. Aaron and K.W. Wedderburn (eds), *Industrial Conflict* (Longmans, 1972), p. 360; the regulation was to have expired in December 1964: Emergency Laws (Repeal) Act 1959, s. 10(2).

34. H.C. Deb., vol. 689, col. 1440.

35. Defence (Transfer of Functions) Act 1964, ss. 1(3), (7), 3(2).

36. Queen's Regulations for the Army ,1975, Annex A (J) to Ch. 1, p. 1 A-1 (QR).

37. Emergency Powers Act 1920, s.1 (1), as amended by the Emergency Powers Act 1964, s. 1.

38. Ibid., s 2 (1).

39. H.C. Deb., vol. 116, col. 1510.

40. H.C. Deb., vol. 198, col. 2540.

41. Col. Wedgwood, ibid., col. 315.

42. J.J. Jones, H.C. Deb., vol. 195, col. 468.

43. Note, however, that the 1921 and 1926 regulations provided that the powers created thereunder 'Shall be in addition to and not in derogation of any prerogative right or other power vested in Her Majesty'.

44. Harold Wilson, *The Times*, 8 June 1966, p. 1.

45. H.C. Deb., vol. 729, col. 37.

46. Ibid., col. 752.

47. Ibid.

48. Bonar Law (Leader of the House), H.C. Deb., vol. 133, col. 1401.

49. Edward Shortt (Home Secretary), ibid., col. 1606.

50. Lord Champion, H.C. Deb., vol. 346, col. 762.

51. Robert Carr, H.C. Deb., vol. 842, col. 1592.

52. Manual of Military Law (1968), Part II, Section V, para. 8.

53. S.A. De Smith, *Constitutional and Administrative Law*, 3rd edn (Penguin, 1977), p. 507.

54. QR J1. 001, J1. 003.

55. *China Navigation Co. Ltd.* v. *A−G* [1932] KB 197; *Chandler* v. *DPP* [1964] AC 763; *Gouriet* v. *Union of Post Officer Workers* [1977] 3 WLR 300.

56. *Chandler* v. *DPP*, p. 791.

57. *Attorney-General* v. *De Keyser's Royal Hotel Ltd* [1920] AC 508, 567.

58. De Smith, *Constitutional and Administrative Law*, p. 295.

59. *Burmah Oil Co. Ltd* v. *Lord Advocate* [1965] 75, 101, *per* Lord Reid.

60. De Smith, *Constitutional and Administrative Law* , p. 501 n11.

61. Ibid., p. 501.

62. Ch. 11, *Queen's Regulations*.

63. Frank Cooper, Prologue to the Queen's Regulations, *op. cit.*

64. J11. 002.

65. J11.002.a.

66. Ibid.

67. QR 1975, J11. 001. Military Aid to the Civil Community in 'Routine Situations' is outlined in a restricted document, see QR 1975, 11.010.

68. Part 1, Section 1.

69. Part 11, Section V, para. 1.

70. Report, Cmnd 7234 (1893-4).

71. QR 1895, reg. 51.

72. Part 11, Section V, para. 5.

73. Para. 4.

74. Para. 2. The authority for this is *Charge to the Bristol Grand Jury* (1832) 5 C and p. 261.

75. R. Evelegh, *Peace-Keeping in a Democratic Society* (Hurst, 1978), p. 8;

presumably there was a duty for military commanders to intervene at Saltley Coke Depot in the 1972 miners' strike when 6,000 demonstrators closed the depot gates despite the police, see p. 91.

76. QR 1975, J11. 002.

77. Winston Churchill, H.C. Deb., vol. 29, col. 2285.

78. Ibid., col. 2286.

79. Ibid.

80. *Attorney-General for Northern Ireland's Reference (No. 1) of 1975* [1976] 3 WLR 235 at 145.

81. At 246.

82. Cmnd 5185 (1972).

83. Any rule of law requiring a person to state the grounds of arrest is complied with if he states that he is effecting the arrest as a member of HM forces: s. 12 (2).

84. Mark, *Policing a Perplexed Society*, p. 30.

85. David Pallister, *Guardian*, 20 March, 1978, p. 2.

86. See D.G.T. Williams, *Keeping the Peace* (Hutchinson, 1967), p. 41.

87. Mark, *Policing a Perplexed Society*, p. 30; for a different view, see H.C. Deb., 16 Jan. 1974, col. 1052.

88. *Stone's Justice Manual* (1973) still refers to the calling of the military by the magistracy: p. 2972.

89. See T. Bunyan, *The History and the Practice of Political Police in Britain* (Freedman, 1976, and Quartet, 1977), pp. 278-9.

90. See Report of the Inquiry by the Right Hon. Lord Justice Scarman OBE on the Red Lion Square Demonstration, 15 June 1974, Cmnd 5919 (Feb. 1975); and *Time Out*, 6-12 Oct. 1978.

91. *The Times*, 10 Feb. 1978, p. 1.

92. Fred Emery, Political Editor, *The Times*, 8 Nov. 1977, p. 1.

93. Some other laws have minor relevance, for example, Army Act 1955, ss. 165-174 (similar provisions in Air Force Act 1955): requisitioning of vehicles, food, etc. when the Secretary of State directs it in 'the public interest', Army Reserve Act 1950, Reserve Forces Act 1966: the use of reserve forces.

94. Para. 7.

8 STEREOTYPING: FAMILISM IN THE LAW

Patricia Allatt

The aim of this paper is to describe and analyse how selective processes occurring in the construction of legal rules, as well as the rules themselves, serve to regulate stereotypes available in the general culture. At a more general level the problems addressed are posed in discussions of ideology as the disjunction between reality and beliefs about that reality and the control of consciousness by the state. Using the concept of stereotypes as formulated by Perkins (1978) I examine, in one discrete area, the association between these legal processes and familial stereotypes which contribute to family ideology.

In theoretical formulations of ideology, the term manipulation may refer to the production of ideas by dominant groups transmitted via the cultural institutions of education, the mass media and so forth.[1] This is juxtaposed to a view which stresses ideology as being lived (Mepham, 1972, p. 19), acted out in material practices (Althusser, 1972, p. 268), incorporated within daily behaviour (Williams, 1973, p. 10). While recognising the importance of the transmission of ideas in the maintenance of an ideology (Allatt, 1977) my evidence suggests that reality itself is manipulated by powerful agencies.

Several empirical studies have demonstrated how an ideology may be mediated by such agencies. They point to a consistent and persistent denial of reality, for example, of the increasing presence of married women in the workforce[2] and their economic family role by welfare legislation (Land, 1976, pp. 116-20) or in the imposition of specific definitions of divorce in French family law (Dezalay, 1976, p. 91) or definitions of maternal instinct (Macintyre, 1976) by the medical and social work professions.

Although Macintyre's study does reveal a discrepancy between professional definitions of behaviour and definitions by clients, often remaining open or implicit in such studies is how impositions which apparently deny the facts of everyday life come to be accepted by many who are disadvantaged as well as by those who benefit. For example, the view that a woman's place is in the home is still held by many individuals irrespective of age, education or gender (Bayer, 1975, p. 392; Marplan, 1977; Goode, 1963, p. 63), and Shaw, while demonstrating how the education system structures girls' failure, also raises the pertinent question,

Do girls really believe that marriage and a family are going to

provide a life-long activity . . . with 42 per cent of all married
women working, and more in the working class, is it likely that girls
are totally unaware of this, especially if they take their own mothers
as models?

or is it that long-term planning is discouraged by marriage and the
accompanying expectations (Shaw, 1976, p. 139)? Dezalay, in a study
of the ideological processes within French divorce procedure, observes,
'the law finds its most important collaborators in the spouses themselves. It is they who institute proceedings and they present, or accept,
interpretations of fault which fit into the stereotype' (1976, p. 100).

The proposition in this paper is that there is a basis for such interpretations which is either part of the individual's direct experience or lies
in available models. Of the above, the clearest example is the reverse of
Shaw's statistic — 58 per cent of married women are not in the workforce. (The case of self-definition is more subtle and forms a major part
of this analysis.)

However, this experience or awareness, it is argued, is only a part of
the whole range of experiences or models available to individuals. What
I suggest, which is indeed supported by these studies is that this total
range is subject to processes which make certain aspects more salient
than others. By the use of a variety of sanctions elements of social life
are selected and accorded structural supports, thereby making them
nodal points of the total experience. Given that social being determines consciousness, the actual living of these discrete though numerous
chunks of reality provides the preselected elements for a selective (but
not necessarily invariant) intepretation of the total reality by both self
and others. This closely parallels Williams's concept of hegemony as
involving the selection of meanings and practices from all that are
available. He further suggests that some of these 'selected meanings and
practices are reinterpreted, diluted, or put into forms which support or
at least do not contradict other elements within the effective dominant
culture' (1973, p. 11). The evidence I cite here suggests that in significant instances such redefinitions also have a behavioural base.

Stereotypes

The selective interpretation of reality is a characteristic attributed to
stereotypes (Perkins, 1978; Jordan, n.d. p.2); for, while they are
generalising concepts, such generalisations are based upon specific and
discrete elements of behaviour. Furthermore, although stereotypes are
simple, the complexity of daily behaviour is not ignored but encompassed by alternative stereotypes. For example, housewife, career

woman, sex siren (or even woman)[3] are, as stereotypes, mutually exclusive. Thus, while based in real behaviour, stereotypes distort by omission, that is, they select only part from the total complexity of an individual's daily experience. Reality is splintered. Consequently, it seemed that this concept might prove useful in exploring the relationship between the behavioural supports I identified in my material and a consciousness which denied or accommodated conflicting aspects of reality.

Additionally, however, the concept of stereotype provides a means of exploring Gramsci's proposition that the state controls thought. That stereotypical images are with some variation widely shared would appear to make them discrete and, importantly, identifiable elements of Gramsci's notion of common sense, which he defines as 'the incoherent set of generally held assumptions and beliefs common to any given society' (1971, p. 323) and which, he argues, 'is under the domination of the State although not in the sphere of general law but wider than purely State and Governmental activity' (1971, p. 195).

Legal material, however, provides numerous instances of constraining regulations which correlate with identifiable stereotypes or common senses. For example, the protective legislation of the Factory Acts and the earlier retirement age of women lend support to the stereotype of the weaker sex despite biological evidence to the contrary witnessed in the greater longevity of women. Women do not work at night (unless engaged in occupational domestic work such as nursing or office cleaning) and few women remain in the workforce beyond 60 years of age. Presumed innate gender differences in conceptual thinking find a place in the existing tax system which is based on the legal premiss that a wife's income, for tax purposes. is 'deemed' to belong to her husband (Slaughter, 1979).[4] The head of the household cannot enact his role as citizen and fill in his tax forms unless his wife tells him how much she earns. Numerous tax and social welfare regulations sustain the stereotype of the male breadwinner.

Such phenomena lend weight to Perkins's (1978) observation that stereotypes are not merely self-fulfilling prophesies but are structurally enforced, and direct particular attention to the role they play in the social control of both self and others.

For stereotypes are not passive descriptions but active placing mechanisms, cognitive tools of social control. They are evaluative, apparently simple, and short circuit analytical thought (Perkins, 1978). From our own experience we know that to invoke a stereotype, whether laudatory or pejorative, is literally to put someone in their place (often with the connotation of back in their place) — in their appropriate position in the social structure with all that this implies. For example, the 'good husband' is placed within the economic and family system predominantly as a reliable worker, just as 'housewife' denotes a sphere of competence and innate attributes[5] which deny a place in, for example, political decision making. What is shared, yet remains latent, in these simple terms is a complex knowledge of the social structure.

The power of such latency and the circuitous resistance of stereotyes is well illustrated when the stereotype itself is challenged. Following the publication of the Beveridge Report, 1942, a formal deputation of the representatives of women's organisations, critical of the status and treatment the proposals accorded women, was led by Mrs M.C. Tate, MP, JP. An internal civil service memorandum, circulated prior to their meeting with the minister, contains the following comment in parenthesis, thereby denoting its special status: 'I gather that Mrs. Tate expects to be able to bustle through it in time to rise for lunch at 1.00 p.m. or soon after!' (PRO. 1944, PIN 8/48, Memorandum, T. Daish to W. Sheepshanks, 18 February).

Mrs Tate is succinctly placed or, rather, rendered *out* of place. By the use of one word, the stereotype of housewife (which the proposals would structurally support) is evoked. It serves two purposes: first it marks out as nonsense any *formal* proposition or criticism offered by Mrs Tate or the deputation, since housewives by definition do not possess the necessary mental equipment; simultaneously the pejorative stereotype of the out-group sustains the solidarity of the group of administrators.[6]

None the less, that stereotypes can be and are challenged, and that everyday reality itself poses such a challenge, suggests a process of continuous reinforcement. If, as Molotoch (1975) argues, while not denying its underlying structural basis, power is a process which must be continuously sustained on a daily basis, the structuring of stereotypes would seem to provide a means of maintaining this power by enabling a control over a consciousness which defines both self and others. The law provides an important source of such structural reinforcement.

In this paper I pursue the process of the fragmentation of reality and the associated stereotypes as they are marshalled to support, and encompass threats to, the ideal model of the single-role family structure with its gender-based division of labour of male breadwinner and domestic/maternal female.

The material comprises legal regulations and pre-legal processes: the Beveridge Report (1942) the recommendations of which were largely incorporated within the National Insurance Act 1946; the evidence submitted to the Beveridge Committee both published (Beveridge, 1942, Appendix G) and unpublished (PRO, 1941-2, CAB 87/76-82); and certain of the associated civil service memoranda (PRO,

1944, PIN 3/48; ibid., PIN 8/69).

These documents were chosen for reasons which, first, relate to the status of the material itself and, second, to the theoretical and empirical implications associated with the technicalities of its production and availability.

Although the material is almost forty years old it is of contemporary relevance in that its underlying assumptions extensively inform today's social welfare legislation (Walley, 1972, p. 40; Land, 1976, p. 108). In this respect it is of significance that the stereotypes with which I am able to illustrate my argument are part of the currency of contemporary thought.

Additionally, the Beveridge Report is of key cultural importance. Beveridge's scheme was intimately related to its societal context, not only instrumentally in its attempt qualitatively and quantitatively to structure a particular kind of workforce, but also because it 'articulated ideas which already commanded a good deal of support' (Harris, 1977, p. 415). This is demonstrated in the evidence submitted to the committee by both men's and women's organisations (Beveridge, 1942, Appendix G; PRO, 1941-2, CAB 87/76-82) and as witnessed by the massive sales of the Report itself (Marwick, 1976, p. 130).

Furthermore, it is of note that this document entered into public consciousness as predominantly radical and egalitarian. While it was viewed by Churchill as a distraction from the war effort, and its early publicity by Brendon Bracken, the Minister of Information, was an embarrassment to the government as a whole, in some official quarters the Report was seen as a means of engendering the commitment of a dangerously despondent and apathetic populace, both civilian (Calder, 1969, pp. 530-1) and military (Summerfield, 1976), to the nation state. It came to symbolise the image of the post-war society for which 'we were fighting' (*Picture Post*, 1943; Directorate of Army Education, 1944, p. 65) in the conception of which egalitarianism was a major theme, largely in terms of class, but, for many women's organisations and individual women, in terms of gender (Beveridge, 1942, Appendix G; Allatt, 1980; *Picture Post*, 10 May 1941, p. 31, 14 Nov. 1942, p. 3, 28 Nov. 1942, p. 3, etc.).

Although this particular conceptualisation of the Report did not pass unchallenged at the time (Abbott and Bompas, 1943; Calder, 1969, p. 530) and although increasingly subject to contemporary criticism (Land, 1976; Wilson, 1977, pp. 148-54; Townsend, 1977), it was possible for Gosden, in a study of education in the Second World War, to write as recently as 1976 that the plan 'was designed to eliminate poverty by guaranteeing a minimum level of subsistence for all in a scheme of compulsory insurance with flat rate contribution and flat rate benefit' p. 207). Yet, as illustrated in this paper, such principles are crucially mediated by gender, marital and economic status in a manner which has implications for everyday interpretations of normality.

The second set of reasons are practical and theoretical. Wartime conditions precluded the publication of the entire evidence and only those memoranda considered to be of general interest, or major issues of social policy, were selected for publication (Beveridge, 1942, Appendix G, *Note by the Chairman*, n.p.). This act of selection nicely fits the process of legitimation described by Habermas as 'directing attention to topical areas — that is of pushing *other* themes, problems, and arguments below the threshold of attention and thereby of withholding them from opinion formation' (1976, p. 70, original italics). Used as a research strategy this division allows an examination of differences in treatment accorded to the various facets of family life and the associated stereotypes in two empirically and theoretically distinct areas.

Such a configuration of texts, it should also be noted, are the most contemporaneous available. The thirty years' accessibility ruling applicable to state papers meant that both the unpublished evidence and the associated documents upon which I draw were unavailable to the general public until 1972 and later.

Finally, before turning to the analysis it is important to note that the enactment of the majority of the proposals in the National Insurance Act 1946 improved the quality of life for many people, and it is in this context of liberal democratic progress, within which Beveridge's views were firmly placed (Harris, 1977, p. 106), that my analysis must be set.

The Analysis

A fundamental fragmentation is immediately apparent. Of the facets of family behaviour which pose threats to the ideal model of the family and are presented in this material, only some are selected as appropriate for economic intervention via social insurace. Broadly, those threats to the ideal with a source external to the family itself — poverty inherent in a wage structure unrelated to family needs, the demand for and existence of women in the workforce, and innate sexuality — are encompassed by the regulations which comprise a direct structuring of behaviour. Those threats which are inherent in the ideal model itself, specifically the hierarchical power structure of the family, are not included but subject to alternative processes of redefinition which appear to give rise to a distinct type of stereotype, and the allocation to other competencies which serve to enforce or support this definition. Most importantly, the juxtaposition of the effects of these processes and available stereotypes serves to bring into sharp focus the extent and penetration of traditional familism into the social structure.

Legal Regulation, Stereotypes and the Ideal Family

The controls exercised over behaviour by legal rules of social insurance comprise many individual items. Tables 8.1 and 8.2 list such items extracted from the proposed regulations of the Beveridge Report and the associated stereotypes. Frequently one item suggests several stereotypes and conversely one stereotype may attach itself to several items.

With regard to the behaviour they endorse, or impose, the regulations fall broadly within two groups. The first consists of regulations which are directly experienced in the behaviour of the individual, for example, level of benefit, access to benefit, differences in the level of contribution. The behavioural constraints in the second group are less obviously felt because concealed within the details of actuarial accounting (although critics of the Report drew attention to their implications).[7] Nevertheless, this is indicative of cultural assumptions which both inform and are structured into the costing.

Turning to a categorisation of the stereotypes themselves, the following broad groups emerge: solidarity and divisiveness, for example catty women, the lads, one of the boys; innate gender characteristics, for example, unreliable women, gold digger, flighty women, sowing his wild oats, approved family roles, for example housewife, good mother, the breadwinner, the worker; threats to the ideal roles, for example working mother, career woman, gossiping women, working for pin money, unmarried mother, the spinster. The categories are not mutually exclusive.

Of the associations I have suggested between regulation and stereo-type, while many are obvious parallels others are more intricately related. Furthermore, one would expect to encounter some of them less within the provisions of social insurance than between the covers of a Barbara Cartland novel or a woman's magazine; for example, the gold digger implied in the regulation stipulating duration of marriage (Beveridge, 1942, p. 343) and personal qualities governing entitlement to a wife's pension, made explicit, incidentally, in Beveridge's comment: 'the social security scheme should not follow the example of the various veteran schemes of the United States, in encouraging marriages of young women with octogenarians or invalids in hope of prolonged widowhood and other benefits' (PRO, 1942, CAB 87/79 Memorandum by the Chairman, 'The Problem of an Income Limit', 10 March). This extensive range is, I suggest, an indicator of linkages between a wide variety of agencies which articulate these stereotypes;

Table 8.1: Prominent Stereotypes (Beveridge Report)

Regulation	Stereotype
Different retirement ages (male and female)	Women the weaker sex
Joint benefit	Man and wife
Subsumed within which is a lower allowance for the wife (husband 24/- wife 16/-)	Head of household Breadwinner The little woman
None for working wife	Got to look after the worker
Male and female benefits irreversible	Woman's sphere, man's world Equal but different
Reduced rate of benefit for married woman	Pin money, jam on the bread Selfish, self-centred
Married women gainfully employed may choose not to contribute	Work for the companionship Gossiping women Working wife Irresponsible worker, unreliable Working mother (latch-key kids) Career woman (eat out of tins) Who wears the trousers Types of women, you never know with a woman
Single women	Equality
Same benefit as single man	Independent woman, solitary woman
Housewife's Policy	The good wife, the good mother Wife and mother, just a housewife The housewife
Eligibility via husband's contribution record	(Dependent on him, grabbing a man (clinging woman, hang on to a man (good worker = good husband/father
Age of marriage	Gold digger, temptress
Pension entitlement of woman related to age and physique of husband	Cunning minx Heartless woman, callous woman A male weakness No fool like an old fool
No compulsory cover for the domestic spinster, national assistance in old age	Pathetic spinster
Lower contribution rate for women than men	Innate differences Women do not pay their way Men's family responsibilities Wife and family round his neck Breadwinner, the worker in the family Wife and family

Table 8.2: Less Prominent Stereotypes (Beveridge Report)

Contribution of all males supports all men and all housewives	(Male solidarity) One of the boys, a real man A man to lean on Need a man
Women not collectively responsible for anything	Women cannot get on together Catty women
Allocation of costs of familial elements in the contributions of men and women	Man's world Woman's world, clinging female Innate differences Male protector Male provider (even after death) Motherly woman Wife and family round his neck
Allocation of cost of maternity between men and women	(Double standard) Got to sow his wild oats Fallen woman Envious jealous women Unmarried mother Unmarried wife The Eve in every woman (temptress) Women cannot get on together
More shifts in insurance status for women than for men	Men safer risks Women unreliable Flighty women Women cannot stick together Catty women
Women do not contribute to cost of own widowhood, guardianship or any male benefits	Financial world of men Helpless women

possibly the tacit interrelationships between the state apparatuses of ideological control, to which Althusser refers (1972, p. 254).

However, to explore the process of fragmentation it is necessary briefly to outline the provisions of the Beveridge Report and aspects of the actuarial accounting. The aim of the scheme was to attack poverty by guaranteeing a minimum level of un-means-tested subsistence to all during interruption or cessation of earnings due to unemployment, disability or old age and to cover the exigencies of marriage, maternity, widowhood, loss of parents (guardianship) and death (funeral costs). To this end the entire population was to be incorporated within a compulsory scheme of social insurance with flat-rate benefit and flat-rate contribution.

The plan was based upon predefinitions of need which were seen as varying with employment and marital status. The following should be seen as isolating discrete elements of such statuses and roles from the total experience of the individual.

Classification

First, classification imposed a distinct economic identity. According to need the population was allocated between six insurance classes to facilitate the 'giving to each need the treatment most appropriate to that need' (Beveridge, 1942, p. 97). Of the four reserved for the population of working age, Classes I and II are reserved for those gainfully occupied and dependent upon income for maintenance. The other two are for those not so dependent. Thus Class III is for housewives, irrespective of any gainful employment they might have, who are defined as married women living with their husbands. Class IV is reserved for others of working age but not employed. In consequence of classification, the principles of flat rate of benefit and flat rate of contribution do not mean that all pay the same contribution or receive the same amount of benefit. Such distinctions act as further differentiating mechanisms between married and single, men and women, and amongst women as a group, the ramifications of which provide the material basis for critical definitions of self and others.

Benefits

While single men and women receive the same amount of benefit (24/-) and are largely treated identically,[8] for the married benefits are gender specific. Married men are treated as providers with a family role additional to a work role; for married women an economic identity becomes subsumed within, or converted into, a family identity. Married men are to receive a joint benefit (40/-) comprising an allowance additional to the single (but set at a lower level on the assumption that the rent element is already accounted for) for his wife or registered dependant. Receipt of this is dependent upon the wife not being in gainful employment, i.e. by implication fulfilling her proper role.

While all fall within Class III (housewives), married women are subject to differentiation the implications of which I discuss later. If not gainfully employed the housewife is covered by the housewives' policy, designed to 'meet the marrriage needs of a woman' (Beveridge, 1942, p. 311). By virtue of her husband's contribution record she is entitled to maternity grant, widowhood and guardian allowances, funeral grant and, as noted above, cover during interruption or cessation of her husband's earnings. If gainfully employed she may choose to contribute at the single female rate but will receive benefit at a reduced rate (16/-) on the assumption that she has no economic responsibility for either rent or dependants. She is eligible for pension in her own right at 60 but on her husband reaching 65 this will be subsumed, at the lower rate, within the joint benefit.[9] Emphasising her ideal role, she will receive maternity benefit for 13 weeks at a higher rate than standard unemployment benefit on condition of her ceasing work during this period. Employed married women choosing exemption from contribution will rely upon the benefits of the housewives' policy but will also be entitled to maternity benefit towards which they have not contributed. The cost is borne by unmarried women, contributing married women and employers.

Contribution Rate

At all ages men are to pay contribution at a higher rate than women of corresponding age in order to pay part of the benefits of housewives (Beveridge, 1942, Appendix A, pp. 18, 23, 29) and, as noted, within the compulsory system of contribution employed married women may choose exemption from contribution.

The constituent elements of the male and female contribution differ according to predefined gender needs and reflect societal expectations regarding the allocation of responsibility surrounding marriage and maternity. Roles are specific and irreversible. Comparison of the single male and female contributions in Class I demonstrates this (Beveridge, 1942, Appendix A, p. 34).

The single male pays for his own risks regarding unemployment, disability, funeral grant and pension. An additional element on each item goes towards the allowances for housewives and dependants. In addition he pays for the maternity grant for housewives, and widow and guardian benefit, none of which can revert to the male should he become a widower. Unless or until he marries this addition to his contribution reverts to the general fund for housewives.

A single female similarly contributes towards her cover for unemployment, disability, pension and funeral grant. These sums pay for part of her housewife's policy on marriage[10] (Beveridge, 1942, Appendix A, p. 18). In addition she contributes towards the marriage grant[11] and maternity benefit, and the maternity grant for unmarried mothers (Beveridge, 1942, Appendix A, p. 24).

Structure and Stereotype

This brief outline shows that many of the correlates I have made between regulation and stereotype are fairly direct. Regulations which support the complementary and irreversible roles of husband and wife (Land, 1976, p. 109) and the associated stereotypes need little elaboration: breadwinner, provider, good husband,[12] housewife, wife and mother, woman's sphere, man's sphere, the good home, are evoked in the extension, and, it must be emphasised, improved provision, of the married man's benefit and the housewife's policy.

However, structured within specific regulations lie constraints relating to power, subordination and devaluation within the ideal they purport to support. The derived and secondary nature of the housewife's benefit is clear. In stereotypical terms the husband 'is her contact with the outside world', a point subscribed to in social theory (Parsons, 1956, p. 151) as well as in family manuals (Wallis, 1963, p. 99). The non-working wife, i.e. the good wife, is dependent upon her husband's contribution record for the good husband is the reliable worker now supported by the state as head of household, the erosion of which was causing concern in several circles.[13] This same fact, however, also facilitates a portrayal of her as the clinging woman, notwithstanding that she has, it would seem, real grounds for hanging on to her man.

Furthermore, because of the distribution of the familial elements between men and women in the contribution, all men must carry the cost of housewives. A woman conforming to the ideal, in the approving words of the representative of the National Labour Organisation 'the woman who has borne children and stays at home to mind them' (Beveridge, 1942, Appendix G, p. 45), is a burden to the male (in fact, as all women are potential housewives so all women are potential burdens). He has in a sense, whether married or single, 'a wife and family round his neck', a foretaste of the restrictions upon his freedom that marriage will bring. An inversion or displacement is apparent here, interesting in view of Perkins's formulation of the operation of stereotypes as turning effect into cause, that is, that the male contribution is defined as carrying the cost of housewives themselves, not the cost of the domestic and maternal services housewives provide and which are noted within the body of the Report.

This discrepancy in contribution between men and women means that structured within the ideal itself is a behavioural element simultaneously conducive to apparently laudatory stereotypes (e.g. the good mother who stays at home with her children) and distinctly pejorative ones (e.g. the clinging wife, the burden of wife and family). The two together subdue threats arising from resentment, egalitarianism, or attempts at independence which arise in the social situation. I suggest they evoke inhibiting feelings of guilt, unworthiness, and parasitism by extracting from the total situation the dependency elements (encouraged by the legislation) of child on mother and both on the father. Furthermore, the stereotype of the good mother, like that of the housewife, is also a mechanism for the devaluation of intellect, thereby creating an impotence to venture challenge as witnessed by such self-definitions as 'only a housewife'.

In addition to these alternative stereotypes of dependency inherent in and serving to maintain the ideal, there are also those associated with threats located in the external social structure. The fact of women's presence in the labour force before and after marriage constitutes such a threat and is encompassed by regulations which structure a particular form of consciousness. 'Every woman on marriage will become a new person' (Beveridge, 1942, p. 339). These mechanisms include a reclass-ification, the physical attachment of a housewife's policy to her insur-ance record, loss of insurance rights gained prior to her marriage, lower benefit than other members of the working population and a change regarding her liability for contribution.

Gainfully employed housewives are the only group of workers not liable for contribution. Should a housewife choose to contribute, the poor economic return on her contribution (and duplication of contri-butions by husband and wife) means that only a small proportion have elected to pay in full (Walley, 1972, p. 119; Land, 1976, p. 124).[14]

This element of choice, further weighted against take-up, can be construed as a formal mechanism for the restructuring of women's attitude towards employment, pressures endorsing a lack of commit-ment to an economic role. Lack of compulsion compounds both an assumed, and possibly actual, lower commitment of women to employ-ment and the negative attitudes taken towards them in the occupational structure by both employees and employers (Brown, 1976, pp. 41-6). In addition this option structurally undermines the legitimacy of econ-omic activity by married women.

That this assumed lower commitment is seen as related to a women's family responsibilities produces two sets of stereotypes: e.g. unreliable workers, work for pin money, provide the jam (although the jam may include shoes for the children); and, working wives, working mothers, they eat out of tins, latch-key kids. Thus, for a married woman, paid work produces stereotypes legitimised and structured by insurance regulations, which deny her competency in either sphere, rather than lauding the double burden she has undertaken.

Furthermore, the enacting of the imposed constraints bites deeply into the social structure in a less obvious way than the examples so far have demonstrated, and sustains behavioural patterns which, while superficially remote, are ultimately linked to a traditional familism. The limits of the paper do not allow the tracing of all such ramifications. I have therefore selected one I consider crucial: the structured social divisiveness based in the underlying familism.

Social Divisiveness

As noted, in the contribution rate men and women are differentiated according to presumed future marital roles. That male and female risks associated with marriage are not pooled implies different spheres of male and female responsibilities in marriage and a major social division between the sexes.

There is, however, a second fundamental difference. In social insurance men are treated as a solidary and stable group; for women, the reverse is true. Men share collective responsibility[15] the whole of their economically active lives, for the maintenance of themselves, housewives and other dependants. They are, furthermore collectively exempt from responsibility for illegitimacy and towards cohabitants. Although a woman may be registered as a dependant, such protection only lasts during the man's lifetime, and the potential sanctions on her are worth quoting in full.

> the unmarried woman living as a wife will get no widowhood benefits. If she is gainfully occupied she will pay contributions for all purposes, including medical treatment, pension and funeral grant which she would get without contribution if married; she will not have the married woman's option of exemption. If she is not gainfully occupied she will be in Class IV and will be required to make contributions for medical treatment, pension and funeral grant which she would get without contribution if married. Though it is proposed that medical treatment should be given without contribution conditions, the legal liability of the unmarried woman in Class IV will remain and be enforced, if she is not exempt for poverty under para. 363. For pension she will have to contribute throughout her working life and if she does not do so she will not be qualified for a pension. The contributions of the man with whom she is living, if he is married to someone else, will go to secure pensions and other benefits for his legal wife; if he is not married, his contributions as a single man will go to support the benefits of married women generally. (Beveridge, 1942, p. 115)

Thus, unlike the husband, the male cohabitant is not accorded any legal or moral responsibility toward his partner.

In addition, a subtle distribution of responsibility is revealed by an examination of the costing of the maternity grant — a sum of four pounds to all married women, and to other women if insured in Class I or II (Beveridge, 1942, Appendix A, p. 4). The Government Actuary writes: 'The lump sum grant on a married woman's confinement is met from the man's contributions . . . and the cost of maternity grant to single women [is] met from the woman's contributions' (Beveridge, 1942, Appendix A, p. 24). Thus non-deviant maternity — that is, maternity within marriage — is costed to all contributing men; women do not share any part of this cost. Secondly, despite their obvious share in illegitimacy, men do not contribute in their social insurance towards this form of marital deviance. While the unmarried father is not defined as deviant, unless the unmarried mother continues in employment she is likely to have recourse to intentionally stigmatising means-tested national assistance, retained within the scheme as a residual means of maintenance.

This structurally reinforced division between men and women in the double moral standard could be construed as feeding into the consciousness of both the individual and others the basis for such sterotypes as Casanova, 'sowing his wild oats', 'man is not a monogamous animal', the unmarried mother (there are no unmarried father stereotypes), the fallen woman, women entice men.

However, this structured divisiveness extends further. Although the cost of the maternity grant is to be met from the women's contribution, this does not mean that women collectively bear the cost of maternity outside marriage. Also relieved of the cost are full-time housewives, i.e. those conforming to their domestic role, and housewives who, although gainfully employed, choose exemption, thereby demonstrating a low commitment to work outside the home; that is, the good wife and mother and those who work only for pin money or companionship. Again notice the duality incorporated within these stereotypes which refer to the ideal. The good wife and mother does not 'work' and the latter two are dilettante.

On examination the cost is borne by women who are potential or actual deviant women themselves. They are single women, i.e. the ones who might have children outside marriage and whose single status itself (after the age of 25)[16] defines them as deviant, or housewives who have chosen to pay the full contribution and are thereby affirming a lesser commitment to the domestic role or at least an alternative identity; furthermore, the use of part of women's pre-marital contribution for this purpose carries the implication that they are potential unmarried mothers who on marriage are exonerated and released from any responsibility towards illegitimacy if they adopt a conformist role. Thus deviant women pay for deviant women.

While such regulations provide supports which deny the legitimacy of a commitment by *any* woman to work outside the home — that career women, working wives and working mothers must pay the cost of their deviance from their alternative and true role, that single women are easy game, that the spinster is to be sanctioned for her unmarried state (the Government Actuary refers to 'where marriage is deferred' (Beveridge, 1942, Appendix A, p. 25)) and that maternity is the goal of every woman – the overriding feature here is that, in contrast to men, women are not collectively responsible for any group or item in social insurance; nor do they collectively enjoy any exemptions.

This fragmentation of women as a group, as well as the fragmentation of the woman as an individual, is also seen in their shifting statuses reflected in their passage between the classes within the social insurance system of classification. Men appear under the following five guises: as single men, husbands, fathers, ex-husbands and cohabitants. However, irrespective of their family or marital status they remain, if willing to work, in insurance Classes I or II with full insurance cover. Women appear in ten varieties: single working women (Class I or II); housewives not in gainful occupation, housewives in gainful occupation but not paying the full insurance contribution and housewives gainfully occupied and not choosing such exemption (all three fall into Class III – the first two are covered by husbands' contributions, the third covers herself); cohabitants who are not in employment, unmarried mothers, domestic spinsters, widows with no dependants, widowed mothers (child-care responsibility is not attributed to males in the system of benefits) and divorced, separarated or deserted wives (all fall into social insurance Class IV with a strong likelihood of dependency on national assistance and possibly moving into Classes I or II on resumption of employment and to Class III on marriage or remarriage).

The materiality of these divisions, compounded by the regulations, serves to contrast the stability, reliability and centrality of men and male stereotypes with the instability, flightiness, enigmatic traits and dependent qualities of women and stereotypes associated with women. The phrase 'you never know where you are with a woman' could be more accurately stated as 'a woman never knows where she is'. More importantly, however, what is set up here are antagonistic interest groups. Men are set against women, the spinster against the married and the widowed, the working housewife against the non-working,[17] the contributing against the non-contributing. 'Parity with the widow', was a pre-Beveridge cry of the spinsters' organisations.

By such provision women are reaffirmed in their antipathetic envious and competing groups (Joffe, 1971, p. 471; Battle-Sister, 1971, pp. 415, 417) which I have subsumed, somewhat inadequately, under the stereotype of catty women. That social insurance regulations structure a reality which validates such an apparently far-removed stereotype as 'women can never get along together' is startling, and demonstrates the legal penetration into the social structure, and by extrapolation consciousness, serving to shore up a traditional familism.

Displacement and Redefinition

Finally, the concept of fragmentation directs attention to areas of family life which posed threats to the ideal model of the family and yet were not (and are not) encompassed by the regulations of social insurance.

A major omission in these proposals is any consideration of the power hierarchy within the family and, specifically its association with the unequal distribution of the family income leading, in some cases, and irrespective of the adequacy of earnings, to lower levels of subsistence for wives and children than for the breadwinner. Furthermore, such unequal access to and control over the family's resources is now consolidated during periods of non-earning by Beveridge's proposals. Given that the central aim of Beveridge's plan was to combat poverty (Beveridge, 1942, p. 444) and given that the fears concerning the declining birth-rate made the health and welfare of mothers and children particularly salient, the fact that no reference is made to the greater poverty of wives and children compared with their menfolk either in the Report itself or within the memoranda of the organisations published with the Report is all the more surprising.

Although Young (1952, p. 309) pointed out that evidence of secondary poverty revealed in the studies by Soutar (1942) and Madge (1943) appeared too late to influence the Beveridge Report, the release of the unpublished evidence, in 1972, to which Young had no access, shows that the existence of differential poverty within families was in fact brought to the attention of the committee.

The problem of superordinate male economic power within the family was raised by Eleanor Rathbone in the evidence submitted by the Family Endowment Society. In presenting the case for family allowances to be paid to the mother she explicitly refers to 'that larger minority of fathers who give their wives a preposterously small amount out of their wages because they regard their wage as something they have earned by the labour of their brains or hands' (PRO, 1942, CAB 87/77, Q 2994, 2 June) and suggests that this selfishness is structurally supported by a wage system whereby maximum earnings are reached early in life when a man has no family responsibilities, thereby engendering 'habits of expenditure on luxuries which are not easily broken and possibly indulged in later at the expense of wife and children' (PRO, 1942, CAB 87/79, 6 May).

Awareness of the ramifications of this power structure is also implicit in the comment of one member of the interdepartmental committee that a father might cut a wife's money by the amount of the children's allowance should it be paid to her (PRO, 1942, CAB 87/77, Q 2994, 2 June). Similarly, in the discussion of separate insurance for the wife, a TUC representative indicates not only his awareness of the position but also that the issue is circulating in the general culture. 'We do not say that the wife is insurable unless the agitation that is going on now that a man's wages should be divided and the wife given a proportion of them, then she would have to pay insurance' (PRO, 1942, CAB 87/77, Q 2266, 6 May).

Such evidence presents a dilemma, for the economic dominance of the father is inherent to the ideal model of the family and alleviation of a wife's situation by economic means, whether by encouraging her to work outside the home or by paying family allowances directly to her, would undermine this ideal. In addition, however, the notion of an egalitarian happy relationship is also a component of the ideal.

The problem, while dismissed from regulation by insurance, is not ignored, nor is it merely defined away as solely a matter for the individuals concerned. Tucked away in this evidence are indications of the processes by which this uncomfortable fact is accommodated and the different type of controlling stereotype which such accommodation supports.

Within the evidence are what can only be described as stereotypes of certain unaccommodating familial actors: 'the really bad father who will abuse an allowance given specifically for the child' (PRO 1942, CAB 87/77, Q 2994, 2 June), the selfish husband, the drunken mother. While such characteristics could be defined as personal traits, as noted, the witnesses of the Family Endowment Society locate some of these, at least partially, in the economic structure; for example, the selfish husband and father supported in his indulgences by a particular wage structure, the inadequate mother finally discouraged by the poverty in which she lives, and the housewife's financial incompetence developed through lack of experience in the handling of large sums of money (PRO, 1942, CAB 87/77, Q 2954).

However, in the evidence of another key group of witnesses such traits are construed in a different manner. The representatives of those who administer welfare draw attention to the lack of skills and the need for education in household management, child management and husband management (orientated particularly, it will be noted, towards women) (PRO 1942, CAB 87/78 Minutes of Meeting, *Representations of the Joint Standing Committee*, Q 7558, 25 August).

> Social welfare must extend to domestic affairs. You may find it necessary to show people how to make beds and how to clean floors and how to cook because quite a number of people have not the faintest idea that there are any cooking appliances other than a frying pan. That is amazing but true. All those things should be included and such things as child management and how to deal with

your husband when he comes home in a bad temper or tired . . . all
these things are very serious points and all come under the heading
of social welfare (PRO, 1942, CAB 87/78, Q 7559)

Thus, in addition to domestic occupational skills, economically
powerless women are to be taught survival skills *vis-à-vis* their husbands.

Furthermore, in pursuance of the request by Sir George Reid, the
Secretary of the Assistance Board, for 'a clear and workable definition
of welfare work' (Q 7558), the following statement is offered:

I suppose one can be said to be well when one is in happy association with things as they are, and the happiness of a home, anyone's
home, I suggest is built up on little things without too much regard
to the big things, and that is the basis of welfare (PRO, 1942, CAB
87/78, Q 7560)

Thus, amongst those responsible for welfare (and who incidentally
suggest the inadequacy of their current expertise) the problems
become defined as personal problems of coping, of inadequate socialisation.

The associated stereotypes are easily identified, ranging from the
poor cook to the battered wife to include, for example, the battered
child, the slovenly wife, the drunken father. It is interesting that in
cases of battering attention is often paid to the early socialisation of
the individuals, the violent homes they may come from, rather than
treating battering as an extreme case of a societal allocation of power.

These special problems of structure, which could be alleviated to
some extent by a reallocation of economic power within the family,
are subject to a double displacement which serves to depoliticise them.
For the denial of the legitimacy of the *source* of such behaviour as a
subject for debate and control in this legal area renders the *behaviour*
available to specific definitions in others.

Such definitions legitimate the allocation of the now personal
problems to other socialising agencies (family law, social work, marriage
guidance, the women's press) which can now assume the task of preven-
tion or cure, can legitimately meet the 'need', and in so doing reaffirm
or continue the process of selectively defining behaviour.

The stereotype of the working mother differs from that of the
inadequate mother. The first stereotype, while implying maternal
inadequacy, also suggests that this lies in her ignoring her real duty, it
implies intent. The second stereotype implies a psychological incapacity
for adequate performance. While the behaviour contained within the
former must be curbed, that of the latter must be helped.

These different kinds of stereotype, I suggest, are related to the different processes by which the behavioural basis is exposed or isolated. While in the legal control of family income by social insurance, categories are imposed upon a total population and behaviour purposively structured, in the displaced sector of family power the individuals themselves assign their behaviour to particular categories or the behaviour of individuals is brought to the attention of the appropriate agencies. The women's press, for example (where incidentally both kinds of stereotypes appear), places its commercial survival on meeting the needs women identify as theirs: the battered and unhappy seek or are directed towards help. Thus the personal and individual nature of the problem is reaffirmed in this activity of self-selection.

Furthermore, the definitions of appropriate behaviour are not merely articulated by these agencies. Dezalay (1976), for example, comments on the pressures social workers exerted on a client to take up sewing classes rather than buy a dress. But even at the level of wishing to vary the daily menu the definition latent in the magazine is enacted by the individual. For the reader who knits the jumper or bakes the cake the definition is incorporated within her life and possibly some sense of discomfort, guilt or recognition of a nostalgic cosiness and security is experienced by those who resist such calls.

Conclusion

To understand the means by which a particular consciousness is maintained, and to render that knowledge capable of application, awareness of the extent and intricacies of the structural supports is essential. Thus, while in order to challenge gross inequalities and anomalies it is necessary to expose the assumptions upon which they are based (Land, 1976, p. 108), it is equally important to trace the extensive structural ramifications produced, in this case, by the selective and fragmentary processes in one area of law which isolate discrete behavioural patterns conducive to partial or inverted interpretations of reality. For taken individually some of the constituent elements are susceptible to being dismissed as trivia. The relationship between access to benefit, cunning minx and sewing a dress is not immediately apparent; and recently the *Guardian* advocated that a married woman's tax form be addressed to the woman herself rather than to her husband as a matter of courtesy. Yet such details cumulatively construct a resistant ideology.

There is a continuing debate as to the effectiveness of law in changing deeply entrenched attitudes and behavioural patterns; and there is much evidence of how the law can be circumvented, for example, in the reclassification of women's jobs in order to avoid the constraints imposed by the Equal Pay Act 1970. Nevertheless, if my analysis suggests that the boundaries which the law legitimates and the minutiae of legal regulation support particular interpretations of reality, it should follow that the law can also serve to produce alternative bases for the formation of a different consciousness.

Consequently, the important questions, latent within this paper, are those concerning social change. What, for example, is the structural basis of change in stereotypical imagery? Are new accommodations made to incorporate the substance of old stereotypes? Do some stereotypes disappear and new ones emerge? And, related to such questions, what is the range of structural bases for the support of different types of stereotypes?

Due to the inaccessiblity of the material, the above analysis cannot be fully replicated on more recent legislation with an apparent potential for change, such as the Equal Pay Act 1970 and the Sex Discrimination Act 1975, or the recent changes in the Social Security Pensions Act 1975, although inspection might disclose alternative discrete areas for such an analysis. Again, only a detailed analysis would penetrate the ramifications and supports for changes in social imagery contained within the rules themselves. Question of change must, therefore, be left open to further research.

Finally, while the important consideration of the relation of law to the distribution of power within society has been omitted, the evidence has demonstrated the extensive and intimate nature of state control.

Notes

1. Mepham (1972, p. 12) refers to Marcuse's (1965) tendency to identify 'the conditions under which people live and think, and which thereby determine *what* they think, with "the prevailing indoctrination" by the "media", advertisements and so on to which they are exposed'.
2. Although Beveridge's proposals for married women were based on the fact that in 1932 only one in eight of married women were gainfully employed, subsumed within this statistical average were wide regional variations. The 1921 census, for example, showed proportions of 2 per cent in the Administrative County of Durham, 13 per cent in London and 42 per cent in Burnley. Furthermore, these figures could be related to the industrial character of the districts and the subsequent availability of employment opportunities. This information is drawn from a published series of broadcast talks arranged by Beveridge himself (Beveridge, 1932, p. 74).

Another example of the use of the statistical average to 'hide' the existence of women in the workforce, in this case those over pension age (60 years) is in the civil service's dealings with the pressures from the women's organisations for the same retirement age for men and women.

(It is odd that as many as 9.2 per cent of manual women are classed in the over 65 grade and only 2.8 per cent of men; this probably represents charwomen and the like.) If, at any rate, no particular age is indicated, there is clear evidence that women retire earlier than men. (PRO, 1944, PIN 8/48, Note, *Age of Retirement – Women*, T. Hutson to W. Sheepshanks, 26 February)

3. Dezalay (1976, p. 102) reports a comment by the French judiciary on a woman who under duress left her children: 'She is a bad mother . . . she is more woman than mother.'

4. The actual words are embedded in section 37 of the Income and Corporation Tax Act 1970 (Slaughter, 1979).

5. Perkins (1978, p. 18) suggests that stereotypes turn cause into effect. She argues that stereotypes of irrationality, illogicality, inconsistency, flightiness associated with women have their basis in the job demands of the housewife which require her continuously to switch skills and attention. This behaviour, however, is attributed not to the exigencies of the job but to innate, negatively evaluated female characteristics.

6. While the administrative machinery for the implementation of the Beveridge Report was under consideration a small co-ordinating staff was set up, drawn from the bodies then responsible for the various aspects of social insurance. They were headed by William Sheepshanks (who was largely responsible for the White Paper 1944) and responsible to the Minister without Portfolio.

Their internal memoranda relating to the criticisms raised by the women's organisations who sought a meeting with the minister abound with crushing stereotypes. They employ alliteration, puns and derogatory images (as noted). The members of the deputation are referred to as 'the women', 'ardent feminists' to whom 'a concession to women is as much an abomination as discrimination against them' and 'unreasonable', and it is doubted 'if anything short of the impossible is acceptable to them'. Distinctions are drawn between 'enlightened women' and 'women generally' and attention is drawn to the dissension within the deputation regarding the pension age of women. The spinsters sought a lower pension age for spinsters whilst the other organisations wanted the same pension age as men. A point is made regarding 'the absurdity of the underlying demand for equality between the sexes' and the ability of women to engage in formal activity is disparaged. The list of demands they submit is criticised as confused and overlapping and in regard to their conduct in the forthcoming meeting a memorandum reads: 'Here are the points which apparently the women are going to raise – but it is unsafe to assume that they will adhere to any agenda and anyhow they have already been told that you [the minister] can only listen' (PRO, 1944, PIN 8/48, *The Woman Citizen and Social Security*, (National Council of Woman) Deputation to Discuss the Position of Married Women under the Beveridge Proposals).

Representatives of the Spinster Association were similarly dealt with. Miss Florence White, who was after all exercising her democratic rights for which we were all fighting (Directorate of Army Education, 1944, p. 16) is referred to as 'an importunate correspondent', and the following weary minutes encapsulate the tiresome finicky spinster. 'Everything that can be said has been said *ad nauseam* but one could never satisfy or silence Miss White' and 'I am afraid that it will continue to be necessary for the Minister to endure representations . . . from the Spinster Association and their spokesmen . . . I do not think the Minister can do anything but listen with patience to what they have to say' (PRO, 1944, PIN 8/69, Note to H.A. Staveley, 1 November; PRO, 1945, PIN 8/69, Minute, M. Riddeldell to Miss Jones, 13 March; PRO, 1944, PIN 8/69, *Notes for the Minister*, 1 December).

That such memoranda could be circulated (the impact on reading this file almost leads me to describe this as frenzied chatter) reflects 'the shared culture and assumptions' of the 'Whitehall Village' referred to by an ex-senior civil servant (BBC2, 1978, *Newsweek*) which are being checked to see if they are intact, reaffirmed and marshalled against the challenge.

7. While there was some criticism of the proposals for women (see note 2 and Abbott and Bompas, 1943) others were fulsome in praise of the Report. *Picture Post* (Hopkinson, 1970, p. 138), for example, a radical journal, and with a wide audience, urged women to work for the full provisions of the Report, describing the benefits as constituting a housewife's charter.

8. A woman could not register an able-bodied man as her dependant.

9. This was altered in the National Insurance Act 1946.

10. In the popular summaries of the Report, the White Paper 1944 and the National Insurance Act 1946, mention of a woman's pre-marital contribution towards her own pension is entirely omitted – a point which contributes to prevailing notions of complete dependency. (See Directorate of Army Education, 1944, p. 564; Owen, 1948; Ministry of Reconstruction, 1944.)

11. The marriage grant was not incorporated.

12. Dezalay (1976, p. 94) notes that French judiciary procedure equates the good husband with the 'good worker'.

13. It appears, for example, in the instructors' notes in the army courses in citizenship.

Do you think that when the father is unemployed, and possibly dependent upon the earnings of other members of the family his position is undermined? Have the changes weakened the family and . . . if they have what is there for us to do about it? (Directorate of Army Education, 1944, pp. 383, 384)

14. Given my thesis it would be interesting to monitor attitudes to work of both employee and employer following the new regulations of the Social Security Pensions Act 1975 whereby a single woman, or one who married on or after 6 April 1977, will pay the same contributions, and get the same benefits, as a man with the same earnings.

15. Delphy (1976, p. 87) refers to 'the collective exploitation of women by men' and 'the collective exemption of men from the cost of reproduction'.

16. The marriage grant was a fixed sum of £10 paid for solely out of the woman's contributions. After the age of 25, on the assumption she had contributed for ten years, there was no return on this element of a woman's contribution (Beveridge, 1942, Appendix A, p. 25).

17. It has been observed that working women find help most forthcoming from other working women.

References

Abbott, E. and Bompas, K. (1943) *The Woman Citizen and Social Security*. London

Allatt, P. (1977) 'A Theoretical Approach to Family Ideology'. Unpublished paper

—— (1980) 'Status, Role and Values in the Articulation of Knowledge: an Analysis of the Published Evidence Submitted to the Beveridge Committee'. Paper read to BSA Libraries and Information Group. Leeds. In press

Althusser, L. (1972) 'Ideology and Ideological State Apparatuses'. In B.R. Coser (ed.), *Education: Structure and Society*. Harmondsworth: Penguin

Barker, D.L. and Allen, S. (1976) 'Sexual Divisions and Society'. In D.L. B⁻ and S. Allen (eds.), *Sexual Divisions and Society: Process and Cha⁻*

London: Tavistock

Battle-Sister, A. (1971) 'Conjectures on the Female Culture Question'. *Journal of Marriage and the Family*, 33, 3, pp. 734-45

Bayer, Alan E. (1975) 'Sexist Students in American Colleges'. *Journal of Marriage and the Family*, 37, 2, pp. 391-7

BBC2 (1978) 'A Secret Society. An Investigation into the Whitehall Village'. *Newsweek*, 9 November

Beveridge, W. (1942) *Social Insurance and Allied Services* (The Beveridge Report). Cmd 6404. London: HMSO

—— (1942) Memorandum by the Government Actuary. Finance of the Proposals of the Report Relating to Social Insurance and Security Benefits. *Social Insurance and Allied Services*, Appendix A.

—— (1942) *Memoranda from Organisations*, Appendix G. Cmd 6405. London: HMSO

—— *et al.* (1932) *Changes in Family Life*. London: Allen and Unwin

Brown, R. (1976) 'Women as Employees: Some Comments on Research in Industrial Sociology'. In D.L. Barker and S. Allen (eds.), *Dependence and Exploitation in Work and Marriage*. London: Longman

Calder, Angus (1969) *The People's War: Britain 1939-45*. London: Jonathan Cape

Delphy, C. (1976) 'Continuities and Discontinuites in Marriage and Divorce'. In Barker and Allen (eds), *Sexual Divisions and Society*

Dezalay, Y. (1976) 'French Judicial Ideology in Working Class Divorce'. In Barker and Allen (eds), *Sexual Divisions and Society*

Directorate of Army Education (The) (1944) *The British Way and Purpose*. Consolidated edn of BWP Booklets 1-18 with Appendices of Documents of Post-War Reconstruction

Goode, W.J. (1963) *World Revolution and Family Patterns*. New York: The Free Press

Gosden, P.H.J.H. (1976) *Education in the Second World War*. London: Methuen

Gramsci, A. (1971) *Selections from the Prison Notebooks*. London: Lawrence and and Wishart

Habermas, J. (1976) *Legitimation Crisis*. London: Heinemann Education Books

Harris, J. (1977) *William Beveridge: A Biography*. Oxford: Oxford University Press

Hopkinson, T. (ed.) (1970) *Picture Post 1938-50*. London: Allen Lane Penguin Press

Joffe, C. (1971) 'Sex Role Socialisation and the Nursery School: As the Twig is Bent'. *Journal of Marriage and the Family*, 33, 3, pp. 467-75

Jordon, M. (n.d.) 'Character Depiction and the Presentation of Stereotypes in Soap Opera'. Unpublished paper

Land, H. (1970) 'Women: Supporters or Supported'. In Barker and Allen (eds), *Sexual Divisions and Society*

Macintyre, S. (1976) ' "Who Wants Babies?" The Social Construction of Instincts'. In Barker and Allen (eds), *Sexual Divisions and Society*

Madge, C. (1943) *War-time Pattern of Saving and Spending*. Cambridge: National Institute of Economic and Social Research

Marcuse, H. (1965) 'Repressive Tolerance'. In H. Marcuse *et al.* (eds), *A Critique of Pure Tolerance*, London: Beacon Press

Marplan Survey (1977) *You Don't Know Me: A Survey of Youth in Britain*. London: McCann-Erikson. Reported in *New Society*, 13 Oct. 1977, 42, 784, p. 73

Marwick, A. (1976) *The Home Front: The British in the Second World War*.

London: Thames and Hudson

Mepham, J. (1972) 'The Theory of Ideology in Capital'. *Radical Philosophy,* 2

Ministry of Reconstruction (1944) *Social Insurance. Brief Guide to the Government's Plan.* London: HMSO

Molotoch, H. (1975) Unpublished paper

Owen, D. (1948) *Guide to the National Insurance Act 1946.* London: News Chronicle Publications

Parsons, T. (1956) *Family, Socialisation and Interaction Process,* London: Routledge and Kegan Paul

Perkins, T.E. (1978) 'Rethinking Stereotypes'. In M. Barrett, P. Corrigan, A. Kuhn and J. Wolfe (eds), *Ideology and Cultural Production.* London: Croom Helm

Picture Post (1941) vol. 11, no. 7, 10 May

—— (1942) vol. 17, no. 7, 14 Nov.

—— (1942) vol. 17, no. 9, 28. Nov.

—— (1943) *Special Issue: Changing Britain,* vol. 18, no. 1, 2 Jan.

Public Record Office (1941-2) CAB 87/76-82

—— (1944) PIN 8/48

—— (1944-5) PIN 8/69

Shaw, J. (1976) 'Finishing School: Some Implications of Sex-segregated Education'. In Barker and Allen (eds), *Sexual Divisions and Society*

Slaughter, J. (1979) 'Chattel's Goods'. *Observer,* 4 Feb.

Soutar, M.S. Wilkins, E.H. and Sargent, Florence P. (1942) *Nutrition and Size of Family.* London: Allen and Unwin

Summerfield, P. (1976) 'Popular Radicalism in the Second World War: the Case of the Armed Forces'. Unpublished paper read at the History Work in Progress Seminar, University of Sussex

Townsend, P. (1977) 'Review of Harris, *William Beveridge: A Biography'* in *Guardian,* 17 Nov.

Walley, J. (1972) *Social Security: Another British Failure.* London: Charles Knight

Wallis, J.H. (1963) *Thinking About Marriage.* Harmondsworth: Penguin

Williams, R. (1973) 'Base and Superstructure in Marxist Cultural Theory'. *New Left Review,* 82, pp. 3-16

Wilson, E. (1977) *Women and the Welfare State.* London: Tavistock

Young, M. (1952) 'Distribution of Income Within the Family'. *British Journal of Sociology,* 3, pp. 305-21

Acknowledgements

The author gratefully acknowledges the permission of the Keeper to reproduce memoranda and the assistance of Mr Michael Roper of the Public Record Office. The early stages of the research were funded by the SSRC, 1974-6.

9 'ALL POLICE IS CONNING BASTARDS' – POLICING AND THE PROBLEM OF CONSENT

Mike Brogden

Introduction

In their discussion of the relationship between the criminal law and the maintenance of a particular class system in the eighteenth century, Hay and Linebaugh[1] emphasise the immediacy of social justice and retribution. Mutilation and the gibbet, the swift justice of the private prosecutorial system for the country landowner, the exemplary punishments and the drama of the judicial public degradation ceremony ensured a constant awareness amongst the lower classes of the legal sanctions over their daily lives.

With the Industrial Revolution, new branches of the state developed, in the legal context as in other forms of political life. The complexity of that new industrial society entailed an obfuscation of statutes and legal procedure. Urbanisation, the new forms of work discipline and the altered forms of social protest made inappropriate the old duality of paternalism and despotism[2] in determining social order. Policing developed – evolved?[3] – in the UK as elsewhere in Europe, in response to the changing relations of the new mode of production, but took on a unique form from the peculiar British tradition – with the impact of the Benthamite legal entrepreneurs and the diffuse nature of reactions to the New Police by both classes and fractions of those classes.[4]

The law itself became more extant, inaccessible – its dramas less visible. The legislation of 1829, of the 1830s and of 1856 institutionalised a new separation of the law and the ruled. Local police forces ('the first significant body of public employees'[5]) inaugurated at various times over the middle of the nineteenth century replaced those public rituals as the new expression of law. Their penetration into the domestic life of city dwellers[6] and offensive incursions into working-class recreation[7] provided a novel and pervasive front-line defence of class society.

Originally monolithic in stark outline structure – if confused in moral cleansing objectives[8] – these forces developed initially (despite resistance from some urban elites that was more apparent than evidential) as the handmaidens of the city middle classes.[9] Often recruited from particular social backgrounds[10] with a bearing hardly civilian despite their sponsors' military disavowals[11] that enforced their separation from the lower classes, in the Victorian provincial cities they contributed a direct agency of urban discipline and control.

A century and a half after the inception of the Metropolitan Police, it is clear that this early economistic model of direct police-class confrontation — with the former pitted against the diffuse working-class groups within the city — provides little assistance in the analysis of that creature of occupational sociology— the 'police role'.

Gradually, in the latter half of the nineteenth century, fissions developed between the arising power of the new Chief (or Head) Constables and that of the local Watch Committees. Splits between local elites — temperance leagues versus brewers, for example[12] — aided by the increased size of establishments and police organisation[13] provided opportunities for political aggrandisement for aspiring commanders. Control by civic dignitaries remained in form but not in substance.[14]

Similarly, the array of duties thrust upon these 'city sanitation experts' made sure that, in some contexts at least, the nature of the power exercised was only tangentially related to class rule. Moreover, the extent to which the urban working classes had already morally — by the Edwardian period — been incorporated into the social beliefs and individuated legal practices of twentieth-century capitalism resulted in a form of police practice more devoted to innocuous social service functions than to the physical repression of industrial disputants.

These various factors gave rise to the development in post-war mainland Britain of a relatively autonomous quasi-national police service, separated internally by the fiefdom-like structure of local forces but unified in ideological form in a distinctive organisational structure — separate from and occasionally conflicting with other state apparatus[15] and, in an unassailable political autonomy, largely freed from the triple taskmasters of Watch Committee, Home Office and the courts.[16]

That relative autonomy has been reinforced both structurally — by the internal colleague reference groups at command level (the Association of Chief Police Officers and the Police Superintendents Association) — and sub-culturally, in support for an organisational and quasi-political ideology, resulting from recruitment, socialistion and occupational isolation practices[17] and by deliberately distancing the service from other apparatuses.

But more than any other factor, police autonomy has come to depend upon the consent of the *policed* to accept that authoritative control over their lives — to give legitimacy to police practices. Crucial to 'police power' is public acceptance.

The Source of Consent

Policing practice in the late 1970s makes a mockery of the crude
interpretation of the police as a repressive state apparatus — Lenin's
'armed men having prisons' or, in Hirst's words, 'the policeman, a state
functionary is necessary for the reproduction of capitalist social relations. He protects the property of the capitalist and others and secures
certain of the conditions of labour discipline',[18] etc., etc. The phenomenal form of contemporary policing lies in its neutrality, not in its
coercive power. Mark is correct: 'the most essential weapons in our
armoury are not firearms, water cannon, tear gas, or rubber bullets
but the confidence and support of the people on whose behalf we
act.'[19] Police power depends upon class consent, not class oppression.
   As Hayes has perceptively argued,

> the unarmed friendly constable helping the aged . . . the young and
> those in distress: the determined but scrupulous pursuer of the
> offender: the neutral protector of life and property, using a
> minimum of violence and intelligent crime prevention techniques in
> the 'public interest'.All these are the dominant images of our time.
> Such images persist because they have a certain validity for all class
> actors . . . we cannot wish that truth away.[20]

Police service, not police power, provides the parameters of most police-
working-class encounters.
   However, not all things are sweetness-and-light. Side by side with
that image of the friendly neighbourhood bobby, there resides another
picture. Bryan Jackson's caricature of different class reactions sums
this up:

> When a policeman appears on the steps of the Reform Club, it is of
> hardly any consequence to the members: when he appears outside
> a Huddersfield working-men's club, the air is tense with protective
> hostility . . . their uniform to many middle-class may be the mark of
> a servant . . . To the working-class, it announces mastery and
> threat.[21]

Or earlier, in Hoggart's Hunslet,

> their relations with the police tend to be rather different from those
> of the middle-classes . . . they tend to regard the policeman
> primarily as someone who is watching them, who represents the
> authority which has its eye on them, rather than as a member of the
> public services whose job it is to help and protect them.[22]

The crucial feature of the working-class view of the police is its ambiguity. On some occasions, the local constable — stripped of his anti-social Panda — is accorded civility based upon personal relationships and service. At other times, he is viewed as a threat — as an agent of other groups within the city with unspecified discretionary powers.[23]

Not merely do such diverse perceptions of the police coexist — indeed, are crucial to the hegemonic mode of domination-subordination and ideological incorporation — but, within the same working-class context, quite different views of police are held by the various groups and strata. The separation out from a fictionally homogeneous working class in the nineteenth century of particular strata, age and ethnic groups — the costers, 'youth' and the Irish, for example, and that amorphous body known to Victorian Chief Constables[24] and certain social historians alike as the 'criminal class' — provides the basis for contemporary variations in police images.

In Belson's[25] study, working-class youths are considerably more antagonistic to the police than are their older contemporaries. Similarly, Shaw and Williamson[26] demonstrate (from a re-analysis of the rose-tinted Royal Commission data) that the lower the strata questioned in such polls, the more hostility and the more suspicion of police actions. The same discrepancy is noted in accounts of police-ethnic relations.[27]

Further, the same individual may hold generalised abstract images of the police as 'good' but nevertheless consider police officers, in practice, to be corrupt, violent to suspects (thus the current graffiti — 'Help the police — beat yourself up!') and generally willing to break the law when it suits their interests. There are variations in images of police over time — brief experience of picket-line confrontation with police officers at Grunwick[28] may have an identical effect in creating hostile impressions to that of prison experience on middle-class dissenters' conceptions of penal institutions during the nuclear disarmament period.

Public perception of the police varies by class, within the classes, over time, and within the same individual's image of the police in the abstract and in practice. Ordinary everyday 'common-sense' views of the police are therefore a medley of contradictions — constantly adapting new experiences to past images. Working-class perception of policing is 'both an historical formation' and also specific to that class in its day-to-day encounters. It 'contains prejudices from all past phases of history at local level'[29] combined with personal experiences of police-public relations.

The general consent to policing is *tentative* rather than absolute. As a distinctive feature of an ideologically incorporated working class, that consent is subject to continuing interpretation, reinterpretation, adaption and negotiation — and endless testing and resolving of the contradictions and ambiguities of the historical and contemporary experiences of the subordinate groups.

Police Service not Police Force

Basic to that contradiction is the common everyday familiarity with the police officer in his social role. Many writers have discussed the social service features of the latter and its functions for imagery. As Lambert says

> the uniformed policeman meets a complainant or a victim. And he has other social duties — diverting traffic, crowd control, helping pedestrians, advising on crime-prevention, road-safety liaison with schools, conveying messages from hospital . . . such tasks arising from the patrolling function of a uniformed officer, require the police to engage in straightforward 'helping relationships'.[30]

Maurice Punch, Cummings and many others[31] offer similar accounts of the service role, suggesting its primacy over the law enforcement function.

A rather different idea of the social services role exists in some police quarters. For example, Blacker,[32] writing in the *Police College Magazine*, argues that the police can be both a law enforcement agency and a social service. He claims that even the French CRS is a social service! — carrying out law enforcement and thereby maintaining 'order' is actually a necessary social welfare function.

The first image of the police officer as a kind of social worker is clearly widely held. Public consent to policing depends upon its viability. It is a tangible role, containing real benefits for members of all classes. Yet somehow, despite the overwhelming evidence of this form of police-public relations, there remains in working-class areas that degree of ambivalence, hesitation and suspicion that casts doubt on the conception of the police officer as a kind of social worker.

Regardless of the pressure to conceive of him as one sort of creature — not merely from personal experience but perhaps more importantly from media presentation of policing — many working-class people are able to filter out that image. A more blurred functionary emerges from the screening process. A mediating barrier prevents full impact.

Now obviously there are a number of contradictions in the social service role itself which contribute to this marginally porous sieve.

Kilby and Constable, and Howe[33] have pointed to the tension between the police apparatus and that of social work. Social workers for the most part do not recognise a social service role for the police. Particular conflicts arise in settings such as the juvenile court and the forms of discretion available to police officer and to social worker are quite different in character and in intent. Tony Judge of the Police Federation quips about one social worker who informed the court that 'this young boy would not have such a bad record if only the police did not keep arresting him'.

Secondly, as Chatterton[34] has postulated, the social function of a police officer is perceived by the recipient to derive not from social expertise but from ultimate powers of arrest. Successful intervention in a marital dispute owes more to the implicit threat than to any skill as a marriage guidance counsellor. Walker,[35] in noting the nineteenth-century origins of the social welfare role, points out that its increasing emphasis in policing gives those officers more 'intervention power' in the life of the ordinary citizen. Indeed, historically, 'the police dispensed social welfare in the same arbitrary manner that they meted out "curb-side" justice — the "undeserving poor" were simply turned away and often threatened with arrest if they did not leave town'.

Thirdly, Lambert, Reiner and others[36] have argued that, within the police service, organisational factors demote social work and 'helping' tasks. Holdaway's[37] discussion of the search for excitement and stimulation in police work-life suggests little glamour in a street-crossing patrol. Community relations has minimal status compared with the twin beacons of CID and traffic. And, finally, of course, no Chief Constable ever justified an increased establishment in terms of the need to help old ladies across the street. Police work is crime fighting.

But the primary determinant of that barrier's mediating effect appears to be that hidden dimension of common sense — indirect historical experience of class-police hostility and occasional conflict. The prejudices regarding policing are passed down from generation to generation in working-class household and community. Ambivalence towards police officers is, in part, a consequence of the specific contradiction in the police role under capitalism but it also emerges from a history seen from below, not, as in conventional police histories, from above.

In other words, there are two sides of the coin in understanding class views of policing. On one hand, one must come to terms with the missing dimension of police history. Not that, as Punch and Naylor would have it, 'the neglected perspective on the police is the historical one'.[38] In Britain, the police studies produced up to the early seventies contained an unstated police history. J.B. Mays[39] and Charles Reith had much in common. Rather, with Platt and Cooper,[40] one should acknowledge the 'a-historical nature of police studies' where the lack of accounts of class experience of policing has resulted in the dominance of the sociology of the police by occupational sociologists. Understanding working-class images of the police depends foremost upon the realisation of the historical experiences of that class.

The other contribution to the picture is equally vital. Due attention must be paid to the way the historical experience — the collective memory — is constantly tested and examined by personal encounters with the service function. The social service mode of policing must be placed under the same microscope — but without the consensual filter. Only when these two contradictory sides are synthesised can one move to a more adequate theory of the relationship between the police and civil society.

Police History — The Missing Dimension

The Peculiarity of Police History

The dominant consensual and social pathological approaches to police history have been amply documented elsewhere.[41] Pre-eminently, they provide a 'history from above'. Three assumptions are generally common to such works:

1. Early opposition to policing was fragmented and not based upon class opposition. There was no substantive economic basis around which hostile elements could cohere. According to Reith, 'only the criminal, the crime industry profiteer, and some of the radical extremists continued to proffer serious opposition'.[42]

2. *Any* early working-class opposition to the police gradually disappeared during the nineteenth century and, by the early twentieth, the lower classes gave general support to most police activities. Moir claims

> in the early years, the police had to suffer a venomous hostility particularly from Chartists and radicals . . . yet in spite of some ignominious episodes when they were attacked, took refuge in the police station or actually fled the town, the police gradually became accepted and the idea that they represented an instrument of class domination gradually died away. By the 1850s, it had become apparent that they were contributing to the improved standards of public order throughout the country.[43]

3. The working class, like the middle classes, benefited from the onset of policing. Robert Roberts quotes sardonically from a 1906 *Times*

leader

> the policeman in London is not merely a guardian of peace, he is an
> integral part of social life. In many a back street and slum, he
> stands not merely for law and order, he is the true handyman of a
> mass of people who have no other counsellor or friend.[44]

There are, of course, discontinuities between the two schools in the
coverage of the specific relationship between the police and the
working class. Reith, for example, perceived the development of
modern British society as a direct consequence of the public learning
civilised habits from the police. Police institutions are the source of
progress and social change and the development of civilisation is dependent upon the degree of recognition given to their virtues. A similar
theme occurs in the work of less able (and less prolific) writers —
Melville Lee, Howard, Selwyn and Coatman[45] ('The English police . . .
is the pith and marrow of the English conduct of democratic government'). These accounts are often buttressed by the autobiographical
nostalgic reminiscences of retired police officers such as Nott-Bower,
Browne and, most recently, St John.[46] To these writers, the police role
was that of a referee, acting impartially at the behest of 'society' to
ensure that immature citizens learnt the rules of the social game.

To the social pathologists, with not dissimilar premisses on the social
order, the police were urban sanitation experts, cleaning up the ills
caused by industrialisation, urbanisation and the population explosion.
The major feature of the city — in Chesney[47] and Tobias[48] — is its
social disorganisation. Police development was not important in itself
but rather as one part of several interrelated reforms. To Critchley[49]
and Hart,[50] policing represented a reformist advance, introduced by
Peel to mitigate the harshness, arbitrary character and inefficiency of
earlier penal and preventative measures in society. As Manning[51] notes,
the main features of the social pathological accounts are the develop-
mental, incremental accumulation of police institutions and their
contextualisation within wider changes in social and industrial life in the
nineteenth century. They share with the earlier school the same
unquestioning conservatism, the lack of attention to the view of the
'policed', the identification of the desires of particular groups with the
'public interest', and the failure to differentiate amongst the groups
threatening 'social order' — the confused notions of the 'mob',
'dangerous classes' and so on.

The Recognition of Class Conflict

Within the work of the historians referred to above, the varying
experience of the lower classes is largely ignored or subsumed under a

general heading such as the 'criminal class'. Only within a few works
does one come across the recognition of class interest in policing.
Critchley's[52] later work argues that police development was based upon
the necessary subjugation of the working class. He gives a poignant
illustration of whose effective ends were served by the police after the
first two decades. He says, that, after the police had shepherded away a
Chartist demonstration in 1848 'that night the middle classes thronged
the streets singing "God Save the Queen". But what they ought to be
singing was "God save our shops" muttered the discontented Chartists.'

Thompson has no doubt about the class nature of policing: after
the initial fractional disputes 'the local bourgeoisie triumphed
absolutely . . . the police was on an acceptable bourgeois-bureaucratic
model'.[53] Of the older generations of police historians, only
Radzinowicz recognises the class interest in police formation. He alone
refers to the economic context of the pressures for more effective
policing. Unlike Critchley, he does not equate the private wishes of the
middle and upper classes with the public interest.

Marxist notions of the relationship of the police to capital are treated
slightingly. In all cases, a straw Marxism of a highly economistic nature
is thrown up in order to be virulently dismissed or, more recently, to be
noted but in no way developed.

Hart,[54] for example, outlines the conflict between the early
Victorian upper classes and the entrepreneurial middle class as a device
for denying such a model. She, like Tobias, argues that the English
police were inaugurated not at the behest of the property-owning
classes but rather in opposition to their wishes. She exaggerates the
way the local manufacturing groups saw the police as the thin end of a
political wedge of centralisation and control. Clearly, with the middle
classes in opposition, the police could not be a weapon against the
lower classes.

Similarly, Whitaker uses a crude class analysis: 'the old Marxist attack
on the police for preventing the re-distribution of property is mis-
conceived.'[55] In both writers, Marxism is equated with a continuous
overt class struggle. Critchley again is more direct. In *The Conquest of
Violence*, he notes a major role for the police in the class struggle. More
recently, Bowden (curiously, given the context of some of his earlier
work) claimed that the 'police were used . . . physically to restrain the
growing power of organised labour . . . clearly taking sides in the class
struggle'.[56]

Marxism fares little better from those recent writings which express
some implicit sympathy with its approach. Manning refers briefly to a
vague 'conflict' approach which appears to cover a diffuse set of
writings from 'critical criminology'. Walker,[57] whose own work is
perhaps the most impressive over-all account of American police

development, adopts a position midway between the social pathological model and a vulgar Márxist interpretation without venturing to
outline the latter. He tests this 'Marxist thesis' by a yardstick based
upon such criteria as the number of police attacks upon strikers and the
extent to which the police acted as the henchmen of local economic
interests. Walker concludes that American policing was highly ambivalent, local forces actually supporting labour unions on some occasions.
Again, Marxism is reduced to a simple statement of class bias in the
genesis and operations of police organisations.

   In brief, no police history examines class relations in other than
crude reductionist fashion. A class conflict model is either dismissed
or partially accepted on the basis of a selective head-counting of the
number of police — working-class clashes. However, it is clear from
alternative historical sources that (a) there was substantially more
physical conflict with and opposition to policing by working-class
groups than is generally appreciated but (b) by far the major form of
police — working-class relations was not that of physical oppression
but rather one of moral discipline — an ideological rather than directly
coercive relationship. The historical filter of class images of policing
should be viewed in the light of these two features.

Police Origins and Form

The inception of the English police owed far more to political and
economic factors than to moral entrepreneurial ones. While the origins
are complex, underlying the gradual acceptance of the 'police idea' by
the urban middle class was the concern of that class with political
hegemony and economic order. As McDonald[58] puts it, once a class
begins to organise — the stirrings of the Chartists in the 1820s and
1830s, the transformation of the London 'mob' from a social nuisance
to a political threat, the growth of combinations of workers — the
dominant class can no longer afford to police the subordinate group in
the old amateurish way, by Bow Street Runners and parish constables.

   Miller argues that the new police arrived at a time of increasing
tension between the classes. The new commercial elites could no longer
afford, particularly in London, the hub of the new exploitative order,
the political instability engendered by street riots. Although Peel gave a
primary justification only of property protection, it is the political and
social relations within the metropolis that seem to have been ultimately
important. Similarly, it was political factors — the recognition of the
threat to 'public' order of street demonstrations — that tipped the
balance towards the organisation of new forces in the provincial cities.
The usual example is the Bristol reform riots of 1832. Parris, for
example, says: 'there seems to have come a point in . . . these towns
when a riot led the authorities to conclude that an efficient police force

was a lesser evil than periodical anarchy.'[59] According to Bunyan, the incorporation of class action by the Municipal Corporations Act left only the streets as the forum for working-class action. The New Police represented an acknowledgement by the dominant economic forces of the political nature of that protest.

It was not merely that the old styles of intervention in civil strife were ineffective but rather that militia were used; in a number of cases cited by Radzinowicz, they were as likely to side with the rioters against a common propertied enemy, even when the militia were themselves serving in alien territory. (In a later context, Storch[60] notes that the urban working class would accept the militia, with whom they had a degree of empathy; it was the police who were the enemy — the 'blue locusts'.)

More effective control of the emerging and increasingly coherent and articulate sections of the working class necessitated an equally coherent policing agency. That body could only be effective when it took on a phenomenal form of impartiality, when contrasted with the traditional association between the old constabulary and the upper classes. Miller, in a detailed study of the early Metropolitan force, claims that the real coercive character of the early police was masked — the deliberately non-military style of bearing, the lack of firearms and so on. Howard[61] elaborates on the problem facing Rowan and Mayne at the outset — how to organise a disciplined force while avoiding a resemblance to the military, in order to avoid alarming a (middle-class) public already sensitised to 'Continental centralized despotism'. Of this impartiality, Miller says, 'the London policeman represented the "public good" as defined by the governing classes concerned to maintain an unequal social order with a minimum of violence and oppression. The result was impersonal authority.'[62]

In the metropolitan area, officers were recruited from outside the city — in the manner of imperial mountain levies — to impose the rule of Empire upon the educated city dwellers of the Victorian colonies; justified by the Commissioners as a means of curtailing bribery and partiality towards kin and friends, it had the objective function of removing police officers from working-class neighbourhood influences and made them less reticent in resorting to force.

Class Relations of the Police

A number of writers outline the two sides of the class relations of the police institutions in their historical development — in their actions on behalf of the local middle class and in the recognition of their class nature by the different classes. A number of instances of police action at the behest of local elites have been documented.

For example, the introduction of beer-house licensing in the 1870s

led to commercial interests influencing police activity against
unlicensed houses (i.e. those bars not controlled by the city's main
brewers). Similar intentions are noted in the control of brothels by the
Watch Committee. As Fosdick observed in 1914,

> Twenty-five years ago, the Chairman of the Watch Committee in
> Liverpool was the attorney for large liquor interests in the town
> while another member was the physician for most of the brothels.
> Needless to say, the activities of the police, in respect to liquor and
> prostitution, were negligible.[63]

Marshall[64] argues that, in the nineteenth century, Watch Committees
were often dominated by local political and commercial groupings who
controlled police prosecutions (until 1905) and influenced police
discretion. On occasion, the police might serve quarrels within the local
elites but, in general, the activities that the police were directed against
were those of working-class people. Parris and Hart have given a number
of illustrations of the control of the police exercised by local brewers
and the patronage of police action by local tradesmen. Some lower-
class groups were particularly susceptible to that action. Evidence from
Watch Committee Minutes[65] from the 1830s to the 1930s shows the
constant demands by local shopkeepers for the removal of street
hawkers — Chesney, Miller and Phil Cohen[66] all emphasise the resulting
deep hostility of the costers to the police.

In an earlier context, Phillips[67] spotlights the collaboration between
police, coalmasters and magistracy in enforcing low wages on the
miners in the Black Country in the 1850s. 'There can be no doubt that
the machinery of law and order operated . . . to the disadvantage of the
working class.' He delineates the extent to which the local control
apparatus — particularly the police — intertwined with the interests of
the middle class and of the local landowners.

Active class support for the police is documented in a number of
instances. Simplistically alluded to by Glover ('public confidence was no
doubt largely engendered by the confidence placed in the New Police
by the shopkeepers'[68] and Mather ('the shopocracy'[69]), middle-class
support was generally obvious in the exhortations of tradesmen to the
police to act against the hawkers, from church ministers against the
disturbance of Sunday recreation,[70] and from factory owners against
thefts from the work-place.[71] It was most apparent at a time of social
and economic disturbance. On such occasions, according to Mather,
'the principal reserve for the recruitment of special constables was the
middle class'.[72] Initial reservations about supporting the police altered
as the class role of the police became more significantly appreciated.

Difficulties of recruitment belong to the early years . . . a remarkable
change in 1848 . . . the almost legendary muster of 170,000 special
constables in the London area was matched throughout the
provinces . . . in Liverpool . . . some 3,000-4,000 selected from the
principal inhabitants . . . Of the large towns, only in Leicester, where
great sympathy existed between the middle and working classes and
in Birmingham, where industrialization had not yet created a marked
social cleavage between capital and labour, was the response poor . . .
The increased supply of special constables . . . reflects the growth in
both size and self-confidence of the English middle classes.

This support for the police has been mirrored on numerous occasions,
especially since the turn of the century. During the 1919 police strike,
members of city business houses enrolled *en masse* to support the
strike-breaking police.[73] 'The business interests in the town made it
clear to their staffs that every able-bodied man . . . was to volunteer his
aid.' 'Typical of the civilian volunteers who signed up with the Specials
. . . were . . . the members of the Hightown (a bourgeois residential
area) Sporting Club who enrolled to help the Lord Mayor out of his
difficulties.'[74] A few years later, after the General Strike, middle-class
support was manifest in a different way — the £240,000 collected for
police charities by readers of *The Times.*[75]
    Equally obvious with regard to the Specials is the tradition of
working-class opposition to them. In 1848, large numbers of Liverpool
dock workers gave up their jobs rather than accept their employers'
demands that they enrol.[76] In 1919, the Liverpool 'mob' had 'nothing
but contempt' for the Specials.[77] In 1926, strikers were more antagonistic to the special constables than to the paid police. Among the
Specials were 'right-wing elements anxious to do anything to destroy
the unions'.[78]
    Various writers have dealt in detail with the articulation of working-
class opposition to the police, and with the consciousness of the role
of the latter. Foster,[79] for example, credits the Oldham artisans with a
realisation of political and economic importance as early as the 1820s.
He documents, over three decades the struggle by those workers to
obtain control over the local police — which they recognised as the
dominant factor governing the relationship between mill owners and
employees. This awareness of the potential of the police as an agent of
labour discipline is illustrated by actions by both classes. Thus, in 1826,
the employers sponsored the Oldham Police Act, against working-class
opposition, as a direct device for maintaining control over both work
and non-work lives of artisans and mill operatives. This bourgeois
dominance over the police was occasionally disrupted by the collective

power of the workers who positioned their own nominees at the head of
the force. They successfully opposed a new local Police Act in 1834
because it removed local electoral control of the police. Finally, the
working-class hold on the police was broken in a direct clash between
the Oldham force and the magistrate and mill-owning-backed county
force, the victory of the latter being interpreted as a major class defeat.

Pelling comments more generally

> gradually by careful training and effective discipline, the force
> commended itself at least to the governing classes and began to
> suppress local disorders in the provinces. But there was an under-
> current of hostility to the force from humbler people, who felt that
> the police were depriving them from their liberties . . . resolved to
> have no police whatsoever until the working classes had a voice in
> making the laws of the land.[80]

Apart from contributing various incisive Edwardian accounts of
working-class police imagery,[81] Storch has documented from radical
newspaper sources the forms of active and conscious working-class
resistance that are markedly absent from the more conservative writers.
He provides examples of the various physical conflicts that arose as
communities resisted the imposition of policing, citing the running
battle between the inhabitants of Padiham — using sophisticated
tactics — and the 'foreign' police in the 1840s and, like Radzinowicz
and Mather, describes the continuing disputes that simmered on
throughout the first half-century of policing. Prominently itemised in
the political manifestos of the day were demands for control of the
police. He argues that in the latter part of the nineteenth century, where
overt conflict disappeared in the relations between working class and
the police, this represented not an acceptance of what James[82] has called
the 'civilising function' of the latter but rather a state of armed truce
which was occasionally broken by an anti-police riot on a public
holiday.

Clearly, from the above material there is substantive evidence that
working-class experience, and consequent image of the police,
contained considerably more oppositional elements than is commonly
portrayed. As in the Edwardian novelist quoted by Storch

> there are two ways of looking at them: from above and beneath . . .
> for the police effectively divide the country into two classes, an
> upper and a lower — those above them whose servants they are, and
> those beneath them who are under their thumb.

Forms of Control

Social order under the new police system depended upon the general preventative ethic enshrined in Benthamite penal thought. In practice, preventative policing involved three interrelated forms of action — patrolling of working-class residential districts, clamping down on the leisure pursuits of that class, and filtration of organised working-class bodies.

McDonald[83] argues that it is in the community that the most essential police functions are carried out. Police concern is with the social conditions under which labour power is reproduced. The introduction of preventative policing by Peel entailed deliberate police actions aimed at disciplining the various diverse strata within the working class. Charles Dickens[84] in Liverpool and Booth[85] in London have both documented the Victorian practice of police sorties into the 'rockeries'. Jack London[86] similarly commented on the importance of the 'move-on' imperative to the unemployed East Ender. What could not be regulated by factory employment and the clock[87] was to be cowed to regular preventative patrolling ('the watching St Giles to guard St James' policy).

Storch, Miller and Phillips all describe the use of the police as a 'lever of urban discipline' and the 'policy of general surveillance'. The police had broad powers of arrest in forays into working-class areas. 'Intruders' into middle-class areas were open to instant arrest on 'suspicion' under the Vagrancy Act.[88] This latter and local by-laws, such as the stop-and-search power in the metropolis, had considerable effects on the movement of poor and marginal members of the working class. These various statutes, justified explicitly by Rowan and Mayne for their preventative effect, gave individual constables substantial discretionary power over the everyday lives of the less powerful members of Victorian society. The changing moral order was instilled into working-class skulls more by insidious threat — rather than use — of police truncheon, and by continual harassment. According to Phillips,[89] in some urban areas the police were sent out 'looking for trouble'. Such conflicts were a means of disciplining workers, as they relieved in expressive activity the tensions and frustrations of the work-place, and also ensured the pliability and submission of the army of unemployed.

Policing intruded upon recreative activities as upon other areas of social life. As Storch and Phillips variously point out, those festive activities of the lower classes that could be viewed as having political connotations — the burning of effigies of local magistrates on 5 November — provided an obvious target. But equally, all forms of street recreation were continually under threat. As Midwinter[90] and Cockcroft[91] show in Liverpool, the major focuses of police action were in clearing the streets rather than in relation to 'crime' (or for that

matter against strikers – only one such action is recorded in the first
25 years of that local force's existence[92]). The Sabbath was the day of
greatest police deployment, putting down games of 'pitch and toss' (a
practice noted by Cockcroft and Judge and Reynolds, in Liverpool, as
prevalent from 1835 to at least 1919) and supervising the chapels and
churches to prevent a 'public' i.e. working-class, nuisance outside. (In
a more contemporary context, Westergaard and Resler[93] argue that the
public leisure context of working-class life means more opportunity for
conflict with the police and an obvious target for a force pro-actively
striving to boost its arrest rate.)

A third dimension of police surveillance of working-class activities
and non-work pursuits was the continuing use of police spies and the
more formal observation of demonstrations by plain clothes officers.
These cases range from the clumsy infiltration of the national political
unions by Sergeant Popay[94] in 1833 to the equally insidious activities
of Detective Constable Dyke[95] a hundred years later in providing an
obsessive and exaggerated account of Communist influence in a weaving
strike in Burnley. At a more sophisticated level, there have been police
spies on the executives of a number of working-class organisations. The
best documented is Hayburn's[96] account of the 'police informer in the
highest circles of the National Unemployed Worker's Movement' in the
1930s and of other informers at lower levels in that amorphous organisation. As Walter Hannington[97] bitterly states in his own history of the
NUWM, the police seem to have received a torrent of information about
the movement and particularly about its Communist Party links. The
partiality of police observational activities is notable – as Stevenson
and Cook say, 'the absence of covert surveillance of the British Union
of Fascists is in striking contrast to their practice with the NUWM'.[98]
Little organised working-class activity occurred without prior police
knowledge and preparation.

Preventative policing was the major form of police-working-class
contact and the basis for historical developments of class images of
policing. In the genesis of that imagery, physical confrontations and
direct coercive experience played a much smaller role than
'intimidation by presence'. Yet the former played some part and this
is most apparent in the evidence from industrial conflict.

The Police and Industrial Conflict

The economistic model attacked by Hart contains within it a conception of two police functions with regard to the employer of labour –
the protection of the rights to property of the employer by prosecuting
workers who 'steal' from the work-place and, secondly, guaranteeing
the rights of the employer in the context of an industrial dispute.
Although there is some evidence of the bias of the police in carrying

out the first function (Phillips), most material relates to the role of the police during industrial conflict.

Illustrations of such police activity are most notable by their absence from police histories. Minimal attention is given to industrial conflict and to the highly discretionary enforcement of the relevant legislation. Only in sources such as Watch Committee Minutes, trade union records, and in the memoirs of labour leaders does one find details of the 'everyday' industrial conflicts of the first century of policing.

For example, all the older police historians distort the nature of the police role during the General Strike. Coatman, Howard and Keeton[99] wax with jingoistic pride as they describe a 'typical' incident during that conflict. 'Possibly no other nation in the world could have witnessed during the progress of a similar crisis, the spectacle of police and strikers engaging in a game of football.' According to Critchley, 'both sides . . . played the game according to unwritten rules, as though the standards of Arnold's schoolboys, had permeated all classes'.[100]

A fuller and rather different account of one such match is provided by Morris. 'The Carstairs Strike Committee took the line that there was no point making enemies of the police.'[101] Similarly, the local Chief Constable, in the best traditions of preventative policing, attempted to cool things by suggesting the sporting encounter. Immediately after the match, a misheard jest led to a police search of the strikers' houses for weapons, with ensuing turmoil and disruption. This latter action, rather than the preceding football match, typified police-worker relations during the General Strike. More common than harmonious encounters is the following from Farman discussing disturbances in Hull: 'The crowd simply looked on out of curiosity when suddenly a large force of police attacked them right and left with batons while mounted police rode into the crowd.'[102] While 'police restraint puzzled people from the Continent, where class struggles tended to follow a more violent course', this was because 'often the police preferred to avoid a trial of strength and retired in the face of mass pickets'. Nevertheless there were many direct clashes between police and strikers and innumerable smaller incidents and arrests of strikers, often on trumped-up charges. As Phillips[103] has noted of the Black Country clashes in the 1860s, in a comment relevant both to 1926 and to the 1970s, where actual conflict between police and strikers disappeared over time, it was not because of less police intervention but because of increased tactical sophistication by the latter.

For a more intense picture of police-labour relations the major sources are the autobiographies of labour leaders. Gallagher,[104] Hannington and McShane[105] provide graphic pictures of the severity of such conflicts. Typical is Tom Mann's account of police intervention in the dock strike of 1911:

If the worst and most ferocious brutes in the world had been on the scene, they would not have displayed such brutality as the Liverpool City Police, and their imported men . . . such a scene of brutal butchery was never witnessed in Liverpool before. Defenceless men and women, several of whom were infirm, and many of whom were aged, were deliberately knocked down by heavy blows from the truncheons of powerful men and even as the crowd fled from this on-slaught, the police still continued to batter away at them.[106]

Of many other examples, Cockburn's account of the attack on unemployed squatters in Birkenhead is one of the best documented by labour historians.

At nightfall the police were sent into the working-class quarters, smashing ground-floor windows and breaking into houses with what could be hoped was pacificatory violence . . . Sporadic fighting continued by day and police incursions by night, these now often being resisted with sticks and iron bars and heavy showers of stone . . . the police moved against the thickly populated tenement blocks.[107]

A number of studies mention the use of 'outside' police in labour disputes.[108] Long before the days of flying columns of pickets, there were flying columns of police, available to be despatched to wherever the brush fire of industrial and political dissent broke out next. According to Mather,

in 1837, some 38 policemen were absent from London for the purpose of suppressing Anti-Poor Law riots in Yorkshire, Essex and the West Country. During the Chartist disturbances of 1839, detachments of Metropolitan policemen were sent to Loughborough, Mansfield, Monmouth, Bury, Bedlington and Cockermouth.[109]

Despite the intense parochiality of some senior officers and Watch Committees, large well-organised forces such as the Metropolitan and the Liverpool were often willing to lend resources to other authorities where local elites felt themselves threatened, almost independently of distance from home base. Thus in 1911 alone, London police officers found themselves in Salford, Liverpool and South Wales. In the period 1883-94, the Liverpool Head Constable sent detachments to defend the Caernarvonshire quarries against strikers, crossed the city boundary to deal with a seamen's strike in Bootle and the Mersey to terminate a Cheshire salt workers' strike, into St Helen's to support an employer against his workforce, to Trafalgar Square for a political demonstration, and to Lancaster for a race-course dispute.[110] The drubbing received by the Metropolitan Police in the Birmingham Bull-Ring in 1848 had only been a temporary set-back to the use of such mobile units.

Police behaviour in industrial disputes was in part a result of their own minimal experience of trade union activities. Reiner's[111] valuable account of contemporary police attitudes towards the unions illustrates the increased isolation of police officers from other workers since the turn of the century.

Prior to the formation of the Police Federation, the contradictory nature of the relationship between the police and other workers was clearly evident. In the late nineteenth and early twentieth centuries, there were several attempts by police rank and file to develop and consolidate their own union structures.

The 1872 strike of the Metropolitan force was symptomatic of disputes by other workers — over pay and victimisation.[112] The 1879 and 1890 strikes by that force were prompted by the same momentum as conflicts in a number of occupations ranging from a postmen's strike to a troop mutiny over pay.[113] In other words, by the early twentieth century, police officers were undergoing the same traumas of economic organisation as other workers,[114] but the 1918 and particularly the 1919 strikes demonstrated the tension between the police and other workers. Where the police union was strong enough to stand on its own, as in the Metropolitan strike of 1918, and where economic conditions were favourable, it was successful. But where it did not have unity in its own ranks, as in 1919, and depended upon sympathetic support by other workers, it failed. As Judge and Reynolds[115] and Picton Davies[116] have pointed out, organised labour, particularly on Merseyside, where its help was most necessary, recognised the police not as fellow workers but as agents of a dominant class who had helped crush the dock strike of 1911 and had for a century continually harassed the leisure pursuits of the working class.

Despite the appeal of some local trade union leaders and some money from trade councils, Liverpool workers almost without exception refused to acknowledge the similarity of the work relations of police officers. That strike, the dismissal of all strikers (Nott-Bower[117] — the former Liverpool Head Constable — expressed his complete jubilation at being able to carry out 'the complete riddance of the whole of the agitators and mischief-makers at one swoop'. It 'was indeed a Godsend'. Commissioner Macready expressed similar pleasure, coupling it with a xenophobic denunciation of 'foreign' leaders of the police union[118]), ensured the development of local police forces clearly outside the realm of organised labour. The Police Union was legally proscribed and replaced with a tame and largely unrepresentative Police Federation. The 1919 strike was deliberately precipitated by the

employers as a means of maintaining divisions between the police and
working-class unionism[119] The affiliations to the TUC and to the
Labour Party disappeared. The contradictory relationship between
police function and class aspirations was formally resolved in a clear
demarcation between police and the working class.

Implications for the Sociology of Policing

Clearly such historical evidence — selective and based largely upon
partisan accounts — in no way proves that most police actions towards
the working class were proactive, in the form of harassment and intimidation. Physical coercion, in particular, was an exception rather than
the rule. Few strike pickets ever found themselves in violent confrontation with police officers and fewer still went to gaol. But, nevertheless,
the collective memory of such occasions — and the general awareness
of the practical implications of preventative patrolling for the lower
classes — is amplified and retained in so far as it reinforces already
held prejudices. Consensual police images do not have such fertile
ground.

Collective memory contributes to police-class relations by
providing a barrier which prevents the easy egress of the model
portrayed by the new police Public Relations Departments of the
1970s. Sociological interpretations of policing within civil society must
start by acknowledging the existence of that barrier, which reflects
real dissent from dominant values. Similarly, the ambivalence of class
attitudes is an empirical fact. The contradictions innate to hegemony
are nowhere more evident than in attitudes to the police.

On one hand, then, it is fallacious to define the police primarily as
a repressive state apparatus. Grunwick, the Liddell Towers case and Red
Lion Square are rare exceptions, not the norm. The evidence of police
violence cited in this paper is not that of everyday experience.
Conversely, an opposite emphasis upon the social service style of
policing conceals considerable contradictions.

However, for some small groups in society (and larger organised
groups, at times of crisis), repression is normal. Working-class youth
(particularly young blacks), left-wing demonstrators, squatters, gays,
amongst others, are disproportionately open to police repression — a
coercion that may well be consented to by ideologically incorporated
members of the working class. However, it is not easy to explain such
experience within a class model. A conception of the police as being
primarily concerned with the reproduction of labour power by disciplining and patrolling the inner city does not provide an easily acceptable
basis for explanation. Not even Spitzer's[120] suggestion that such groups

are a 'problem population' for the capitalist state can provide a sufficient analysis of the need to over-police a twilight area largely irrelevant to the capitalist mode of production.

A more tempting model is one that locates the rationale for police action in the context of a relatively autonomous organisational ideology — one with roots in the juridicial notions of individual rights under capitalism, but distorted by its organisational setting and development. For example, Watch Committee evidence from the 1919 race riots in Liverpool[121] provides some justification for an analysis of present police action under the 'sus' laws within the context of police ideological formation over time.

In practice, the use of the police as a coercive apparatus signals the breakdown of consent and may be dysfunctional for capital. According to Gramsci, 'lapses in the administration of justice make an essentially disastrous impression upon the public: the hegemonic apparatus is more sensitive in this sector, to which arbitrary actions on the part of the police . . . may also be referred'.[122]

Where the phenomenal form of law provides for equality of treatment and conceals the hidden relations of inequality, police blunders draw attention to that inequality. As Poulantzas[123] argues, law under capitalism separates groups into individuals with individual rights before reconstituting those individuals into the 'nation'; the practice of law depends upon the principle of universality. Consent rests on the belief in equal treatment before the law. Arbitrary action threatens that consent. Policing is most effective in its consensual, not in its coercive, mode. Reith was correct: 'the chief element in the power of the police is the approval of the community, and their success depends upon their power to retain it.'

However, that consent is not readily given. Not merely are there contradictions in both the organisational life of the police officer and his position as a state functionary, but the backcloth to his actions in the community is historically formed. Working-class experience of policing may consist in the main of passive, 'helping' encounters, but within that experience there exists a collective memory of policing redolent with suspicion and occasionally reinforced by arbitrary police action. The reports of police officers such as Chapple[124] in Kirkby cannot be understood without reference to the types of historical experience noted in this paper.

This is not to argue that all historical memories of the police contain primarily antagonistic elements. The part-mythological, part-real, 'village bobby' is an important reference point. Working-class experience of policin has always been characterised by ambiguity and ambivalence.

But what is clear in early sociological studies of the police in the UK is their dependence upon a latent version of the second conception as the basis for interpretation of the 'police role'. The vitriolic attack by Rosenberg[125] upon Banton's work, in the path-breaking 1971 paper, was justified in that it drew attention to the failure of the police socio-logists to examine the historically and structurally formed class relations of the police. But where Rosenberg failed was to dismiss, almost *in toto*, those insights from organisational sociology which provide a valid — if partial — contribution to the sociology of the police. Similarly, Rosenberg paid only lip-service to duality of consent and coercion — giving more emphasis to the latter and failing to recognise the cruciality of consent. Indeed, further, one could argue that a major failure in the writing of such sociologists as Quinney has been their inability to appreciate that in police work, as in other forms of managerial activity, 'there are those elements of management and super-vision that are necessary to a given . . . level of production i.e. tasks of organisation and co-ordination, and those that are particular to its forms within the capitalist mode of production'.[126] Socialist as well as capitalist societies require policemen.

There is clearly a conceptual problem in separating those two functions. But what is clear is that successful performance of the first necessary function provides the ideological support for the performance of the second. The continual challenge to that duality is apparent, finally, from the (apocryphal?) account of the Kirkby schoolboy who is asked by his teacher to write an essay on the police. All that results is the one-line sentence 'All police is bastards'. A week later, the local Police Juvenile Liaison Officer visits the school and gives the assembled children a talk on the welfare function of the police. After the visit, another essay is requested. The schoolboy obliges with a similar one-line production: 'All police is conning bastards.'

Notes

1. D. Hay *et al.* (eds), *Albion's Fatal Tree: Crime ad Society in Eighteenth Century England* (Allen Lane The Penguin Press, 1975), chs by Hay and Linebaugh; and M. Foucault, *Discipline and Punish: the Birth of the Prison* (Allen Lane The Penguin Press, 1975).
2. T. Bunyan, *The Political Police in Britain* (Friedmann, 1976), appendix.
3. J.J. Tobias, 'Police and Public in the U.K.', in G.L. Mosse (ed.), *Police Forces in History* (Sage, 1975). For a critical discussion of the general evolutionary approach to law see S. Hall *et al.*, *Policing the Crisis* (Macmillan, 1978), p. 193.
4. W.L. Melville Lee, *A History of Police in England* (Methuen, 1901), p. 128; L. Radzinowicz, *A History of English Criminal Law* (Stevens and Sons, 1956) vol. III, pp. 168, 217, 472.
5. B.D. White, *A History of the Corporation of Liverpool* (1951), p. 20.
6. W.R. Miller, *Cops and Bobbies* (University of Chicago Press, 1977).

7. H. Pelling, *Popular Politics and Society in Late Victorian England* (Macmillan, 1968), p. 70; D. Phillips, *Crime and Authority in Victorian England* (Croom Helm, 1977), p. 84; R.D. Storch, 'The Plague of the Blue Locusts: Police Reform and Popular Resistance in Northern England, 1840-1857', *International Review of Social History*, 20 (1975), pp. 61-90, and 'The Policeman as Domestic Missionary: Urban Discipline and Popular Culture in Northern England, 1850-1880', *Journal of Social History*, 9 (Summer 1976), pp. 481-509.

8. A. Silver, 'The Demand for Order in Civil Society', in D.J. Bordua (ed.), *The Police: Six Sociological Essays* (Wiley, 1967), or in Douglas's discussion of Foucault: 'police work – a totality of morally sanctioned ideas and practices aimed at "rationally" controlling the lower classes so that they would work and not endanger the lives and interests of the upper classes', 'the bureaucracies of official morality': J.D. Douglas, *American Social Order* (Collier-Macmillan, 1971), p. 51.

9. S. Walker, *A Critical History of Police Reform* (Lexington Books, 1977), p. 7, notes, amongst other things, a distinction which many other writers ignore, particularly Miller, that the Metropolitan Police have always been distinct from the provincial forces. 'A creature of the Home Office; it was essentially an extension of national government.' Indeed, the Metropolitan Police have just announced their intention to carry out their own annual inspections, internally.

10. Miller, *Cops and Bobbies*, pp. 26-7.

11. G. Howard, *Guardians of the Peace* (Odhams), p. 123, notes the various problems in the attempt to avoid a militaristic bearing. However, as late as 1867, Anthony Trollope, in *Last Chronicle of Barset,* points to the failure of that attempt: 'a policeman pure and simple with the helmet-looking hat which has lately become common, and all the ordinary half military and wholly undesirable outward adjuncts of the profession'.

12. F.L. Mather, *Public Order in the Age of the Chartists* (Manchester University Press, 1959), p. 117, and H. Parris, 'The Home Office and the Provincial Police in England and Wales 1857-70', *Public Law* (1967).

13. Many writers have emphasised the post-war expansion in the local force – roughly 1-500 population now compared with 1-1000 in 1919; see, for example, L. McDonald, *The Sociology of Law and Order* (Faber, 1976). The force mergers of the post-war period have greatly increased the size of individual forces. C. Ackroyd *et al., The Technology of Political Control* (Penguin, 1977); G. Picton Davies, 'The Police Service of England and Wales Between 1918 and 1964', PhD thesis University of London.

14. John Arden's Chief Constable Feng puts it best, ' . . . I said that I

Derived authority for my high office not
From the jerk and whirl of irrelevant faction-
. . . your democratic Punch and Judy –
But from the Law, being abstract, extant, place'

(*The Workhouse Donkey* (Faber, 1964), p. 124).

15. There are an increasing number of published criticisms by members of different apparatuses on one another. See, for example, R. Mark, 'Minority Verdict' in his *Policing in a Perplexed Society* (Allen and Unwin, 1977); T. Judge, 'Social Worker and the Citizen', *Social Work Today* VII, no. 8 (8 August 1970); and the chs by R. Kilby and T. Constable, and by K. Howe in J. Brown and G. Howes (eds), *The Police and the Community* (Saxon House, 1975).

16. R. Moodie, 'The Use and Control of the Police', in R. Benewick and T. T. Smith (eds), *Direct Action and Democratic Politics* (Allen and Unwin, 1972); M. Brogden, 'A Police Authority – the denial of conflict', *Sociological Review*

(May 1977); G. Marshall, *Police and Government* (Methuen, 1965). T. Bowden claimed that Home Office control has increased considerably: 'Guarding the State: The Police Response to Crisis Politics in Europe', *British Journal of Law and Society*, V, no. 1 (1978), p. 77. One would like to see some evidence to support this assertion. (T. Critchley in *A History of Police in England and Wales* (Constable, 1979 edn) makes a similarly unsubstantiated claim.)

17. L.W. Sherman, 'The Sociology and the Social Reform of the American Police 1950-1973', *Journal of Police Science and Administration*, II, no. 2 (1974), pp. 255-62.

18. P. Hirst, 'Marx, Engels on Law Crime and Morality', in P. Walton *et al.* (eds), *Critical Criminology* (Routledge and Kegan Paul, 1975), p. 58.

19. R. Mark, 'Keeping the Peace in Britain', in Mark, *Policing in a Perplexed Society*.

20. M. Hayes quoted in F. Pearce, *Crimes of the Powerful* (Pluto Press, 1976), p. 63. As early as 1830, Edwin Chadwick had argued, according to Miller (*Cops and Bobbies*, p. 107) 'that the police should seek public support by appearing more frequently in a service role-helping to prevent and assist at accidents' and by 1868, according to Chadwick, 'this service role had become the mainstay of police legitimacy'.

21. B. Jackson, *Working-Class Community* (Pelican, 1968), p. 118.

22. R. Hoggart, *The Uses of Literacy* (Pelican, 1958), p. 73.

23. A. Blumberg and A. Niederhoffer, *Ambivalent Justice* (Holt, Rinehart and Winston, 1976), p. 3, say 'most of us do not fully comprehend the awesome power that the police possess in their exercise of discretion to arrest . . . can be a powerful weapon . . . a form of summary punishment'.

24. Watch Committee records show a constant use of this form of reification by nineteenth-century Chief Constables: Liverpool Watch Committee Minutes, 1835. J.J. Tobias, *Crime and Punishment in the Nineteenth Century* (Penguin, 1972), p. 68, finds the term 'acceptable' but note the excellent discussion and critique of the concept in Hall *et al.*, *Policing the Crisis*, p. 121.

25. W.A. Belson, *The Public and the Police* (Harper and Row, 1975).

26. B. Shaw and W. Williamson, 'Public Attitudes to the Police', *The Criminologist*, VII, pp. 18-37, note also the earlier attack on the Royal Commission on the Police, data in B. Whitaker, *The Police* (Eyre and Spottiswoode, 1965).

27. D. Humphry, *Police Power and Black People* (Panther, 1972). J. Lambert, *Crime, Police and Race Relations* (Oxford University Press, 1970).

28. J. Dromey and G. Taylor, *Grunwick: the Worker's Story* (Lawrence and Wishart, 1978), Ch. 9.

29. A. Gramsci, *Selections from the Prison Notebooks* (Lawrence and Wishart, 1971), p. 374.

30. J. Lambert, 'The Role of the Police in Race Relations', in S. Zubaida (ed.), *Race and Racialism* (Tavistock, 1970).

31. M. Punch and T. Naylor, 'The Police as a Social Service', *New Society* (17 May 1973), E. Cummings *et al.*, 'Policeman as Philosopher, Guide and Friend', *Social Problems*, XII, 3 (1965).

32. J. Blacker, 'Policing or Social Service', *Police College Magazine*, XIV, 1.

33. Brown and Howse (eds), *The Police and the Community*.

34. M. Chatterton, 'Police in Social Control', in J. Kine (ed.), *Control Without Custody* (Cambridge Institute of Criminology, 1978).

35. Walker, *Critical History of Police Reform*, p. 55.

36. R. Reiner, 'The Police Class and Politics', *Marxism Today* (March 1978).

37. S. Holdaway, 'Changes in Urban Policing', *British Journal of Sociology*, XXVIII, 2 (1977).

38. Punch and Naylor, 'Police as a Social Service'.

226 *'All Police is Conning Bastards'*

39. J.B. Mays, 'A Study of a Police Division', *British Journal of Delinquency* (January 1953); similarly, G. Gorer, *Exploring English Character* (Criterion Press, 1955), contains many Reithian assumptions on the relationship between the police and social change. According to Mays, 'the attitude of present-day police officers is tending to approximate to other social service workers'.

40. A. Platt and L. Cooper, *Policing America* (Prentice-Hall, 1974), Introduction.

41. P. Manning, *Police Work* (MIT Press, 1977), Ch. 3; Walker, *Critical History of Police Reform*, Ch. 1; and the excellent paper by D.D. Robinson, 'A Look at the Way some Police Historians Look at the Police' (Pennsylvania State University, 1976, Bramshill Library).

42. C. Reith, *Police Principles and the Problem of War* (Oxford University Press, 1940), p.69.

43. E. Moir, *The Justice of the Police* (Pelican, 1969), p. 143.

44. R. Roberts, *The Classic Slum* (Pelican, 1971), p. 100.

45. Melville Lee, *History of Police in England*; Howard, *Guardians of the Peace*; A. Selwyn, *The English Policeman* (Allen and Unwin, 1935); P. Coatman, *Police* (Oxford University Press, 1959), p. 9.

46. W. Nott-Bower, *52 Years a Policeman* (Edward Arnold, 1926); D.G. Browne, *The Rise of Scotland Yard* (Harrap and Co., 1956); I. St John *One Policeman's Story* (Barry Rose, 1978).

47. K. Chesney, *The Victorian Underworld* (Penguin, 1972).

48. Tobias, *Crime and Punishment*.

49. T. Critchley, *A History of the Police in England and Wales 1900-1966* (Constable, 1967) and *The Conquest of Violence: Order and Liberty in Britain* (Schocken Books, 1970).

50. J.M. Hart, *The British Police* (Allen and Unwin, 1951).

51. Manning, *Police Work*.

52. Critchley, *Conquest of Violence*.

53. E.P. Thompson, *The Poverty of Theory* (Merlin Press, 1978), p. 52.

54. Hart, *British Police*, p. 27.

55. Whitaker, *The Police*, p. 34.

56. T. Bowden, *Beyond the Limits of the Law* (Penguin, 1978), p. 21. Note his paper for the Institute of Conflict Studies, 'Protest and Violence: The Police Response', no. 75 (September 1976), which appears to reflect a significantly different standpoint.

57. Walker, *Critical History of Police Reform*, p. 17.

58. I. McDonald, 'The Creation of the British Police', *Race Today*, V, pp. 331-3.

59. Parris, 'Home Office and the Provincial Police'.

60. Storch, 'Plague of Blue Locusts'.

61. Howard, *Guardians of the Peace*, p. 127; note Foucault, *Discipline and Punish*, on the early French police.

62. Miller, *Cops and Bobbies*, p. 15.

63. R.B. Fosdick, *European Police Systems* (Patterson Smith, 1969), p. 53.

64. Marshall, *Police and Government*.

65. Liverpool Watch Committee Minutes.

66. P. Cohen, 'The Legal Subject in the City', National Deviancy Conference, January 1979.

67. D. Phillips, 'Riots and Public Order in the Black Country', in R. Quinault and J. Stevenson (eds), *Popular Protest and Public Order* (Allen and Unwin, 1974).

68. E.H. Glover, 'The English Police' *Police Chronicle* (1934), p. 62.

69. Mather, *Public Order in the Age of the Chartists*, p. 111.

70. Liverpool Watch Committee Minutes – roughly half of all complaints processed by the Watch Committee between 1836 and 1872 were from ministers urging action against Sabbath disturbances by the local working class.

71. Phillips, *Crime and Authority*.

72. Mather, *Public Order in the Age of the Chartists*, p. 84.

73. Liverpool Watch Committee Minutes

74. A. Judge and G. Reynolds, *The Night the Police Went on Strike* (Weidenfeld, 1968).

75. Whitaker, *The Police*, p. 33.

76. Mather, *Public Order in the Age of the Chartists*, p. 82.

77. Judge and Reynolds, *The Night the Police Went on Strike*, p. 162; Whitaker, *The Police:* 'members of Hurlingham Polo Club could be seen dressed in their kit of boots, spurs and topees cantering off to fresh sport swinging their riding crops', p. 24.

78. M. Morris, *The General Strike* (Penguin, 1977), p. 54.

79. J. Foster, *Class Struggle and the Industrial Revolution* (Oxford University Press, 1973), pp. 55-61.

80. Pelling, *Popular Politics and Society*, p. 69.

81. Storch, 'The Policeman as Domestic Missionary'. The Edwardian working-class account of policing referred to by him – Reynolds *et al. Seems So* (Macmillan, 1911) – is an exceptionally vivid representation of class feeling.

82. L. James, 'Police and Public Relations for an Open Society', *J.P. and Local Government Review* (13 February 1971).

83. McDonald 'The Creation of the British Police'.

84. C. Dickens, *The Uncommercial Traveller* (Poor Mercantile Jack).

85. C. Booth, *Life and Labour of the People in London*.

86. J. London, *The People of the Abyss* (Isbister and Co., 1903).

87. E.P. Thompson, 'Time, Work and Industrial Capitalism', in T.C. Smout and N.W. Flinn (eds), *Essays in Social History* (Macmillan, 1974).

88. Mentioned by Miller but also emphasised in a much earlier police history: C.H. Clarkson and J. Richardson, *Police!* (Field and Tuer, 1889), p. 202.

89. Phillips, 'Riots and Public Order in the Black Country'.

90. E.C. Midwinter, *Old Liverpool* (David and Charles, 1971), Ch. 3.

91. W. Cockcroft, 'The Liverpool Victorian Police', MA thesis, University of Bangor, 1968.

92. Liverpool Watch Committee Minutes.

93. J. Westergaard and H. Resler, *Class in a Capitalist Society* (Heinemann, 1975), p. 184.

94. Critchley, *History of the Police*, p. 55.

95. A. Bullen, 'Watching and Besetting', *North-West Labour History Bulletin*.

96. R. Hayburn, 'The Police and the Hunger Marchers', *International Review of Social History* (1972).

97. W. Hannington, *Unemployed Struggles* (Lawrence and Wishart).

98. J. Stevenson and F. Cook, *The Slump* (Jonathan Cape, 1977), p. 243.

99. G.W. Keeton, *Keeping the Peace* (Barry Rose, London, 1975), p. 166.

100. Critchley, *History of the Police*, p. 202.

101. Morris, *The General Strike*, p. 56.

102. C. Farman, *The General Strike* (Panther, 1974), p. 246.

103. Phillips, *Crime and Authority in Victorian England*. Miller makes a similar observation.

104. W. Gallagher, *The Rolling of the Thunder* (Lawrence and Wishart, 1947), pp. 118, 129.

105. H. McShane and J. Smith, *H. McShane: No Mean Fighter* (Pluto Press, 1978), p. 106.

106. K. Coates, *Tom Mann's Memoirs* (Macgibbon and Kee, 1967), p. 220. Critchley provides some corroboration.

107. C. Cockburn, *The Devil's Decade* (Sidgwick and Jackson, 1973), p. 64. Curiously, none of these events − by far the most tumultuous in its development − are mentioned in the official history of the Birkenhead force: S.P. Thompson, *Maintaining the Queen's Peace* (Birkenhead, 1958).

108. J. Hart, 'Reform of the Borough Police, 1835-1856', *The English Historical Review* (July 1955).

109. Mather, *Public Order in the Age of the Chartists*, p. 107.

110. Liverpool Watch Committee Minutes.

111. R. Reiner, *The Blue-Coated Worker* (Cambridge University Press, 1978).

112. M. Tomlin, *Police and Public* (John Long Ltd).

113. Keeton, *Keeping the Peace*, p. 162.

114. A. Judge, *A Man Apart* (Arthur Barker Ltd, 1972).

115. Judge and Reynolds, *The Night the Police Went on Strike*, p. 154.

116. Picton Davies, 'The Police Service of England and Wales', Ch. XX.

117. Nott-Bower, *52 Years a Policeman*.

118. N. Macready, *Annals of an Active Life* (n.d.) vol. II, Ch. XII.

119. Picton Davies, 'The Police Service of England and Wales'. R. Bean, 'Police Unrest, Unionisation and the 1919 Strike in Liverpool' (forthcoming *Journal of Contemporary History*) provides an excellent analysis of the Liverpool strike.

120. S. Spitzer, 'Towards a Marxian Theory of Deviance', *Social Problems*, vol. 225.

121. Liverpool Watch Committee Minutes. This evidence to the Watch Committee by the Head Constable attributes the riots to 'arrogant and over-bearing conduct of the Negro population . . . and by the white women who . . . cohabit with the black men boasting to the other women of the superior qualities of negroes as compared with those of white men . . . In nearly all cases, negroes have been aggressors' Analysis of the police action which Humphrey (*Police Power and Black People*) describes in Liverpool in 1971 must, in part, be based upon the development of such racist attitudes within the local force throughout the twentieth century.

122. Gramsci, *Prison Notebooks*, p. 246.

123. N. Poulantzas, *Political Power and Social Classes* (Sheed and Ward, 1973), pp. 277-9; Hall *et al.*, *Policing the Crisis*, pp. 205-8; A. Hunt, 'Law, State and Class Struggle', *Marxism Today* (June 1976).

124. N.L. Chapple, 'Community Relations in Kirkby New Town', *Police Journal*, XLJX, no. 4, pp. 290-301.

125. D. Rosenberg, 'The Sociology of the Police and Sociological Liberalism', mimeo, University of Bristol, 1973.

126. A. Hunt, *Class and Class Structure* (Lawrence and Wishart, 1978), p. 97.

NOTES ON CONTRIBUTORS

The editors of this volume were the members appointed to organise the 1979 Conference by the BSA Executive.

Bob Fryer	Department of Sociology Warwick University
Alan Hunt	Assistant Dean (Law), Middlesex Polytechnic
Doreen McBarnet	Centre for Socio-Legal Studies, Wolfson College, Oxford
Bert Moorhouse	Department of Sociology, Glasgow University, and BSA Executive Committee

Patricia Allatt taught for several years in primary and secondary schools. She studied sociology at University College Cardiff and the University of Keele: BSc (Econ.), MSc. (Statistical Sociology). She was formerly Research Fellow, Senior Research Fellow and Lecturer at the University of Keele, and is author of 'Friendship and Membership' in Murray (ed.), *Youth in Contemporary Society* (National Foundation for Educational Research, 1979). She is currently completing a study of family ideology in the Second World War.

Mike Brogden is Principal Lecturer in Sociology at Liverpool Polytechnic. He has published research on varied topics from international organisation and town-twinning to social work and policing. He is currently preparing books on the social workers' strike and the development of autonomy by police organisations in Britain.

Philip Corrigan is a Lecturer in the Department of Sociology, University of London Institute of Education. He is author with Harvie Ramsay and Derek Sayer of *Socialist Construction and Marxist Theory* (Macmillan, Monthly Review Press, 1978) and *For Mao* (Macmillan, Humanities Press, 1979); jointly edited and contributed with Michele Barrett, Annette Kuhn and Janet Wolf to *Ideology and Cultural Production* (Croom Helm, 1979); edited alone *Capitalism, State Formation, and Marxist Theory* (Quartet, 1980).

Roger Cotterrell is a Senior Lecturer in Law at Queen Mary College, University of London, where he has taught courses on legal institutions, sociology of law, legal theory and political sociology. He has written on sociological theory and sociology of law in a variety of social science journals and has contributed to law journals on topics in legal theory, public law and the legal framework of social policy.

Bob Fryer is Senior Lecturer in Sociology, University of Warwick. He has undertaken research in connection with redundancy, including a study of the collapse of Rolls-Royce on behalf of ASTMS, carried out with Professor Dorothy Wedderburn. Recent work includes a detailed examination of the organisation and structure of NUPE, which was funded initially by the union and subsequently by the SSRC. He is currently initiating a study of the organisation of a major civil service trade union, the SCPS, together with Peter Fairbrother, funded by the union itself.

Derek Sayer was born in London in 1950. He has a BA in Sociology from Essex University and a PhD from Durham University. He is Lecturer in Sociology at Glasgow University. He has published articles in *Radical Philosophy, Capital and Class, Socialist Register, Sociological Review* and *Sociology,* and is author of *Marx's Method* (1979) and co-author with Philip Corrigan and Harvie Ramsay of *Socialist Construction and Marxist Theory* (1978) and *For Mao* (1979).

Iain Stewart studied law at the University of Exeter and in the International Faculty for the Teaching of Comparative Law. He has had various jobs, with trade union involvement. He was Tutorial Assistant at the University of Dundee, 1976-80, and is now Lecturer in Law at the University of Hull. He is interested in public law and the philosophy, sociology and anthropology of law.

David Sugarman is Principal Lecturer in Law, Middlesex Polytechnic. He is a graduate of the Universities of Hull, Cambridge and Harvard. At Harvard he completed a socio-historical study of the role of Anglo-American company law in the facilitation and legitimation of the modern company and industrial capitalism, 1750-1930. Other current research includes: critical evaluations of Max Hartwell's, Morton Horwitz's and E.P. Thompson's work on law, economy and society; and legal, empirical and historical studies on the regulation of 'insider trading'. He is co-editing an historical anthology on the relationship between law and economy in England, 1750-1930, and a series of essays on critical legal theory; and is writing a text on company law.

Christopher J. Whelan read law at the London School of Economics; between 1975 and 1976 he was a Visiting Research Fellow at the Institute of Industrial Relations, University of California at Berkeley. Since 1977, he has been a Research Officer in Law at the Centre for Socio-Legal Studies, Wolfson College, Oxford. He will shortly complete a PhD on national emergency industrial disputes in the US and the UK.

NAME INDEX

Albrow, M. 61
Althusser, L. 11-12, 95, 185
Anderson, P. 10
Arnold, T.W. 115
Attlee, C. 162

Balbus, I. 55, 96
Bentham 71, 202, 216
Bernstein, B. 36, 38, 45n27
Beveridge, W.H. 140-1, 144-9, 180-3, 185, 190-3, 197
Blacker, J. 206
Boorstin, D.J. 71
Booth, W. 216
Bowden, T. 210
Browne, D.G. 209
Bunyan, T. 212

Cain, M. 37, 79, 94
Campbell, C. 9
Chapple, N.L. 222
Chatterton, M. 207
Chesney, K. 209, 213
Churchill, W. 160
Clegg, H.A. 143
Coatman, P. 209, 218
Cockburn, C. 219
Cockcroft, W. 216-17
Cohen, P. 213
Constable, T. 207
Cook, F. 227
Cooper, L. 207
Critchley, T. 209-10, 218
Cummings, E. 206

Danzig, R. 96
Darwin, C. 112
Davies, P. 228
Dewey, J. 114
Dezalay, Y. 178, 196
Dickens, C. 216
Diplock, Lord 171
Dobb, M. 89
Durkheim, E. 9, 107
Dworkin, R. 117

Engels, F. 33, 36, 39, 81

Farman, C. 227
Ferguson, R.B. 96
Flanders, A. 144
Fosdick, R.B. 213
Foster, J. 214
Foucault, M. 17
Friedman, L. 77, 96
Fuller, L. 13, 64

Gallagher, W. 227
Genovese, E. 83-4, 96
Glover, E.H. 213
Goodrich, C. 143
Gouldner, A. 10
Gramsci, A. 10-11, 43n19, 71, 82-3, 87, 179, 222

Hall, S. 9
Hannington, W. 217-18
Hart, H.L.A. 13
Hart, J.M. 209-10, 213
Hartwell, M. 73-4, 77-9, 80-1, 97
Hay, D. 84-5, 87-91, 93, 96-7, 103n102, 202
Hayburn R. 217
Hayek, F.A. 99n26
Heath, E. 172
Hegel, G.W.F. 30-1, 112-13
Hindess, B. 44n25, 56, 96
Hirst, P.Q. 44n25, 55-6, 96, 98, 204
Hoebel, A.E. 107
Hoggart, R. 204
Holdaway, S. 207
Holmes, O.W. 113-14
Horowitz, M. 74-8, 80, 97
Howard, G. 209, 212, 218
Howe, K. 207
Hunt, A. 37
Hurst, W. 74, 77

Jackson, B. 204
James, L. 215
Jenkins, R. 167
Judge, A. 217, 220

Kafka, F. 124
Keeton, G.W. 218

233